To

Brice Marsh.

Bless you for
all you have
accomplished.
It's a joy
to be your friend

Bob Graham
Governor Fl.

MAPS OF THE GARDEN OF EDEN

- Where was the Garden?   *The foot of Mt Ararat*
- When was the Garden?   *Before 4004 B.C.*
- Where is the Garden now?   *You'll find out.*

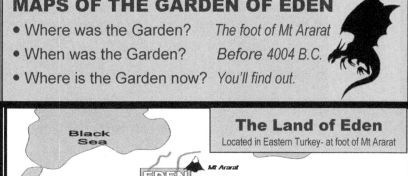

The Land of Eden
Located in Eastern Turkey- at foot of Mt Ararat

Black Sea

EDEN

Mt Ararat

TURKEY

IRAN

Tigris

Euphrates

IRAQ

Mediterranean Sea

ISRAEL

EGYPT

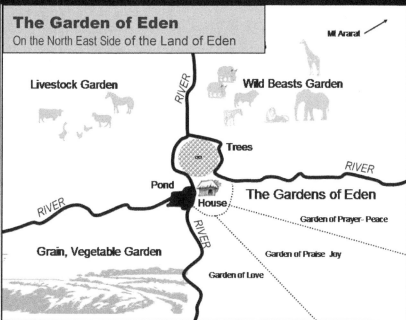

The Garden of Eden
On the North East Side of the Land of Eden

Mt Ararat

Livestock Garden

RIVER

Wild Beasts Garden

Trees

RIVER

Pond

House

The Gardens of Eden

RIVER

Garden of Prayer- Peace

Grain, Vegetable Garden

RIVER

Garden of Praise Joy

Garden of Love

THE GARDEN OF EDEN

Bob Curlee

JONAH  PUBLISHERS

Printed by CreateSpace
International Standard Book Number- 1517148936
Printed in the United State of America, 2009

CONTENTS

Maps of Eden 3
Prologue 11
Introduction 12

PART 1- CROSS+ROADS 13
1- Welcome to CROSS+ROADS 13
2- First Baptist Church.......................................15
3- Cross Park, Thursday Night 24
4- Preparation for Time Travel 32
5- The Door in the Cross......................................38
6- The Villain Appears 41

PART 2- FIRST HEAVEN 45
7- Through the Open Door.....................................45
8- The Earth 46
9- Another Look at Cross-Roads 47
10- Back Through History 48
11-Would You Like to See God?.............................50
12- The Creation of Gabriel..................................54
13- What Color is God? 57
14- Was God Lonely? 62
15- History is His Story 65
16- Smell, Taste, Sound and Feel of Heaven 69
17- A Tour of the Holy City 73
18- Lucifer Arrives 78
19- Lucifer Begins the Uprising 85
20- War in Heaven...93
21- The Wrath of God...95

PART 3- THE BIG BANG 99
22- What in the World Was That? 99
23- Planet Earth is Born......................................105
24- The Six Phases of Creation.............................108

PART 4- CREATION OF LIFE 123
25- Life Begins 123
26- Watch Our for Dinosaurs................................131
27- Man Takes the Stage 136

PART 5- THE GARDEN 141
28- The Garden of Eden.......................................141
29- Adam and Eve 144
30- A Special Creation- Eden and Adam................147

31- Where was Eden? 151
32- Adam is Created 153
33- Adam Goes to Work..155
34- The Tree of Life 157
35- Animals Are Made for the Garden 159
36- Eve..161
37- How Long Were They in the Garden?....................164
38- A Tour of the Gardens 169

PART 6- THE SERPENT **187**
39- The Snake in the Garden 187
40- The Last Day in the Garden.................................193
41- The Tree of Knowledge of Good and Evil 195
42- Adam and Eve Eat the Fruit 199
43- The Curses 205

PART 7- OUTSIDE THE GARDEN..................................**209**
44- God Always Provides 209
45- Cain Teaches Abel a Lesson................................214
46- Adam and Eve Make a Comeback 217
47- Cain Finds a Wife in the Land of Nod....................219

PART 8- NOAH AND THE ARK **231**
48- Adam and Eve Have a Visitor 231
49- Enoch and Methuselah 235
50- Methuselah Lived Until the Flood.........................238
51- Noah Builds an Ark 240
52- The Animals Board the Ark 242
53- Was it the Earth or the Land of Eden that was Flooded?...245
54- The Ark Lands..249
55- A Last Look at the Garden 251

PART 9- EASTER SUNDAY..**253**
55- Church 253
56- Easter Evening at Cross Park...............................256
57- I Think Therefore I'm the Result of a Thinker 261
58-Temptation...263
59- The Angel Back at the House 268
60- If Your Hand Offends You 273
61- God Always Provides a Ram.................................277
62- One Last Question 281

Reasons I Believe in God, Creation and Intelligent Design .**283**
By Chris Christian, Sandra Hall and Sonny Miller

Creation Time Line **287**

DEDICATION

Years and years ago, I dedicated my life to Jesus Christ.
Now I dedicate this book to Him and His Creation.

Also I wish to thank the teachers in my life:

Sue- my wife, who taught science until retirement
and lived the Christian life every day.

Jamey, my son, who teaches science
and firmly believes in the Creator and His Creation.

Marie Duncan, who taught English for years
and has been a example of faithfulness.
Now she edits my writing.

And to all Christian teachers everywhere-
who may not be able to preach in the class room,
but who teach the love of Christ by their lives.

THE GARDEN OF EDEN
PROLOGUE

Adam and Eve were very real to me when I was a child. I also thought God rode around on a cloud and turned on a faucet to make it rain. But my faith grew up! When I was saved at age nine, my view of God changed to understanding He made the laws that made the rain. Adam and Eve remained as real to me as Roy Rogers and Dale Evans- though I had never met either one of them.

Even at a Baptist College my faith was shaken when I learned of the huge distances of stars, the size of galaxies, and the age of the earth. If the world was made in six days and Adam appeared in 4004 B.C., it seemed we had a problem. But Faith won out. Sometimes I felt Adam was merely a symbol for all mankind, but deep inside I had to believe Adam was a real man.

As years passed, Science added billions of years to the age of the earth. but Adam was still stuck at 4004 B.C. It didn't bother my faith, for it is in Jesus Christ- not Adam. But this did cause others to struggle.

Today it seems as if there is an all-out war to prove there is no God, no Creator and no Intellectual Design. No concept of a Creator God can be taught in public schools.

The Garden of Eden is a novel of creative writing that dares to accept the facts of science and the dates of the Bible and blend them together into an hypothesis of faith, fact, and fiction that places a real Adam and Eve in the Garden of Eden in 4004 B.C. And, oh yeah, it also tells of a real Noah, in a real flood, in the year 2348 B.C.

This book is written to help you come to know the first Adam in his Garden of Eden. I pray you will also come to know the last Adam as He has gone to prepare a place for His followers in Paradise.

Bob Curlee

+ + +

INTRODUCTION

Placing his tools down gently, he slipped through the door, tiptoed behind her and placed his strong hands over her eyes. "Guess who?" he murmured in a sensuous voice.

She giggled then answered, "It can't be Mr. Bear, because he has claws for fingers. And it's surely not Gabriel, he's too polite for such a move. Who could it be?"

She spun around quickly and kissed him on the nose. "What a surprise, it's Adam!"

Laughing, they hugged each other. He backed off a few feet and said, "Hey, I've been working with the livestock all day- you should have guessed I was Mr. Pig."

"Then why don't we take a quick bath before supper?" Eve suggested as she raced out the door. She sprinted across the front porch, dashed down the pier and made a perfect dive into the pond. When she emerged, her golden hair floated around her like a golden sunrise against the virgin blue sky. "Come on in," she said seductively, "the water's fine."

"The water is always fine in the Garden," Adam laughed and dove in beside her. She splashed water at him and he flipped some back at her.

They did not know I was watching them from another dimension and another time. And I knew what else they did not know: tomorrow was their last day in the Garden of Eden.

+ + +

PART 1 CROSS+ROADS

CHAPTER 1
WELCOME TO CROSS+ROADS

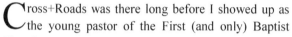

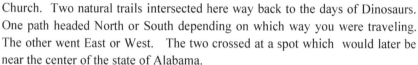

Cross+Roads was there long before I showed up as the young pastor of the First (and only) Baptist Church. Two natural trails intersected here way back to the days of Dinosaurs. One path headed North or South depending on which way you were traveling. The other went East or West. The two crossed at a spot which would later be near the center of the state of Alabama.

Guess I ought to introduce myself because I'm going to be your tour guide on the wildest adventure you're ever seen. I'm Chris Christian. Now I know that sounds like a character from Dick Tracy- but my dad was a deacon and my mom headed up the mission work for the church, and they wanted a son to enter the ministry. So they named me Christopher Columbus Christian. How I survived with a name like that, I'll never know. It was soon chopped down to Chris and like Jonah I ran from God as fast as I could- but his legs were just too long for me. When I was fifteen I was called to serve him full time, I surrendered and never looked back.

This is my first church- and I'm their youngest pastor ever. I've been here a couple of years, long enough to see babies come from marriages I performed. Now the young folks who used to fill the choir on Sunday nights are filling the colleges and universities across the state.

I have one wife, Shirl, and God has blessed us with four little ones: Chuck, Betsy, Christy and little Johnny. They are twelve, ten, eight and two.

The town looks like something from a Norman Rockwell painting. Alabama needed a new county in that area after the war, so the people decided to place it at the crossroads and name the new county Cross County. That tickled the folks who owned land there and they built a city and named it CROSS+ROADS. Then they bragged that they were the only town in Alabama and probably the whole United States that had a real cross in their name.

By the middle of the Nineteenth Century, a quaint little town had grown up. It radiated out from where the two roads had crossed. In order to go North or South or East or West, one had to detour around the Cross County Court House which was built right smack dab in the middle of where the roads crossed. There the old men played checkers during the day or just sat around and talked about the weather or the government or how the whole country was going to the dogs since prayer and God had been taken out of the public schools.

The town was quite proud of the huge clock that sat atop the court house. It's four faces looked out on the four directions of the compass. Unfortunately none of the four faces ever showed the same time. This may have been caused by a mechanical failure or by a squirrel trying to bury some nuts in the machinery that controlled the time. After several attempts failed to fix the problem, the town folk just laughed and said that people relied on clocks and time too much anyway.

One block south of the courthouse, I had talked First Baptist Church of CROSS+ROADS to build the Cross Park. It was a place where you could meet and not worry about wealth or denomination or race. And in the center of the park stood an old rugged cross.

None of the almost one thousand residents had any idea that here Science and Religion were about to clash head on. The issue would be "Evolution versus Creation" Some of the mysteries of time would be revealed in the shadow of the four-faced clock.

+ + +

Bro, Chris

CHAPTER 2
FIRST BAPTIST CHURCH
The Thursday Before Easter

"**B**rother Chris, (chomp, chomp,) there's some guys here to see you." Billie Nelle, the church secretary, shouted into the old fashioned, out-of-date intercom system at First Baptist Church, CROSS+ROADS, Alabama.

I replied, "Billie Nelle, I'm not outside, you don't have to talk so loud. But do I smell chocolate over the intercom?"

Silence on the other end, then a swallowing sound. "You can't smell chocolate over a telephone."

"I can smell chocolate over television. I told you I don't mind your eating all the time if you will half it with me."

"How about a third?" the oversized secretary responded. Billie Nelle, like many women, was proud of her cooking, and unlike most ladies equally proud of her weight which was the result and evidence of her good cooking. Outwardly she seemed rather drab and cold, but she possessed a dry wit and loved for her pastor to kid her. She wore a cotton dress with an old shawl around her shoulders. Fortunately she was so plain looking no one would ever accuse the pastor of having an affair with this church secretary.

I asked, "Did you say there are some guys here to see me?"

"Well, honestly, there's one guy and one gal, uh, I mean girl."

"Are they the local caterers bringing more food?"

"No, they are two of your favorite young folks home for the Easter holidays from college," she replied as the sound of a cookie crunched in the background.

"That must be Sonny Miller and Sandra Hall! Tell them to take that plate of cookies from you and come in to see me. Then get us all a Diet Coke. Some of us need to lose some weight, hint, hint."

Billie Nelle mumbled on the other end of the intercom, "My doctor says my weight is all right, I'm just not tall enough."

'How tall did he say you need to be for you weight?'

"Seven foot four, if it's any of your business," was the giggled reply. "I'm sending in one guy, one gal and one almost full plate of double chocolate chunk cookies."

I turned off the Solitaire game I had been playing on my computer, clicked on my Bible Study program, slicked back my hair and headed to the door. I wasn't bad looking but neither had I won any beauty contests. Tall and thin through high school and college, I had added thirty pounds in three months after I married Shirl. Blue eyes sparkle over my Roman nose. Folks say my smile is genuine and the people at my church love me: and I'm having a wonderful love affair with my first flock. That day, the Thursday before Easter, I wore a blue denim shirt with the name of the church printed over the pocket. Blue jeans and comfortable shoes completed my outfit. On Sundays, I still wear my coat and tie, though many of the younger pastors had chosen the "casual look.' I opened the door and Sonny Miller reached in and gave me a bear hug. "Preach, you look great!"

I gasped for breath as the six foot two Alabama running back squeezed me. "Sonny," Sandra laughed, "Don't crush the preacher to death, not at least until we squeeze some answers out of him." The beautiful Samford student gave me a warm hug.

Sonny Miller

Sonny and Sandra made the perfect couple. He had been short until his sophomore year in high school. Then like the proverbial weed he shot up to six foot two. Black hair accented his olive complexion and happy brown eyes. Proudly he wore a crimson Alabama muscle shirt with a cross over his heart. Naturally he wore jeans. He was a hunk of muscle with almost no body fat. Yet he was a gentle giant who would take time in the summer to do mission work with under-privileged children. At the University of Alabama he had become a starting running back his freshman year. His speed was unmatched and his scoring ability almost unbelievable. He had just finished his junior year and was a Heisman Trophy candidate. Tim Tebow, the talented quarterback at Florida, had taken home the prize. Tim and Sonny were close friends and both spiritual leaders on their football teams. But Sonny Miller was the favorite to win the Heisman his senior year at Alabama.

Pro teams were licking their chops waiting for this super talented young runner to finish his last year. Although no team could legally court him, it was common knowledge in all the sports circles that Sonny Miller could probably be the number one in the draft if he had chosen to drop out after his Junior year. But the young athlete from CROSS+ROADS, Alabama, was persistent in his desire to earn his degree and then decide how God wanted him to serve Him.

Sandra Hall was a hometown girl who looked like she should be on the front cover of a fashion magazine or a Sunday School book. Golden hair, sparkling blue eyes, gorgeous mouth, perfect figure added up to a sure fire finalist in the Miss Alabama Beauty Pageant the summer before. Laughing she had told her followers, "I might have had a chance if I had had any talent!" Had they accepted brilliance as a talent, she would have been Miss Alabama and Miss America. Nothing but A's filled her report cards in school and now in college. She walked off with the Miss Congeni-

Sandra Hall

ality Award, the result of her love for people and her love for her Lord. Wearing designer jeans, she reflected the current fashion with a yellow blouse with something like a short slip over it.

I eyed both of them and then grinned, "Questions? Questions? Like Radio Shack, 'You got questions, we got answers.' Questions about the Bible, prayer, morals, I can answer, but if you're into college courses, I'm not so sure. You may have to ask my wife. Anyway, sit down and let's talk about it. Care for some cookies?"

At that moment Billie Nelle waddled into the office with three Diet Cokes and a couple of paper towels. "We're out of napkins," she said as she flopped them down and wobbled her way back out.

Sonny grabbed a cookie, sniffed it as James Bond smells a vintage wine, then put the whole thing in his mouth. A smile of contentment came over his face as he whispered, "It don't get no better than this. Not even in Heaven."

Sandra nibbled on a cookie, sipped on her coke, punched Sonny playfully and added, "Sonny, Heaven is a whole lot better than Billie Nelle's cookies. Heaven's even better than my mama's homemade coconut cake."

Sonny smiled a dreamy smile, reached over and held her hand in his. "Promise me that after we've graduated from college and gotten married, you will cook as good as your mother."

"Ha," I replied, "Just pray that after you're married she won't get as big as Billie Nelle."

"I heard that," the intercom squawked, "and I *represent* that, uh, I mean, I *resent* that remark."

"I knew you were listening and I'm only kidding," I laughed. "Just turn off the intercom and find something to do."

"It's time for lunch," she grumbled.

"Go eat lunch, then. These young folks need to talk to me about something important, I imagine." I clicked off my intercom, turned to the young couple and asked, "So, what questions do you have? Are you worried about cookies in Heaven or getting married here on earth?"

Silence. Sonny looked at Sandra. She sighed, lifted her eyes, sniffed a bit and said, "Brother Chris, uh. We've got a problem."

"Good Lord," I jumped up and said, "surely you're not pregnant?"

"No, No, No!" they both said together, then laughed. Sonny added, "You know we are Christians, and we've taken a vow to save ourselves sexually until we are married."

"Whew!" I said as I sat down. "So, what's the big problem?"

Sonny turned his bronze face toward Sandra as if wanting her to pop the question. As I waited, I remembered how Sonny Miller had shown up one morning at the Cross Prayer Garden. He turned out to be a record breaking runner, and then he turned football player as he got older and bigger and ready for college. Quite a few schools wanted him, especially from his home state, Florida. But he had gotten saved, fallen desperately in love with Sandra Hall and accepted a scholarship to the University of Alabama. He was pretty disappointed when Sandra went to Samford University, a Baptist School, in Birmingham. But they decided true love not only waits, it can travel the forty miles between Birmingham and Tuscaloosa. Besides, she won a Miss Alabama Scholarship to the religious school.

"So," I repeated, "what's the big problem?"

Sonny dropped his dark eyelashes, then looked up at me and said, "Well, Brother Chris, you know I love the Lord, uh, even more than I love football."

"That's a lotta' love," I replied.

He hesitated, rubbed his long muscular fingers through his jet black hair, then continued, "Evolution. Uh, that's my problem- Evolution. Sandra doesn't have a problem with it, because she's so well grounded in her faith. The Devil couldn't knock her beliefs out of her with a baseball bat."

He sighed, "There's a little Baptist church in Tuscaloosa a few of us attend when I don't go home on the weekend, or when I can't see Sandra. The preacher there told us if we believed in Evolution we would all go to Hell."

"To Hell?" I asked. "Surely, he meant at least purgatory! I believe the only reason people go to Hell is when they don't accept Jesus as Lord."

"That's what I believe or I have believed- salvation depends entirely on Jesus. But this preacher said that Adam was born in 4004 B.C. " Sonny shrugged his shoulders as he told me, "But my professors at the University said the first man, or woman, goes back to almost three million years ago. And, uh, the professor tells us there is no God, and Adam wasn't born in 4004 B.C."

I did a little head scratching as if trying to figure out how to tell both of them what I knew but had pledged to keep secret. "First, Adam was not born in 4004 BC," I paused then added, "he was created." "Does that make a big difference?" Sonny asked. 'Absolutely! But I will tell you one of my favorite stories." I took a cookie, then a sip of my Diet Coke and settled back as if I had the final solution. "There was this ex-marine who went back to college to get his degree. He was a big tough guy, but a Christian, just like you, Sonny. This professor in one class made fun of church and the Bible. He told them there was no Adam and that there is no God. The ex-marine just sat there holding his temper until one day the professor got carried away and cried out, 'There is no god. If there is a god, let him come down now and smack me on the nose.' The ex-marine got up, went to the front of the room, rared back and threw a punch right on the professor's nose. The professor fell to the floor. The ex-marine bent over and said, 'God's busy, so he sent me in His place.'"

Sandra roared. It took Sonny a minute to catch on, then all of us joined in the laughter. Finally Sonny calmed down enough and gasped, "That's a very good idea, Preach, but I'm afraid if I did that, I'd get kicked out of school and lose my scholarship."

"You're right, that's not a solution," I said. "But it is a good joke. Sandra, you're studying to teach science. How do you handle this supposed contradiction between evolution and creation?"

Her golden hair fell across her face as she leaned toward Sonny. She put her arm through his and looked at him with those blue eyes that would melt an igloo. "I guess, I just look at evolution as being science's answer to how life began on earth. But Adam and Eve are faith's answer to that same question."

Sonny blinked a couple of times, then asked. "So you believe in both of them?"

"Yes, " she answered. "Many scientists use a different definition for evolution than I do. To many people evolution means everything started from scratch. Somehow life emerged on its own and evolution pushes it forward. But I believe God created Heaven and Earth. The Six Days are six phases of his creation, maybe taking millions of years."

Sonny nodded but added, "Evolution is confusing to me. Something about survival of the fittest."

"Or sometimes it's survival of the fattest," I added as I patted my tummy.

That broke the tension. Then Sonny looked at both of us and said, "I don't see how a protein molecule could end up looking and thinking like a man. But my professor made me look like an idiot as he explained that evolution is the only scientific answer. All other hypotheses are wrong. He told us evolution works two ways. The first is *Natural Selection.* What does that mean, Sandra?"

Sandra paused then said, "Science teaches that changes come through *Natural Selection*- which believes the traits which are helpful for survival can be inherited and passed on through reproduction. But it also makes sure harmful traits become more rare. Thus animals with good features are more likely to reproduce and have lots of good traits in their offspring."

"To put it simply, Sonny," I chipped in, "they teach that you are the product of good traits of looks, physique, and energy. Your tribe will increase. Those with bad, fat traits like Billie Nelle and I have will soon be as extinct as dodo birds."

Sandra laughed, "It takes longer than a few years for a trait to disappear. But over many generations- adaptations occur through a combination of successive, small, random changes in qualities. Natural selection chooses variants best-suited for their environment. Or that's what they now teach."

She paused waiting to see how her boyfriend absorbed all of this.

He blinked and said, "Is that all?"

"Well, there is also another process at work called *Genetic Drift.* This produces random changes in traits. It's somewhat like mutations. Over time, like a million years, these changes can result in a new species."

"And you believe that?" Sonny asked.

"Well, some of it. Do you remember when we talked of *Intelligent Design?*"

"Um, yea, but I forget what it means."

Sandra flashed that eat-your-heart-out smile at him and said, "*Intelligent Design* is the belief there is an intelligence behind all of creation and evolution. We Christians believe that force is God."

Sonny replied, "I thought I used '*Intelligent Design*' the first Sunday I came to church. Remember my tailor-designed clothes?"

She snuggled closer to him and smiled, just as she had the first Sunday he came to church with an oversized sports coat, an ugly tie wrapped around the collar of one of his shirts, and a hat that must have belonged to some Mafia member. When Sonny Miller showed up that first Sunday at First Baptist, I had almost laughed and wanted to tell him he didn't have to dress so formally. But Sandra Hall had seen him, sized up the situation, greeted him, and said, "Sonny! Sonny Miller! I know you from school. Wow, look at this cool outfit you wore today. I love it."

Then she grabbed him by the arm and escorted him into Sunday School. When I preached that morning and gave the invitation, Sonny jumped up and ran down to the front- complete in his tacky outfit- and told the church he wanted to get saved. Like the dog named Rover who dies and he died all over, Sonny Miller was saved all over- he completely turned his life over to the Lord.

All the church boys were envious of the way Sandra had befriended Sonny.. So they all showed up the next Sunday with similar Sonny costumes. But Sonny had caught on and arrived in jeans and a muscle building tee shirt. Naturally, Sandra greeted him and said, "Sonny, now that outfit is really hot! You know how to dress like a real he-man."

Sonny blushed at these memories from a few years ago. He put his hand over hers and said, "I don't think I can ever thank you enough for the way you accepted me that first Sunday. I had never been to church, so I didn't know what to wear except what I had seen in old movies. Maybe I don't know enough about *Intelligent Design.*"

Sandra kissed her finger, then put it to his lips. "If you had not worn that eye-catching outfit, I might never have noticed you," she laughed.

"Well, I had already noticed you at school and figured you were way out of my poor league. Why would a beautiful girl like you care for a no-nothing guy like me?"

"God takes those of us who are no-nothings just like we are, and then He turns us into some-somethings just like He wants. And he has turned you into the greatest guy I know."

"Is that Evolution?" Sonny asked.

"Nope, that's regeneration," I popped back quickly.

"What is this *Intelligent Design* you were talking about? Doesn't it just mean evolution has to be intelligent?" Sonny asked.

"Glad you asked," Sandra answered. "Now, how can I put it? *Intelligent Design* is the belief certain features of the universe and all living things can not be explained by natural selection. Instead there is a force of intelligence which best explains the creation of the universe and life."

"Isn't that what we call '*Creationism?*'"

"Similar, but in *Creationism* we believe God created the universe and all living things and directed their development. *Intelligent Design* just says there seems to be an intelligent force behind all of it, not necessarily God or a god. This is a genuine theory of life that could be taught in school. The courts will not allow teaching about a Creator God."

"Sorta'- like in Alcoholics Anonymous," I piped in. "*Intelligent Design* has to believe in a Greater Power, but you don't have to call the power God."

Sonny asked, "So, you believe in *Creationism* which took millions of years and you also believe in Adam who just showed up on the front porch a few thousand years ago, Preacher?"

"Well, yea. It's kinda' like believing in Santa Claus and the Baby Jesus at Christmas."

"Which is the fictitious Santa Claus: Evolution or Adam?" Sonny retorted. "Or is this something like the Holy Trinity which makes no sense to me?"

"Uh," I backed up. "Good point. Bad illustration. Trinity? Hmm, let's see. How about if I tell you I am a father, a son, and a husband?"

Sonny thought a moment, then asked, "So you are Brother Chris- but you also have three different roles?"

"That's it," I exclaimed.

"But do you pray to yourself as father? Or when you were baptized did you crawl up in the ceiling and shout down to yourself, 'This is my beloved son, in whom I am well pleased?'" Sonny asked as he stood up and looked out the windows. "That must be some kind of answer as how there is a triune God. How can God be three in one?"

Sandra replied, "Sonny, I can tell you how I had to deal with the problem. I told my Vacation Bible kids the trinity is like water: it can be liquid as in water, solid like ice, or vapor like steam."

Sonny shrugged, "But isn't one plus one plus one always three?"

Sandra said, "Not in chemistry, you can taken one oxygen atom plus two hydrogen atoms and you have one water molecule."

"That's chemistry," Sonny said, "and God is not just a chemical compound."

"If instead of adding, what if you multiply?" I asked. "What is one times one times one?"

"One times one is one- and times one again is one," Sonny said. "That's sharp, but God is no chemical reaction nor is He a mathematical equation."

Holy Trinity
$1 + 1 + 1 = 3$
or
$1 \times 1 \times 1 = 1$

I moved over beside Sonny, placed my arm around his shoulder and said, "Sonny, there are just some things we can't answer. When I was young, it was questions like 'How many angels can stand on the head of a pin?' or 'Can God make a rock so big he can't pick it up?'" I gave Sonny a big hug and said, "Sometimes we just have to take the thirteenth."

"The thirteenth?" Sonny looked at him puzzled. "Don't you mean the fifth?"

"No, I mean the Thirteenth Chapter of First Corinthians, verse 12,

"Now we see but a poor reflection in a mirror;
then we shall see face to face.
Now I know in part; but then I shall know fully,
even as I am fully known. (NIV)"

Sandra stood and walked over beside Sonny. Slipping her arm inside his, she whispered, "Sonny, a lot of things we just can't understand. We just have to do like the black preacher told us at church one Sunday. 'When I reads something in the Bible I don't understand- I just believes it and goes on.'"

Sonny wiped a tear from his eye. "I am so lucky to have both of you- and the Lord." But then he shook his head and said, "I just can't think like you do. I don't understand three gods in one. To me, it's got to be either Evolution or Adam. Both can't be right. The two just don't match up. Maybe if I had just gone to a Christian school like Samford..."

I sighed, "Sonny, it may help you to know when I went to Samford, I was utterly confused about faith and evolution. I doubted my salvation and even thought about giving up on my preparation to become a preacher."

My eyes misted over as I remembered the terrible pain in which I was torn. "But someone came along and helped me through it. I now believe God created everything and guided evolution. I believe Adam was created- and he and Eve appeared about 4004 B.C. No problem at all!"

"Someone helped you?" Sonny asked. "Who was it?"

"Uh, I was afraid you would ask that. It's a secret and I can't tell you."

It was pitiful to see the big muscular athlete pull his arm away from Sandra, then drop his face into his hands as if defeated. "Preacher, if you can't help me, and Sandra can't help me, then I, I don't know what to do."

Standing up, I put my hand on Sonny's head. "Hey, pal. We're going to do everything we can to get you through this crisis. Tell you what, let me talk to my, uh, that somebody and see if he will help you, like he helped me."

Sonny's head snapped up., He smiled, jumped up and hugged his preacher. "Oh, Brother Chris, if you can get that guy, or gal, or whoever, to help me through this, I'll love you forever!"

It was refreshing to see a college student so hungry for the truth. I told him, "Well, I'm going to love you forever, and so will Sandra. Tell you what, let me do a little, uh, calling and I'll meet you at the Cross Park tonight. Remember it was at the cross where I first met you several years ago."

"Good deal," Sonny said. "We had planned on being at the Park tonight anyway. We love it and we were just going to sit there and talk about our yesterdays, our todays and all of our wonderful tomorrows."

I, the reverend Chris Christian, watched the two as they walked out arm in arm. They were so much in love they looked liked my wife Shirl and me when we were first dating. But then I sympathized with the young athlete in his search for the truth. I yelled, "See you at the Cross Park about eight."

+ + +

CHAPTER 3
CROSS PARK- THURSDAY NIGHT

Azaleas usually bloom once and turn the Park Garden into a sneak preview of Paradise- or perhaps a lingering memory of Eden. The Garden of Eden seems to be imprinted in the minds of every culture- either something to remember or some place to anticipate. The azaleas were in full bloom, mixing Ruffle Pinks with Alabama reds. The Pride of Mobile blossoms blended into the recreation of the famous garden of the Bible. To add to the bouquet some of the ladies had planted jasmine and wild honeysuckle. The result was a heavenly aroma.

Water tumbled over the manmade rock waterfalls, splashed into the four foot pool, then was recycled through an underground pipe back up to the foot of the cross. There it wiggled and giggled its way down again.

To add to the near perfect scene, a full silver moon beamed down it's light upon the young couple sitting on one of the benches. Sandra leaned on Sonny's strong shoulder. He finally broke the silence by saying, "That pink rose bush over there is in memory of my brother, Curtis. I'll never forget him, he was one of the most loving men I've ever known."

"Good old red headed Curtis. He had a life-threatening stroke down in Florida. He was not supposed to live, but he fooled the doctors and stayed alive long enough to come up here and get saved and baptized," she sighed.

"Then, he was gone, just like that!" Sonny reached over, picked off one of the pink roses and showed her the little red cross on each pedal. "Curtis was a true believer. He never worried one bit about Adam and Eve. He said he just believed the Bible from Genesis to Revelation, and he even believed the maps in the back. I wish I had his simple faith."

"That other bush over there is for my dad, Smiling Sam. A great guy. He got saved after Curtis died. They're up in Paradise now, probably praying for Alabama to win all of its football games."

"They're very proud of you," Sandra said. "It's good you planted a bush for each of them on either side of the cross. They're like the two thieves on the crosses beside Jesus." She realized this didn't sound quite right, so she added, "Well, they're both like the thief on the right who believed and met Jesus later that day in Paradise."

"Look, Sandra, there's a butterfly fluttering over Curtis's rose," Sonny said. "That's odd. I don't think I've ever seen a butterfly at night before." Sandra gazed at the golden work of art flitting from blossom to blossom, then said, "You're right. I never thought about it. Where do butterflies go at night?" Sonny sighed, "This place is so beautiful. If there were really a Garden of Eden, do you think they had roses and waterfalls and butterflies and rainbows?"

Sandra laughed, "Yes to the first three, no to the fourth. They didn't have rainbows in Eden because they had no rain. Rain and rainbows didn't show up until Noah and the flood."

The butterfly flew away as the rose bush started shaking. Sonny jumped up to examine, "What's wrong with that plant? Does it think it's going to burst into a burning bush?"

Just then there was a loud sneeze and the bush shook off a few pedals.

"Brother Chris, what are you doing hiding behind the rose bush?" Sonny asked.

Embarrassed, I looked like I had just been caught with my hand in the cookie jab. Pulling out my handkerchief, I wiped my nose and said, "This pollen and my allergies just don't go together."

"You haven't answered why you were hiding."

Sniffing again, I looked at the two and said rather quietly, "I had hoped he would show up and talk to you by himself. He doesn't need some preacher trying to theologize everything."

"He? Oh, you mean the guy you were going to ask to meet us?" Sonny looked around, "Did he tell you he would be here?"

"No, unfortunately calling him is like most phone calls today. No answer," I said.

Sonny replied, "Hey, maybe it's like praying. Sometimes you don't get an immediate answer, you just have to leave a message."

"Who is this person?" Sandra asked. "Is it a college professor? A wise old preacher? A scientist who is a Christian?"

"No. No. No. You could never guess and if I had told you who he was, you probably would not have come tonight," I looked down the street. Then I even looked up in the air as if I expected the guest to drop in on a parachute. "And it looks like he's not going to make it tonight. He's pretty busy these days."

"How did you meet him?" Sonny asked, looking down the street, up in the air, and even behind one of the rose bushes.

+ + +

I sat down on a bench that faced the one they had been occupying. I waved them down beside me and said, "It was a night just about like tonight- right before Easter. I didn't go home for the holidays because I had a job and a lot of work to do my senior year at Samford. The problem of evolution was eating my guts out. Excuse me, Sandra. But I couldn't sleep well, couldn't think of anything much. Here I was about to graduate and planning to enter the seminary- and I wasn't sure if I even believed there was an Adam. If Adam is just a story, symbolic or not, how do you know that Moses was real? How do we know the ten commandments were given by God; what if they were just made up?"

Sonny interrupted, "Yea. That's a problem I've got. So many of the guys and gals at the University sleep with each other and laugh about it. When they ask me why I'm still a virgin, I respond that God commanded us not to commit adultery. It's a sin. They laugh at that and then they laugh at me. They say the Bible's just a book for fools."

"They've got it backwards," Sandra replied. "The Bible is a book for people who are not fools. The Bible informs us- the fool says in his heart there is no God."

"Good for you, Sandra." I continued, "That night I had prayed and prayed for God to give me some sign or some knowledge as to which was right- Evolution or Creation. In my room I told him to answer me- just to turn on the light in my room. I had turned it off to try to sleep. Being unable to sleep I was sitting at my desk in the dark. "Show me a sign, Lord, show me which is right. Let there be light!"

I stopped, looked at the ground, at the cross and then at the couple.

"What happened, Preach?" Sonny asked.

Sandra was spell bound. "Did the light come on?"

"Yep," I smiled and answered looking up in the sky again. "That light came on just as sure as I'm sitting here. It stayed on about thirty seconds than it faded out."

"What did you do then?" Sonny asked.

"Believe it or not. after the shock was over, I started laughing."

"Laughing?"

"Yea, I realized what a great God we have, how powerful He is and what a great sense of humor He possesses. You see, I told God to turn on the light. I forgot to tell Him whether a lit light meant Creation was correct or whether Evolution was right."

"You had a miracle take place and didn't know what it meant?" Sonny snorted with laughter. Sandra joined in as they all added the sound of joyful laughter to the gurgling water and the smells of springtime.

Finally I calmed down and said, "I was lucky to get by with a thirty second light flash. God gave Paul a light and it blinded him for three days. You know, we have miracles take place all around us and too often we fail to see what they mean. Like tonight- see that moon up there following God's laws so completely that it turns full on an exact schedule. See how these roses are so beautiful and smell so wonderful. And there's both of you, examples of young life at its best. Miracles. Unfortunately, many believe all of this just happened when good traits were passed along and bad traits became extinct."

"Did the light experience solve your problem about Adam?" Sonny asked.

"No. It took more than that. That was just God's way of letting me know He's still around. Something else happened that night and I haven't told a living soul." I stood to my feet, and looked as if I were going to leave without even telling them.

"Aren't you going to tell us the rest?" Sonny pleaded. "That hasn't helped me. No light has come on in my brain."

"God works with different people in different ways. He burned a bush for Moses- closed the mouths of the lions for Daniel- and gave Isaiah visions of the coming Messiah. He gave tongues of fire at Pentecost and even a great light for Paul. But He doesn't do any of those for just everybody. Most people just have to live on faith." I turned and started back toward his house. "I'm sorry, Sonny, you'll just have to work it out yourself. I'll pray for you."

+ + +

Sonny sat down dejectedly next to Sandra. She put her arm around him and tried to console him when all three of us heard the voice at the same time. Sonny thought it was someone passing by; Sandra thought it was the preacher joking with them. At first I was sure it was his old deacon, One-eyed Jack, playing a prank on all of us.

The voice was clear. It rang out once again, "Chris Christian, why don't you tell them what happened that night?"

The man was standing by the cross at the top of the fountain. He just appeared out of nowhere. We had not heard footsteps nor rose bushes rustling.

At first he looked at me and winked. As he turned, Sonny and Sandra saw two blue-green eyes staring at them as if he had known them for a long, long time. The kindest smile they had ever seen decorated his face. Silver hair fell shoulder length and radiated an aura of light about his head. We could see a smile glowing between his bushy beard and mustache. With the perfect posture of an English butler, he walked down on top of the waters of the fountain. Sandra thought he must be one of the painters who had been at the courthouse that day, for he had on a solid white shirt and pants and shoes. But there was not a drop of paint on them. Again, there was a glow from his garments, his face, his hands. He had long hair and a beard, but seemed young and spirited.

Sonny wondered if it were the Lord appearing- he wanted to see the nail prints in his hands, but the man laughed and said, "I know who you think I might be. He turned his palms toward him. Not a scar. I am not worthy to bear the pain and sin he bore."

With that he turned and shook my hand then hugged me with a strength greater than the young football player.

I smiled like a silly child as I said, "I didn't know if you got my message today or not."

"Oh, we get all the requests. Some we answer 'No,' some 'Yes' and some, 'Wait a while.'" He turned and once again radiated his smile and gaze and love toward the young couple. "Ah, it does me good to see folks in love again. There is so much hatred in the world. Bless both of you, my children."

"Thanks," Sonny said. "But who are you?"

"Oh, forgive me," I blurted out. "This is the person who helped me. He popped up that night at Samford. He explained to me the hidden mysteries of God."

"God has hidden mysteries?," Sonny asked.

"Sure," the smiling man explained, "God chose to hide the great things of this earth so man would have to discover them He hid gold and silver deep in the ground along with jewels of all kinds. Pearls were buried in oysters in the deep sea. For the reason that God alone knows, He hid the great secrets of life and death for man to discover. The Law of Gravity was as plain as the nose on everybody's face but was unknown until Newton discovered it. What about electricity? It had been around since creation, but it took Benjamin Franklyn to explain it to you. Because Einstein was a genius, he was the first to figure out that energy and matter are connected."

"$E=mc^2$," Sonny raised his hand.

The man grinned, "But that's not the whole equation of matter nor energy. Nor is it the answer to the Universe. God hid treasures to be found down through the years. So now man has found Evolution and some of the mad scientists are quite pleased with themselves and are saying, 'Eureka, we have found it!' It seems they would be smart enough to know they have only found a small part of 'IT.' Why, they have even discovered black holes and the big bang. But they have no idea who makes black holes nor who the Big Banger was."

He sat down on the bench, stretched his arms and legs, then said, "Now where was I? Oh yes! You have scientists who think they are the most brilliant people on the planet- yet they believe in a Creation and Creatures without a

Creator. Utter nonsense. When you ask them what was before the big bang, they hum-haw around and say that they cannot know. If you ask them how life arose, they beat around the bushes and finally admit they don't have the faintest idea."

"But you revealed some secrets to Brother Chris. Why hasn't he told us all about them?" Sonny asked, looking from the man in white to the preacher.

"Did you know that Copernicus knew the world was round, but that if he told anyone he would be burned by the church?" I answered.

"Yea, but that was way back then. People were cruel and intolerant then. Now things have changed."

"Men haven't changed that much. Unfortunately, neither has the church. If Chris were to tell all that he knew about Creation and Adam, he would probably not be burned- but he would be thrown out of the church."

"No way, not you- Brother Chris. Why?"

"Because just as there was war in Heaven and war on earth, there is forever a war going on in the church. Often it's Catholic versus Protestant, or Calvinists against the Free-willers, and always it is the Conservative at war with the Liberals. You might as well know there is an ongoing war today between the Evolutionists and the Creationists."

"But all that is important is the truth."

"Not so. All that is important to any side is THEIR TRUTH. We're right and you are wrong. You see this attitude running rampart today with Christians, Jews, Moslems and Hindus. Even the peaceful Buddhists are becoming terrorists and demanding their way is the 'True Way'. If you don't believe as I do, I'll bomb you!"

Sonny slowly nodded his head in agreement as the man began talking, "So you see, my son, some truths have to be kept hidden until mankind is ready to accept them. Jesus was Lord way back before time was split in two. He was born hidden in a manger in a little known town called Bethlehem. God has all the time in the world, and He waits for the right time to reveal things to His people."

Sonny shook his head and turned back to Sandra. She just smiled and gave a little shrug of the shoulders affirming what was being said to her boyfriend.

"O.K. Let's say the time is right, but why are you going to tell me these great secrets?" Sonny asked.

The man said, "Simple. You are going to be a great football player. Very great. You will hold your faith and these secrets in high regard. When you have reached the right time of popularity, you will share these secrets with the world. Sandra will help you for she will become quite famous in the scientific world."

"And if I refuse?"

"God will find someone else. He burned many a bush in the desert before he caught Moses eye. He loves you and Sandra."

"What about Brother Chris?"

"Alas, he won't be real famous. But he will be a part of the team and be a witness to what you will discover. Is that all right with you, Reverend Chris Christian?"

"As Mary said, when you talked with her, "I am the Lord's servant. May it be to me as you have said,"" I said as I nodded toward the un-introduced man. "I think that's what he wants you to say now, Sonny."

"Brother Chris, who is this guy?" Sonny eyed the stranger then pointed to the man in the white outfit.

"Oh," I laughed. "Excuse me! I forgot to formally introduce you. This is my friend I met that night at Samford. He helped me. He will help you. I call him 'Gabe.'"

"Gabe?" Sonny asked out loud. "Gabe? Good Lord, you are the Archangel Gabriel, and I'm talking to you like you're some common man on the street."

Sonny fell to his knees. Gabriel walked over to him, patted him on the shoulder, then helped lift him up. "If I show you these mysteries, will you keep them along with Chris and Sandra? Then, when I tell you to share them with the world, will you do so?"

With a big grin, he shook Gabriel's hand and said, "Like Mary said, oh gosh, I forgot what she said. But whatever God wants me to do, dad gum, like my football, I'll do the best I can."

Gabe took his arm, hugged him close and said, "That's all God asks of everyone."

+ + +

Gabriel

CHAPTER 4
PREPARATION FOR TIME TRAVEL

G abriel motioned us to stand back as he said, "We hav[e]
tion for a little traveling."

"Do you mean time travel?" Sonny asked, as he looked around to see if Gabriel had some type of Orson Wells' Time Machine hidden behind the rose bushes.

"Um, you could call it that; however, where we are going there is no time as you know it- it's called Eternity."

"Are we going to die?" Sandra blurted out before she thought how that sounded.

Sonny grabbed her arm and said, "Thanks, but no thanks, we had rather stay around for a while. Why don't you just tell us the secrets of the universe- and we'll be satisfied."

"You're not going to *die*, you might say you're going to *fly*," I joked. When nobody laughed, I continued, "You mean we're going to fly to Heaven?"

"I was only putting it in terms you might relate to. Actually we are not going to fly, but we are going into another dimension- that of eternity."

"Eternity?" Sonny exclaimed. "But don't you have to die and go to Heaven for eternity?"

"That is the usual process. But you recall that Paul had a sneak preview in Second Corinthians 12:2-4.

> '*I know a man in Christ who fourteen years ago*
> *was caught up to the third Heaven.*
> *Whether it was in the body or out of the body I do not know--*
> *God knows.*
> *And I know that this man-- whether in the body or apart from the body*
> *I do not know,*
> *but God knows-- was caught up to paradise.*
> *He heard inexpressible things, things that man is not permitted to tell.*
> *(NIV)*'"

I interrupted and told the two young college students, "I had often wondered if Paul were talking about someone else or himself in that passage. But after you met with me years ago, Gabe, I now know that it was Paul who took the trip to third heaven- he just didn't want to sound arrogant."

"Plus, he probably feared people would worry him to death asking about details of Heaven," Sandra said.

"Or if he happened to see their mother-in-law there," Sonny laughed.

It was so good to say Gabriel again, so I laughed along as Sandra and Gabe looked at the young athlete pleased that he would make mother in law jokes at a time like this. I put my arm on Sonny's shoulder and said, "A preacher met an old friend one day and said, 'How is your wife?' The man answered, 'She's in Heaven.' The preacher stalled a moment and then said, 'Well, I'm sorry.' He thought that didn't sound right, so he said, 'Uh, I'm glad.' That didn't go over really well either so he cleared his throat and said, 'Well, I'm surprised!'"

While Sonny and I howled with laughter, Sandra tried to keep a straight face but Sonny's laughter was contagious. First she smiled then laughed out loud. We all stopped when Gabriel cleared his throat, rather loudly.

We looked and were glad he wasn't angry, he was smiling. "It's O.K. to laugh about death and Heaven, especially for us Christians. But did you know the reason there are so many jokes about death and graveyards is that we laugh at things we fear?"

I cleared my throat, shook, my head and said, "You know, that's right. We are afraid of death, so we laugh at it as a defense measure."

Gabriel nodded approval and said, "You three are not going to die- yet. Your body will die someday, of course, but your name is written in the Lamb's Book of Life not with pencil- but with the blood of the Lamb. So, as I told Mary and Joseph, 'Fear not.'"

He continued, "We are going into eternity. The reason is simple- here on earth you are bogged down with sins of the flesh, and your mind hops around like a bouncing ping pong ball. Plus, you humans have learned to doubt. You doubt everything and anything. Of course, you have had so many snake doctors, car salesmen and politicians, I'm surprised you can believe anything anymore. In eternity you will be free of sin, and your mind will be focused on the truth."

"Hmm, that explains a lot of things about my fragmented prayer life,' Sonny said.

"Mine, too," Sandra confessed.

"But how do we get to Eternity?" Sonny asked.

+ + +

"That is the easiest questions you've asked all night," Gabe responded. Suddenly the cross that usually stood twelve feet tall in the garden began to grow. The post in the ground stretched outward to about ten feet. Then it soared up and up into the Heavens. There was a pause. The arms of the cross began to elongate out and out and out until they disappeared from sight.

"It looks like the cross is reaching up to Heaven and all the way around the world," Sonny said.

"Correct."

At the point, a door opened in the cross just above the fountain. It looked like the door to Noah's ark. The base of the fountain began to rise until it stood about ten feet tall. The recycling water poured even faster down toward the pool which still stood at our feet. The waters then parted- one stream going to the left and one flowing to the right. Up from the ground then rose what looked at first like an old fashioned phone booth under each stream. The water poured into the top and sprinkled down inside.

"It's a shower," Sonny responded, "we're going to have to take a shower before we enter eternity. But I don't need one, because I showered and shampooed my hair just before I came over. Here, Gabe, take a whiff. I smell fresh as a daisy."

He held out his hand to the angel.

"Really?" Gabe asked.

Sonny looked- then his gaze turned into horror. His hand was rotten and smelled like a backed up toilet. Dirty pus-stained rags covered the leprous hands. He had come to the garden with a fresh shirt and a newly ironed pair of blue jeans. They were either gone or now covered over with an old army jacket that looked like he had been the prodigal son eating, sleeping and wallowing in the pig pen. As he pulled it up to inspect it, there was the smell of rotten eggs.

Sandra screamed as she looked at her once handsome boyfriend. His face was scarred, open sores dripped from his jaws. One eye was blackened shut, the other so red it looked as if it would burst open at any moment. In his hair were bugs and worms curling in and out.

Sonny turned to look at her and his mouth dropped in shock. His beautiful girlfriend looked like the witch in Snow White. Warts grew on her nose, mud was caked in her hair, ugly acne covered her once porcelain face. Her fingernails were broken and the smell of dog poop came from them. She had come to the park in a spring dress and light blue sweater. Now she wore an old overcoat like that of a homeless man she saw on television. It was ragged and dirty and reeked. Putting her hand into the pocket she pulled out a decomposing fish.

"What is this?" Sandra yelled at Gabriel.

"This is your sinful flesh," Gabriel stated. "You can't go into eternity like this."

"But she was saved when she was young," Sonny retorted. "I can see where I look like the garbage man- for my life was dirty before I was saved."

"And since..." Gabriel said.

"And since," he bowed his head. "I have ... yea... I have slipped many, many times. The internet makes pornography so available for us young hot blooded guys. And I, uh, looked at some of it."

"And..." Gabriel repeated.

"Sandra, you don't need to hear this. I am honest, I have kept myself from any woman, or man, for you. But, oh gosh, Gabriel- this is embarrassing. I would look at the porno in my room and I would ... oh boy... I would play with myself like boys do. I know that's a sin."

Sandra blushed at his openness, but I broke in with some Christian sex education, "Sonny, I should have talked with you. Masturbation is not a sin. It can become a sin if you practice it too much or if you practice it with other guys. But masturbation is something God gave you to control your sex drive. It is a form of satisfaction for the sexual river that runs within us men."

"So, it was not a sin?"

"You sinned because of the lust you created. Plus pornography will warp the normal sex drive into making you want to do abnormal things to satisfy your lustful drive. Pornography is wrong- it's a sin and should be shunned at all costs."

"Huh," Sonny smiled. "At least that took care of the guilt part I carried around about that, uh, part of my private life. Is that all?"

"Heavens, no," Gabriel said. "If all your sins were poured on you, you would be crushed to a bloody spot."

"What have I done to look like this?' Sandra asked. "I've tried to live a good life."

"And you have," Gabriel explained. "You are to be rewarded greatly for your good works and righteousness. But do you remember what Sonny said after he was saved?"

"He said something about he knew good works were just dirty rags but when he got to Heaven he wanted to present God with a whole truck full of them."

"Good, or as the Bible states it in Isaiah 64:6: "All of us have become like one who is unclean, and all our righteous acts are like filthy rags; we all shrivel up like a leaf, and like the wind our sins sweep us away. (NIV)"

"So these dirty bandages on my leprous hands are my good deeds, trying to cover my sin?" asked Sonny.

"Exactly. Sandra you have lived a good life but like the Bible states, 'For all have sinned and fall short of the glory of God, Romans 3:23 (NIV).'"

"So my sin is falling short?"

"Yes. And sometimes you don't even realize you have sinned. For example, your senior year you wanted to be Miss CROSS+ROADS for the Junior Senior Prom"

"She won it," I smiled.

"But before she won it, she was afraid Lily Mae Thompson might win," the angel answered then turned to Sandra. "Isn't that correct?"

Sandra blushed again, worse than she had when Sonny confessed one of his sins. "Lily Mae was very popular with the boys, if you know what I mean. And, uh, somebody told me she was having an affair with one of the black football players."

"Lily Mae was having an affair with Speedy Johnson? " Sonny asked.

"Well, Gabriel, sir, you need to know both of them had bad reputations."

Gabe nodded, "I know, but that rumor was not true. Sandra, you not only heard it, you told one of your best friends and made her promise not to tell. But she did, and then others told others. Lily Mae not only lost Miss CROSS+ROADS to you, she dropped out of school. Do you know why?"

"She, uh, no, I never really knew why."

"One of your friends told the rumor to her father, and he beat her with a belt. He told her that no daughter of his was going to have sex with any black man, so he threw her out of the house her senior year before graduation."

Sandra had tears in her eyes, "I never knew why…"

"Oh, that's not the end. Lily Mae Thompson went to Birmingham. Without a high school degree she walked and worked the streets. She contacted the HIV virus, developed AIDS and died in Atlanta in a home for girls like her."

Sandra was weeping, now. "Oh, my God, I am so sorry. Oh, Lord, forgive me. I should never have repeated that gossip. I should not even have listened. And I should have stood up to whoever told me that and said, 'I don't believe it. You and I will go and tell Lily Mae what is being said.' Then we could have stood up for her- whether it was true or not. I am so, so sorry."

Sandra sobbed loudly into her filthy hands and wiped them with her dirty sleeve.

Gabe put his hand on her. "Now, God will forgive you. That's the difference between Christians and non-Christians. Christians weep when they have sinned and ask God's forgiveness. Non-Christians either deny it, ignore it or are even are proud of their transgression."

Sonny knelt beside her, looked up at the cross towering into the heavens and said, "Oh Lord, forgive my many, many sins. Especially my sin of doubt."

"Those are good words both of you have said: 'I'm sorry,' and 'Lord, forgive me. But I want to teach you something.'"

Sonny and Sandra looked bewildered as Gabe said, "Now you surely can't get into eternity and Heaven looking and smelling like that So, I suggest both of you take a shower and clean up first."

Sonny took Sandra's arm as they started for the booth on the left. I grabbed his arm and said, "Separately!" Then I guided Sonny to the other shower, pushed him in and said, "Hurry up, I'm next."

Each lumbered into the booth where water from the fountain was spilling down like an old fashioned sprinkler. Sandra yelled, "There's no soap, no shampoo!"

"You won't need any," I answered remembering my first encounter with Gabriel years ago and the shower, then.

Sonny was filthy. He reached up and splashed his face. Surprised, he blinked his closed eye- and it opened. He felt his chin. The bruises and boils seemed to melt away. Then he washed over his rotting hand and found his fingers growing back, stronger than ever. He yelled out, "Sandra, wash yourself. Something is happening when you shower!"

The grime was so thick on him it looked like dirty water pouring over his hand and his clothes. He looked closer and discovered it was not water at all- it was blood- pouring over him. This blood was washing away the grime, the dirt, the sin and the guilt. Before his eyes the old coat evaporated and was washed down the drain. His pants and filthy underclothes foamed like carpet cleaner then slid down his legs where his shoes began to disappear.

Sandra cried out, "Sonny, it's the blood! It's the blood of Jesus and it's coming from the cross and washing away our sins."

Sandra sang out, *"What can wash away my sins?"*

Sonny answered, *"Nothing but the blood of Jesus."*

I joined in, *"What can make me whole again?"*

Sonny came in cue and on key, *"Nothing but the blood of Jesus."*

Gabriel joined then and we all sang out:

"Oh, precious is the flow that makes me white as snow.

No other fount I know, Nothing but the blood of Jesus."

"Sandra, I'm clean. It's wonderful. The sores and filth are gone. I wish you could see me, but, uh, I don't have any clothes on.," Sonny yelled from his shower stall.

"I don't have on anything either," she replied. "But I am not ashamed. This must be how Adam and Eve felt before the fall."

Sonny was silent for a moment, then said, "Yea, it's probably how they felt if there really had been an Adam and Eve."

Gabriel laughed. "It didn't wash all your doubt away did it? You would be surprised how much you two look like the original Adam and Eve. She was blonde- he had jet black hair. However, Adam's hair was a bit longer, and he had a handsome mustache and beard. But here, I can't have both of you bouncing around Heaven in your birthday suits. Put these on."

He reached through the curtain and gave Sandra the most beautiful gown she had ever seen. It glowed with cleanness- it radiated with purity. She took it and held it close to her face. "So this must be like the white robe that will be given to us in Heaven."

Sonny yelled, "Say, Sandra, this is some more outfit. It's better than the tacky coat I wore my first day at church. This is even better than my graduation robe."

Sandra emerged, and the two were undoubtedly the best looking couple CROSS+ROADS, Alabama, had ever seen. With a hand on her hip, Sandra displayed the robe like a French model walking down the runway at a fashion show. Sonny and I applauded.

"Your turn, Chris," Gabriel pointed to me.

"But, I have already been washed …" I stopped as I looked down at my sin-stained hands and felt my mouth fester with blisters. My shirt and pants were ragged; my shoes were worn; and the soles had dropped off. For some reason over my regular clothes I had on an old robe that was tattered and torn. I then confessed, "Like Paul, I forget- I, too, am the chief of sinners. Sandra, I heard about Lily Mae Thompson and the rumor about the affair. Since she didn't attend our church, I did not try to contact her nor her parents. Hmm, I didn't even attempt to find the football player. Later, I heard something about her father's running her off. But my sin was doing absolutely nothing. I didn't start the rumor nor did I pass it. But I didn't do anything to stop it. I often commit the damning sin of failure to do anything about a problem."

Looking at the shower stall, I walked in, pulled the curtain and sang,

"There is a fountain filled with blood, drawn from Immanuel's veins.
And sinners plunged beneath that blood, lose all their guilty stains."

+ + +

38

CHAPTER 5
THE DOOR IN THE CROSS

Sandra sighed as I stepped forth in my white gown, "Brother Chris, you look like Jesus emerging from the grave on Easter morning,"

"I smelled more like Lazarus before I went in," I replied.

At that moment a door opened at the foot of the cross. "Look at that!" Sonny exclaimed. "That must be the door leading into eternity. You have to go through the cross."

Sandra studied it, then said, "But it's not like a door into your house that swings horizontally. This door opened from top to bottom and is now stretched out before us like a bridge for us to enter. Oh, I get it. That's like the door to Noah's Ark. I've seen pictures of the animals parading in, two by two. They walk up the door and then are safe inside."

Sonny pondered then asked, "Brother Chris, didn't you tell us one time that the ark was built large enough for every person who lived at that time?"

"Yes, some theologians believe that."

"So when men refused to get on board the ark- animals had to be substituted?"

"It could have been something like that."

Sonny shrugged his shoulder inside his shiny white robe. "I forgot to tell you, I don't believe in Noah, either. My professors pointed out that no boat could hold two of every animal that existed then."

"What about two of all the animals in the known world?" I asked.

"Uh, the known world? I don't know anything about that. I never even thought about the animals in the Garden of Eden, except for the serpent."

"If Gabriel will take time, he may show you Adam in the year 4004 BC- and also let you take a glimpse at Noah, 2348 B.C."

"Will we have time?" Sandra asked.

"Time is no problem for me," Gabriel smiled. "We shall see what we shall see. First, let me explain about the door before you. We will enter on the first level, First Heaven. You will see the Big Bang which would blind you, and the light from Eternity would leave you sightless for all your life. But you won't have any trouble because your bodies were transfigured when you were washed in the blood a moment ago."

"Like Jesus at the transfiguration?" Sandra asked.

"Exactly. The Bible tells us Jesus was transfigured, but Moses and Elijah had also been transfigured so they could enter eternity."

"Jesus' robe shone just like mine," added Sonny Miller.

Gabriel interrupted, "Sonny, reach over and pick up that park bench for me." Puzzled Sonny walked over to the bench where he and Sandra had been sitting only a few minutes ago. He reached down to grab the back but his hand went right through it. He looked back at Gabriel then used both hands to grasp the unmoving bench. Both hands sliced through it like a knife cutting through butter.

"What in the world?" he mumbled.

"You are transfigured," Gabriel explained. "Sandra, do you remember studying atom and molecules. The center was the nucleus and the electrons spun around it, correct?"

"Yes. But there was a great deal of empty space between the electrons. If you burned off the electrons like some stars do, the whole earth would be reduced to the size of a ball, but weigh so much no one could lift it. Suppose you could remove the electrons but keep the space there?"

"The body would retain it's size, but without the chemical and electrical properties of the atoms and molecules, there would be nothing to hold it together."

"But if some kind of energy could hold the nuclei of the atom together and retain the space of the electrons, would it stay the same size?"

"Probably, but…"

"Then if that empty space in Sonny's hand were filled with energy instead of its natural makeup, what would his hand do when it reached out for an object."

Sonny scratched his head but it didn't disappear into his brain. He asked, "A transfigured hand could go through the open spaces in the object. So Jesus told Mary not to touch Him, because He had not yet gone to the Father. Was that because He had been transfigured?"

"Close," Gabriel said. "I'm very proud of your insight. But Jesus was Transformed at the Resurrection. Someday you will have transformed bodies in Heaven. But those are permanent. We are just using the temporary form to let you take a look at eternity. Remember at times the light will be very bright. However, you will not need *sun* glasses to see the *Son* of God. Little joke. Needless to say, your bodies would also be burned quickly into tiny ashes without transfigured bodies. So, are you ready to enter eternity?"

At that moment a meteorite flashed across the sky splintering the evening with its golden tail. With a bright explosion it disappeared. We all watched in awe, then Sandra said, "What a pity. That meteor must be several million years old and then to end up in a flash of light and then ... nothing."

Sonny laughed, "Don't feel too sorry for it, save your tears for the mayfly. The poor critter doesn't have a mouth, all it does is have sex, live one day and then it's gone, without any flash of light or explosion. Plus, nobody cares, not even it's a mayfly mama."

Sandra said, "I never realized time is so strange. If you could talk to a may-fly he would not believe we humans live an average of seventy years- over twenty five thousand days. That would seem impossibly long. But if we could have a conversation with the meteor who was millions of years old, he would say we were less than a mayfly."

Gabriel stood silently while the questions of time and space whirled around the minds of the mortals. Then he said quietly, "Follow me."

"What about my mom? Shouldn't I call and tell her I'll be gone for...- How long will we be gone?" Sandra asked.

"In Meteor life, we may be gone millions of years," Gabriel smiled. "But in Mayfly time, we will be back in a few minutes. Everything will be all right."

The angel walked quickly through the door in the cross and vanished. I ges-tured to both of them to follow me. Then I went through the door.

Sonny turned to Sandra and said, "Wow, just like in Star Wars. One minute you're here and the next you are light years away. This is exciting, let's go."

The football player grabbed the hand of his beautiful girlfriend and they marched boldly across the lowered door and through the opening. They disap-peared off the face of the earth.

+ + +

CHAPTER 6
THE VILLAIN APPEARS

Beelzebub

The figure stepped out of the shadows in time to see the cross rapidly shrinking back to its original size- twelve feet tall. The door had closed as surely as the one on Noah's ark. Everything looked just as it had- the roses bloomed, the night smelled of nature's perfume, the moon looked down on planet earth as it had a billion times.

Dressed in black leather pants, tight black shirt and a strange black headband, the man stood over thirty feet tall. He looked down at the small cross beneath him, then seemed to realize his size was inappropriate. In slow motion his features shrunk down to five feet ten. But that seemed to bother him, so he swelled back up to six feet five.

His black hair was slicked back and fell in a pony tail. The eyebrows were thick and met each other over his crooked nose. Thin, tight lips sneered from beneath the straggly mustache and the messy beard. Red flames danced within his black eyes. He smelled of putrid sulfur. If anyone from the little town had seen him, they would have thought him a left-over from a Halloween party.

In the Old Testament even the Jews had worshipped him at times and called him the Baal. When the Scriptures were translated from Hebrew to Greek, the Septuagint called him *Baal Myian*, "Lord of the Flies." In the third chapter of the Gospel of Mark, verse 22, the Pharisees accuse Jesus of driving demons out by the power of Beelzeboul, prince of demons. Later his name would change into the one by which we know him- *Beelzebub.*

Thanks to John Milton's *Paradise Lost*, he was exposed as one of the many fallen angels, second in command only to Lucifer. In John Bunyan's famous *The Pilgrim's Progress*, Beelzebub shows up as a main character. Whatever his name, he was good buddies with Adolph Hitler and was known to hang out with Ted Bundy, the Mafia and even had friends among many of the intellectuals who called themselves scientists. He had shown up in many "Christian" groups which were merely cults and sects led by false teachers and prophets.

The man in black raised one finger with its long black finger nail to his nose, scratched it, drew some blood, sniffed it, then licked it off with his long black tongue. Walking over to the cross, he spat on it, then declared in his rasping voice, "You stupid cross. You betrayed us. My Lord Lucifer and I had planned the perfect trap for Jesus. 'Jesus,' where did he get that silly name? From that blundering Joshua who fit the battle of Jericho? When I knew him in Heaven before the fall, He was the Son. I never liked him- so loving, so kind. Yuk! Lord Lucifer and I almost overthrew Him and his Father and the Spirit in their complicated Godhead that nobody could ever understand."

"But you- you crooked cross, you let us down!" He kicked the wood as he said this, then howled in pain. Anger sparked from him in bursts of blue lightning because he was so upset that he, the Prince of Demons, had stubbed his toe on the cross. "You were set up to be our sign of victory- stupid wood. You would have become a well worshipped god if you had done your business correctly. All our planning and scheming resulted in the Final Solution. We would kill God the Son in the most humiliating way, crucifixion. Even the priest and religious leaders were in our plan- this Jesus was to die and stay dead. "

Shaking his fish toward Heaven, Beelzebub rambled on. "What a party we had that Friday afternoon. All of us fallen angels were sure we had cut off the redemptive part of God. Oh, we remembered when The Creator created those wretched human creatures. We rejoiced when Lord Lucifer tricked Adam and Eve and they fell from Paradise. At the crucifixion we had a great celebration- we had killed off the human's god."

"On Saturday, lost angels from all over space came to make merry with us. It was undoubtedly the grandest of all Hell's festivities. We even planned a holiday for these pitiful humans to celebrate. We would call Friday 'Xmas.' The 'X' would stand for Christ whom He thought He was, but we demons had 'X'ed him out, got rid of him once and for all. He dared become flesh, so we killed that flesh. Then Saturday, the first day we were free of their goody-goody rules over us, we would name it 'Lucifer Day.' I had personally wanted the next day, their Sunday, to be named 'Beelzebub Day.'"

Then he raised his head back and howled like a wolf and cried out, "But then came Sunday, and He ruined it all of me and for us. Who ever could have imagined He would be resurrected? He fooled us and his dumb disciples. The stone was rolled back and he walked out into the Garden and into eternity. And you, you stupid cross, became the symbol not of our win but of His victory. Oh, how I hate you."

He was so angry he kicked the cross again, then yelled because he stubbed another toe. Hobbling over to the bench, he sat and fumed and thought and thought. "Lucifer sent me here to this hick town, CROSS+ROADS. Ugh, I hate your name, 'CROSS-Roads'. But my lord sent me here to find out why Gabriel had come to earth. We remember that tragic day when he visited Miss Prissy Virgin Mary. Ha, he would have a hard time now finding a virgin. But this Sandra Hall fits the bill. Is Jesus going to be born of a virgin again for the second coming? Our Devilogians can't figure out how or when He's coming back. Will it be on a cloud, on a horse, in the middle of the night? Lucifer laughed and told us it would be on a Monday, for it would be a day when no man thinketh."

He stood and smelled the roses. The petals withered up and died. Kicking them he yelled again as a deep thorn was now embedded in his stubbed toe. Carefully he picked it out. *"A thorn in the flesh.* Paul had one. Some think it was his eyesight but I like to think it was me. I was assigned to that know-it-all apostle and kept trouble stirred up for him from the Philippian jail to the crowd in Ephesus. They were disturbed because they were worshipping my sister, the fallen angel, Artemis, or as the Romans called her, Diana. I almost had Paul murdered in Jerusalem, like his Jesus. But no, he got away. With Paul in chains in Rome, we figured we had shut him down or at least shut him up. But he wrote and wrote and wrote all those letters that God inspired. When Nero had him beheaded we celebrated- but it was like destroying a pumpkin by rolling it down to crash on the hillside. Out popped all kind of seeds that would sprout and grow up in Rome and then around the world."

"So what is Gabriel up to now? Is he here for the virgin Sandra? Or could it be that goofy two-bit preacher, Chris Christian? What a heretical name! It couldn't possibly be that football jock, Sonny Miller! I was standing close enough to hear their conversation, but the goody-good Angels caused some kind of interference so I couldn't hear most of what they said. What harm could a football player do to us? Or what good could he do for God?"

"I'll just wait around for them to return. Maybe I can figure out what this is all about. Unfortunately I can't do anything to Gabriel, but the boy and the girl! Maybe we can use this cross here in this dumpy town for something other than a decoration."

Beelzebub snickered as he walked back across the street and elevated himself back up to his thirty feet. It was just in time as a car came around the corner, its headlights shining through the park and lighting up the cross. A young voice called out, "Oh Daddy, look! The cross! I just love the cross of Jesus."

As the car sped away, the Prince of Demons cursed and punched the big oak tree. He bruised his hand.

+ + +

PART 2 FIRST HEAVEN

CHAPTER 7
THROUGH THE OPEN DOOR

Once the door to the cross slammed shut behind us, we floated rather than walked up a dark passageway. In the distance we could hear dull thunder, then a speck of light appeared like the first star of the evening. Sonny was the first to react. "Hey look, just as the Scripture says, 'There is a light at the end of the tunnel.'"

"That's not in the Bible," I explained to the young athlete as we seemed to accelerate in speed. In the darkness stars appeared, glowed brightly, then disappeared. Comets flashed by. Galaxies unwound from the center, stretched beyond our imaginations, then collapsed back into themselves as if swallowed by monstrous black holes. Now the lights were flying by so fast that Sonny yelled out again, "I think we are about to reach the speed of light! This is faster than I've ever been. Wheee!"

The light was growing brighter and larger until soon it filled both horizons. We stopped with a jolt. Whatever magic carpet or ray of sunshine we had been traveling either ran out of energy or reached it's destination.

We all were standing in midair. Sandra looked down and screamed as she realized there was nothing under her but space. Sonny grabbed her and then he looked for something to hold. But they didn't fall. I smiled an I've-been-here before-and-you-haven't smile.

In a few seconds all of us hovered over a blue planet.

CHAPTER 8
THE EARTH

I recited very slowly and very clearly,
*"In the Beginning God created
the Heaven and the Earth."*
Then I said, "Sandra and Sonny, that Scripture was read to the entire world on December 24, 1968."

Gabriel remembered it well. He quoted, "Apollo 8, the first manned mission to the Moon, entered lunar orbit on Christmas Eve, December, 1968. America was about to receive a unique Christmas present. That evening, the astronauts, Commander Frank Borman, Command Module Pilot Jim Lovell, and Lunar Module Pilot William Anders, did a live television broadcast from Lunar Orbit, in which they showed pictures of the Earth and Moon seen from Apollo 8.

"Lovell said, 'The vast loneliness is awe-inspiring, and it makes you realize just what you have back there on Earth.'

"They ended the broadcast with the crew taking turns reading from the book of Genesis. William Anders read, 'For all the people on Earth the crew of Apollo 8 has a message we would like to send you'.

'In the beginning God created the Heavens and the earth.

"Others read until the Creation story until Commander Borman added, 'And from the crew of Apollo eight, we close with good night, good luck, a Merry Christmas, and God bless all of you - all of you on the good Earth.'"

I breathed a sigh and then said, "Wow! They wouldn't be allowed to make those religious statements now. They sure couldn't read from the Bible. They would probably have to wish everyone a Happy Holiday, and end up asking the force to bless all of us."

+++

CHAPTER
A LOOK AT CROSS+ROADS

The view was spectacular!

"Would you like to take a look at CROSS+ROADS before we begin out journey?" Gabriel asked.

"Sure," Sonny said, as the planet began to grow larger and larger, until they could see continents and oceans. Then America could be discerned by its shape. Finally we saw clouds covering out little town but we burst through them.

"There's the church!" Sandra exclaimed. "I can see the Cross Park where we stood a few moments ago.

Sonny added, "And there's the football field and the school."

"Look at that!" I stated. "In the backyard I can see my kids playing. Wow, I wish Chuck could be with me, he would love the adventure."

"What about your daughters?" someone asked.

"Oh, they would be scared to death, and screaming to get down and back in their house."

"Say 'Good-bye' for a little while," Gabriel smiled. "We are going back thirteen billion years to the big bang- and then travel around in eternity."

"Thirteen billion years!" Sonny shouted.

"When we get back, everything will be gone- CROSS+ROADS will probably be a ghost town and the football field will be a corn field.

"But the church shall remain," I said with a spiritual overtone! "Earth and heaven shall pass away but my word will remain forever!"

"Relax," Gabriel said. "In earth time we will only be gone a few minutes.

"So I will be home in time for a midnight snack?" Sonny asked.

"Promise," Gabriel said.

+++

CHAPTER 10
BACK THROUGH HISTORY

The world whirled beneath us as we started our backward search. Beneath us satellites circled the world. Smoke and the flare of battles blurred past. Huge explosions sent mushroom clouds spewing into the air. We heard screams. Often the smell of death and rotting flesh rose up toward us and made us gag. Independence Hall raced beneath us as we saw images of the forefathers signing the Declaration of Independence. Puritans stepped forth on Plymouth Rock.

Huge cathedrals rose magnificently in the sky dedicated to the glory of God.

Sailing ships crisscrossed the seas. Realizing we were soaring backwards, we searched until we spied three ships with Spanish flags landing on an island beach and claim the New World for Spain and the Lord.

Thousands of men journeyed on Crusades to recapture the Holy City. Barbarians roared through villages and towns. The sun rose in the west and sank again and again and again in the east. Swimming across the sky were meteorites and comets. Hurricanes smashed against islands, and volcanoes exploded spewing ash halfway around the world.

We slowed down over what is now Israel and saw three crosses against the sky. Soldiers gambled as blood dripped down from the center figure. Crowds of people rushed back and forth following the Carpenter from Galilee. A star blazed in the Heavens, three wise men on camels trotted toward the east. Angels sang. Shepherds ran. A cave was spotted with an unusual glow and Sandra cried out, "Stop, please stop. We have to see the birth of our Lord. Stop and let's look at the baby Jesus."

"Not now," Gabriel explained as the scene disappeared. "Maybe later."

Thousands of men and women lay on battlefields. Villages burned. Temples rose from ruins, stood and then fell apart as workmen shuffled about. We saw Israelites being dragged from Jerusalem to foreign lands.

Below us an angry sea split in two, and thousands of people marched onto the dry land. An old man with a gray beard led them safely to the far side. The Exodus then disappeared in the sands of time.

Egyptian pyramids were spotted. Cavemen grunted and hunted in what would one day be Europe. We slowed as we saw an ark sitting among some mountains near the Black Sea. Gabriel let us fly low enough to see a man and woman coming out of a beautiful garden.

"Stop," Sonny said. "There they are. We can stop here and find out the truth."

"Not yet," Gabriel shouted through the whistling wind. "We have to go way, way back beyond here."

Now we zoomed faster and faster into the past. Vegetation began to disappear as the earth looked more and more like the dark side of the moon. A monstrous explosion threw water and land into the air. Then we could see the cause, a meteorite miles wide. Jungles covered the earth, dinosaurs roamed and fought and killed.

Light and time and history blurred past us until we saw a molten earth glowing red. A young sun spread light on us. Our minds boggled at how fast we were flying into history and exactly how far back we had gone. There were no calendars, no one to ask, "Say, would you mind telling me the time of day. And while you are at it, could you tell me if we are four million B.C. or five billion B.C.?"

Gabriel guided us to the edge of the universe and we watched a scene we had witnessed earlier. Stars and galaxies stretched beyond our imagination. In seconds they were sucked inward. Whirling and flashing they grew smaller and brighter until they imploded into the Big Bang.

"Wowee," Sonny whistled as everything quieted down. "If Six Flags could make a ride like that, we would become millionaires. Is this the end of the ride?"

"Heavens, no," Gabriel answered. "We have only come a very short way. We are going to stop reviewing time and space. Now we must enter Eternity. We can't go back to the very first because there is really no beginning. Don't worry, I'll try to explain that later. We are going to whiz past Lucifer and his group being downloaded form Heaven. I'll tell you about that in due time."

With that, we hurdled backwards so fast, nothing could be seen. When we slowed down, angels filled the air like stars. Love and peace seemed to fill the air around us. We could hear the angels laughing and feel the joy that radiated around us like the smell of fresh cinnamon rolls that fill the whole house.

A glow much brighter than any Super Nova ever seen. As we four zoomed closer, Sonny cried out, "It's a man! A gigantic man made of pure burning energy!"

+++

CHAPTER 11
WOULD YOU LIKE TO SEE GOD?

Rapidly the angels disappeared, then there was only light. As far as we could see there was nothing but radiant, dazzling streams of light. There were no dark spots, no blackness, no night. In the midst of all this there was a pulsating form that looked like a man!

Gabriedl smile then asked " Sonny and Sandra, would you like to see God?"

It was a sight never seen before. Three tiny dots of human beings, accompanied by a teeny Gabriel, hanging in space before a Being larger than a galaxy. All was so bright that we could not see any details of the face but the arms and legs were shrouded in a gleaming gown that resembled the Milky Way.

"Wow!" Sonny said. "Is this the very beginning? Is this where it all started?"

"Of course not!" Gabriel said a bit louder than he had intended. "This is where I began. But there is no starting point for God. He was. He is. He will be."

"That doesn't make any sense," Sonny said.

"So when does everything have to make sense to us? We are only humans," I answered. "Gabriel explained it to me this way. Let's say we were back to CROSS+ROADS and you decided to go north. How far north can you go?"

"Well, I haven't been very far. Let's see, we did go up north to play the University of Tennessee at Knoxville last year," he answered. Then he grinned, "And we beat the dog out of them."

"Sonny, you went to Lexington, Kentucky, last year with the team," Sandra added. "I've been further north than Sonny. My parents took me to Canada to see Niagara Falls."

Sonny laughed, "At school, we call it Viagra Falls."

Sandra gave him a quick look and nodded toward the huge form of God looming in the distance.

"Uh," Sonny stammered, "I mean some of the other guys called it... Heck, I don't want to lie in the presence of God, I made the joke up. And I must confess, we had a lot of other Viagra jokes."

Sandra whispered, "This is not the time nor place."

"Right," Sonny said. "So, Preach, what does traveling north have to do with God? Are you trying to tell us He hides out at the North Pole like Santa?"

"Absolutely not!" I answered. "I am trying to help you understand that if you did travel all the way to Santa's land, or the North Pole, which direction would you take from there?"

Sonny scratched his head again, remembering he had done a lot of that since early afternoon. "Well, I guess if you are at the North Pole, any direction you take would be south."

Applause rose from the other two, and Sonny took an exaggerated bow.

"But," I continued my geography lesson, "If you traveled west from CROSS+ROADS, how far west can you go?"

"That's easy," Sonny answered. "you can go west all the way to California. I've been there when we were underdogs to Southern Cal. I remember well. Trailing five points, we were behind with the clock winding down. We were at the five yard line with five seconds left. A field goal would not be enough. We had used our last timeout but we had a special play. I posted up as a wide receiver, the ball was snapped, the quarterback rolled to his right as if to throw a pass into the end zone. Southern Cal had us covered, but I took off running left; the quarterback faked the ball to me, then pulled his arm back to pass. A huge defensive tackle zeroed in on him and tackled him. The California crowd stood to cheer, but what they hadn't seen was a new version of the old Statue of Liberty play. Just as the quarterback was jolted down, I turned around and ran behind him. He flipped the ball to me. I raced around the right end and into the end zone. Ta da! We won!"

Gabriel was quiet for a moment. "I know, I was there."

"You go to football games?"

"Only if one of God's chosen has to make a big play at the end of the game."

"You didn't have anything to do..."

"Quite contraire, my dear young hero," Gabriel smiled softly. "If you must know, that ball would have been fumbled as your quarterback went down. I was there, to, uh, give it a little tap to bounce it up into your hands. Plus, Southern Cal's defensive back could have tackled you easily ."

"Yea, I remember. He saw me coming around the end, but he shook his head as if he had lost me. Maybe the sun got in his eyes."

"You could say that," Gabriel responded. "Something distracted him. Hmm, I wonder what or who it could have been?"

"You throw ball games?"

"I wouldn't use that term," Gabriel blushed. "Let's just say, on occasions we help our team members out."

"Wow!" Sonny said. "I mean, thanks. Uh, I sure don't understand God very well."

Reflecting, Gabriel said, "Perhaps the best way you can understand God and time is to think of a stick with only one end."

Sonny scratched his head and tried to picture a stick with only one end. Finally he shrugged realizing there were things beyond his mentality. Behind us the giant form continued to vibrate as if shaken by humongous earthquakes. We all turned and looked as a crimson circle appeared in the solid white figure. Brilliant red bursts exploded throughout, then the bright white light returned.

I said, "O.K., Sonny, you've been west all the way to Los Angeles. We all watched the game on television, and my wife was so excited when you scored she jumped up, hit our lamp, knocked it over and broke it. But it was worth it."

"What about heading west?" Sandra asked.

"Oh, yea," I continued. "Sonny, you can go further west than California."

"I forgot about Hawaii," he answered.

"You're missing the point," I said. "You can go west all the way to China, then into Europe, back across the Atlantic, make your way through Georgia, come back to CROSS+ROADS, Alabama, U.S.A. Now if you continue going west, when will you be going east?"

Sonny was quiet as if trying to remember which direction you go on a pass play. Putting his left hand out before him, he drew a line across it with the index finger of his right hand. Using his fingers, he tiptoed up his fingers to the top and said. "Now I can go north to the North Pole but when I pass it I go south toward the South Pole." He walked his fingers down the back of his hand and under his palm. "But when I cross the South Pole, I go north again. " Then he finger walked across his palm, "And I can go west to the Pacific." Turning his hand over, he continued, "Then I can continue west through Asia and Europe and the Atlantic and Georgia and Eastern Alabama. But..." his eyes lighted up as if he had discovered a cure for cancer. "But I can't ever reach east by going west, it goes on and on and on forever." With that he swung his right hand around and around and around his left.

"So?" I asked. "Can you now see that we humans are bound by North and South? We can only go so far. It's that way with time. We start, we go, we stop. There are goal lines at each end. But God is East-West. He goes on and on forever."

"I don't fully understand it," Sonny confessed, "but I see what you're saying."

Sandra nodded her head in agreement, then asked, "Gabriel, why did you say that this was your beginning? I thought angels like God had just been around forever."

"No, we were created, just like you human beings. We have eternal life through Jesus, God's only begotten Son, because He created us in His image. You humans were created in His image but you fell and sin marred your resemblance to Him. With his death on the cross and His resurrection it is now possible to be recreated into His image. Through faith in Him you may have eternal life.

"That burst of red in the figure of God we saw a minute ago," Sonny asked. "did that have anything to do with your birth?"

"As a matter of fact it did," Gabriel answered. "I'll try to explain the colors of God in a little bit, but we need to deal with this in a better perspective. Now we are sized down to approximately that of an atom compared to God as being the world." The angel searched around on his robe until he seemed to discover another button. "Here, let's equalize this situation."

As he pushed the invisible knob, God began to shrink at a massive rate of speed until He was almost our size.

"Is this something like the incarnation?" Sandra asked. "Did we just see an example of the word not becoming flesh, but sizing down so we could understand better?"

"I couldn't have improved that definition myself," Gabriel beamed.

+ + +

100 Billion B.C.

Gabriel

CHAPTER 12
THE CREATION OF GABRIEL

As we watched, we saw an exact replica of Gabriel standing beside the brilliant white form of God. Gabriel wasn't moving- his eyes were closed.

"You aren't even breathing. You, I mean that other Gabriel, uh, the one over there that we are looking at, the original Gabriel." Sonny said a bit louder than he should have in the presence of God. "Come to think of it, I never realized angels breathed before. I knew you could talk, but... Oh well, live and learn."

"Of course we live and breathe." he answered. "In this history you are watching, I haven't taken my first breath yet. I'm, uh, the original Gabriel is in the process of being created."

"The process of creation?" Sandra asked. "I thought God could just say a word, 'Let there be an angel,' and there would be, well, an angel!."

"Of course, He can, if He wanted to. But God is in no hurry. He could say 'Light' and the sun could appear out of His mouth. For that matter all the stars could come tumbling out in one big breath of God. But that's not the way God usually works."

"I think we are about to get a lesson in creation and evolution," Sonny said.

"Evolution is a word man made up- you won't find it in the Bible," Gabriel explained. "To quote the popular internet encyclopedia, Wikipedia:

'Evolution is change.
It is a change in the inherited traits of a population
of organisms from one generation to the next.
These changes are caused by a combination of three main processes:
variation, reproduction, and selection.'"

"Television programs and science professors make Evolution sound like the Force from Star Wars," Sonny said. "Evolution is the driving force. Evolution caused us to grow eyes and ears. Evolution forced us to walk and be able to hunt. Evolution is..."

"Evolution has become a god," Gabriel said. "Quite honestly, if you listen to all they are saying, they are trying to explain all of God's creation by accidents and mutation."

"So God made angels, you are not the product of evolution?" Sonny asked. "That is a silly question," I answered this time. "But some teach God is the result of a type of evolution. As man's brain developed so did his thinking and his fears. He could not understand how the sun rose and the moon set. Because he had no explanation for all that exists, they say that man made god up as a reason."

"So," Sonny said, "we have man-made gods instead of god-made men."

"Exactly!" I replied. "Bless their hearts, they are trying so hard to prove God doesn't exist they will not even allow Intelligent Design to be taught in the class room."

"Let's make sure I've got that one down pat," Sonny said. "At the University they told us that Intelligent Design was a no-no- it was false, it was an unscientific explanation for creation."

"Did they also teach you that we angels just evolved in Heaven from cloud fluff and stray moon beams?" Gabriel grinned.

"I don't think they believe in angels but if they did, I'm sure they would say some spiritual molecule learned how to fly and grew a body and wings and a white robe and a halo around itself," Sandra laughed. "But they would insist it took at least six billion years."

"That's about what it took," Gabriel said, "if you are thinking in earth years."

"Earth years?" Sonny asked. "You mean there are earth years and Heavenly years?"

"Not exactly," the angel explained. "Heaven is without time and space. Better, I could explain, Heaven is not limited to time and space."

"That, I do not understand."

"O.K., do you remember in the Bible where it states..."

Sandra interrupted, "I remember the Bible says that a day to the Lord is like a thousand years."

"Close," Gabriel replied, "In Psalm 94, verses 1 through 4:

Lord, you have been our dwelling place throughout all generations.
Before the mountains were born
or you brought forth the earth and the world,
from everlasting to everlasting you are God.
You turn men back to dust, saying, "Return to dust, O sons of men."
For a thousand years in your sight are like a day that has just gone by,
or like a watch in the night. (NIV)

"Or," Gabriel continued, "Old King James put it well,

*'For a thousand years in thy sight are but as **yesterday** when it is past,'"*

Sonny and Sandra looked at each other, then she stated, "'For a thousand years are but as yesterday.' That's interesting the way it is worded. It's like God is saying, 'Once upon a time, long, long ago, one yesterday was like a thousand years.' Could that be part of our time problem with evolution?"

"Good thinking," Gabriel said. "But we'll take a closer look when we get back to creation of time and space and man. Right now, I want you to understand I was not just a last minute thought by God."

As he was talking, a bright red figure slipped out of the white figure of God. The figure was shaped like a man and He reached out as if to tidy up the original Gabriel. Two red hands reached over the ears just as Jesus would one day heal the deaf. Nodding His head as if everything was ready for final approval, the scarlet hands reached out grabbing a handful of light.

Gabriel said quietly, "That is pure energy He is gathering. Now watch as he molds energy back into matter."

On cue, the red image rolled the crackling energy as it spat out lightning and sparks. When it calmed down and cooled down, we saw two eyes. They were the same blue-green color of Gabriel's. Carefully they were inserted into the sockets. The red fingers pulled two eyelids over them. The crimson figure nodded his head as if all were finished.

The red figure dissolved back into the white form of God. Bright blue lights exploded in the white form. Red lights blinked in response. There was a pause, then the most beautiful yellow light came on softly and slowly. There were three short bursts of red, yellow and blue.

+ + +

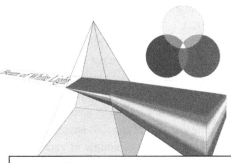

CHAPTER 13
WHAT COLOR IS GOD?

Sandra turned to the real Gabriel and said, "It looks like the blue said something to the red. Then the yellow said something and all three, well, it looked like they laughed!"

Sir Isaac Newton Discovered that White Light is composed of Red, Yellow and Blue Light.

"My, my, the secret is out," sighed Gabriel. "I didn't think humans would ever figure it out. The three short bursts of all three colors? You are very sharp to discern that was laughter. God has a sense of humor.."

"I had figured that one out after meeting some of his creatures," I said.

"What did they laugh about? I mean what did He laugh about?" asked Sonny. "This is terribly confusing."

"It was laughter of approval- all three lauded my Creation!" Gabriel laughed a hearty chuckle. "God made me in His image, just as He made you. Now take a good sniff and tell me what happens. "

All three humans took a deep breath. Smiles appeared on all faces. "It's like apple pie and ice cream," Sonny blurted.

"More like an expensive perfume," Sandra added.

I sniffed again and said, "Fried chicken, mashed potatoes with gravy, turnip greens, fresh cornbread, and coconut cake. I had forgotten that Heaven has a sweet, sweet smell."

"Why do you think the Catholics and a lot of other religions are always burning incense?" Gabriel asked.

"Hold on a minute and watch this and maybe you will understand a little more."

The Red Form reemerged, grabbed a handful of energy, ground it into the form of a nose and placed it in the center of the angel's head. His crimson mouth hovered over the inactive nose. Bolts of lightning of all three colors shot forth into the Angel's nostrils. The first Gabriel's body quivered. The Son's hand patted him on the back like a new born baby, as the first Gabriel sucked in a deep breath of Heavenly air.

Blue-green eyes opened and looked into the face of the Son. Smiles appeared on the faces of both angel and the Son. They looked at each other for a moment then two white arms of light reached out and hugged the original Gabriel.

"Wow, that is really sweet," Sandra said. "I knew God loved us humans, but it never dawned on me that God loved the angels."

"God is love," was the reply.

"What about the light show? What was that?" asked Sonny.

"In time," Gabriel answered. "Let's review. What you just experienced was the creation of the first angel, mainly me. Remember this was not done in a few earth minutes, a couple of earth hours, or even several earth years. Six billion earth years went into my creation."

"Why so long?"

"Not long at all for God. You can't imagine how extensive eternity is. Everything had to be created correctly. God the Son took a small piece of energy, molded it into a bit about the size of one of your atoms. He had to do this with many different types of matter, to create a foundation for angel life. Then those atoms had to learn how to form Celestial molecules. That's not easy, you know. After a billion earth years or so, the Heavenly matter had progressed to where it could bond with other bits of matter. God had to teach it how to reproduce. For you humans that doesn't seem to take too long, but have you noticed that a new baby cannot replicate itself. A baby has very little interest in sex at all until curiosity takes over in pre-teens. Even at teenage, the interest is not in birthing but in pleasure."

"That was a mistake God made with you. We angels don't reproduce, but our Heavenly atoms had to learn how. Subsequently there were little squiggly bits of matter after another long period of your time. Much of this took place in the Glassy Sea."

"You have a sea in Heaven?" Sonny asked.

"Haven't you ever read Revelation? We have a Glassy Sea plus rivers and trees. It's quite beautiful, you know. In fact, the Garden of Eden was really just a colony of Heaven on Earth. Jesus even told you to pray that God's Kingdom would come again on earth as it is in Heaven."

"Gee, I always thought of Heaven as being rather, uh, ..."

"Dull?" Gabriel finished the sentence. "When you have a God who approves the creation of angels, don't you think He can come up with some fun times for all his children?"

"So you have fun in Heaven? Did it start when you were created?"

"No. The Triune God has always been happy. He is Love, Joy and Peace. What you call fun, we call Joy. It's happiness with as many zeroes beside it as there are light years in the universe."

"But did God have joy before you were created?"

"Glad you asked. Now comes some new lessons in theology," Gabriel said. "Before I was created, there were billions upon billions of what you call earth years. It was kind of like…"

"East and west!" Sonny said. "Eternity is like a circle, no beginning, no ending."

"Very good." Gabriel answered.

We watched God and the newly created form of the original archangel Gabriel drift away into the white space. "Let me see if you can get this. God is a Triune God. He is Father, Son and Spirit."

"I know that but I don't begin to understand it," answered Sandra. "Remember, Pastor, I used the analogy of water being one, but it can be experienced as liquid water, solid ice or gaseous steam. I thought that was pretty good."

"We were taught that God is three persons," Sonny chimed in. "It's like the old actors could play three different parts in a drama by putting on three different masks."

I added, "We also were taught that just as I am a father to my three children, I am also a son to my parents, and a husband to my wife."

"Those are all good examples- for humans," Gabriel grinned. "We angels were made from pure light and pure energy, so it was easier for us to understand how God can be three in one. In fact, it makes so much sense, Chris, I am surprised you haven't shared this with your church members the facts of John 8:12:

When Jesus spoke again to the people, he said,
"I am the light of the world.
Whoever follows me will never walk in darkness,
but will have the light of life."
(John 8:12 NIV)

"So, God is light," Sandra said, "I have no problem with that."

"That's right, you are preparing to teach science. So you can tell Sonny a few facts about light," Gabriel said.

"To be honest, light is still an enigma. Some say it is energy, some say it is matter. It is unique. For years science thought that light was white. But Sir Isaac Newton used a prism…"

"A prison?" Sonny asked.

"No, silly, a prism. You know, a piece of glass that allows light to shine through it."

"I remember now. All the colors of the rainbow are refracted through the glass, and they shine on the wall or whatever," Sonny said quite proud of his knowledge.

"True. Sir Isaac Newton, however, went a step forward and found that there are three pure colors in the light," Sandra answered.

"Red, yellow and blue," Sonny replied. "All other colors are mixtures of those three."

"True, again. But that was not known before Sir Newton shone the light through a prism until it broke into all the different shades of the rainbow. He then isolated the red and made an amazing discovery: red cannot break up into other colors. For example, green is caused by a combination of ..."

"Blue and yellow," Sonny had the answer again. "I learned that in kindergarten."

'Sure, but Newton found you cannot separate or break down the colors of red, yellow and blue. So he concluded that white light is the presence of all colors. And red, yellow and blue are the primary colors. When all the colors are present, you have white."

"And I'll bet you a nickel," Sonny looked at the pastor, "*if* I gambled, that the absence of all color is black."

"You catch on quick," said Gabriel. "Now you understand why God and good are associated with light- and the Devil and evil are connected to darkness."

Sonny wandered over closer to Sandra and said, "I'll bet you a doughnut that the three colors we saw in God have something to do with the Trinity."

Sandra exploded with delight. "The Trinity. I think I understand. You take the three primary colors, red, yellow and blue, combine them and you have white."

"So God is made up of three colors?"

"Heavens, no." Gabriel laughed. "God is made up of three persons of light. God revealed to you a few minutes ago how the Son can separate from the Godhead to create an angel."

"So if a blue figure comes out, that is, uh," Sandra pondered, "that must be God the Father?"

"Through your human eyes, let's say God is represented by a Blue Form."

"Then the yellow light we saw is God the Spirit, as best we can visualize Him." Sonny was excited. "The White God is the Godhead- three in one. He can manifest Himself as the One, or He can separate out into the Red Son, the Blue Father or the Yellow Spirit."

Gabriel applauded happily. "Yes. But you must remember God is not Red, Yellow and Blue. Neither is He Red, White and Blue as Americans may think. To best understand how HE is three in one, you think of how three colors blend to make one."

"Is that the great secret you said you would reveal to us?" she asked.

"One of them," Gabriel stated. "Remember God is a mystery, and there are areas of Him you and I can never understand. We are Creatures, He is the Creator."

THE GOD HEAD
White Light

FATHER   SON   SPIRIT
Blue   Red   Yellow

The Triune God is Light.
Just as Red, Yellow and Blue
combine to make White-
so Father, Son and Holy Spirit
Unite to Form the Triune God.

CHAPTER 14
WAS GOD LONELY?

Love   Joy

Peace

I spoke up again, "So, Gabriel, God existed many billions of   light years before He created you."

"Wasn't He lonely?" Sonny asked.

"Now you are getting there," Gabriel remarked. "No, God did not get lonely for He is three in one. He has the perfect blend of Love, Joy and Peace. All three love one another with all their being. There is a perfect peace for each other in the presence of the other two."

God is a

Perfect

Blend of

Love,

Joy, and

Peace.

Sonny said, "We saw how they have fun, uh, joy with each other."

Gabriel explained, "They were never lonely, not at all. There came a time when they wanted to share their love, joy and peace with others. Their big problem was ..."

Sonny popped in, "There were no others. So God decided to create you."

"That's right. Love just has to be shared to be love. He wanted some creatures that could experience His love, whom He could love, and who could love Him," Gabriel explained.

"I was the prototype, or you might say, the guinea pig. I wanted you to see this moment in the history of eternity in order that you might better understand the creation of man."

"How long before, they, uh, He created other angels," Sandra asked.

"In His time or your time?" Gabriel laughed.

"Whatever," she answered.

"Not long. He was so pleased with His creation He made millions and billions of us. Each one was carefully planned and uniquely created," Gabriel smiled remembering the good old days. "It was wonderful. Where you have overnight parties, we had millennium parties. Everybody cared about each other. We were all head over heels in love with God. I know it sounds strange, but we loved equally the Father, the Son and the Spirit. When humans reminisce about the 'Good Old Days,' they are feeling just a tiny fraction of what I long for. All of us angels desire a return to those experiences."

"My memories do not go as far back as yours, Gabriel," I said. "I remember the days when I was young. My mom and dad loved me so much. There was a time when it snowed and we were all snow bound for several days. No electricity, no television, and you young folks cannot imagine, but we had no video games!"

"Good grief! That would be boring!" Sonny said as he drew a square with his hand. "How could you exist without cell phones and I-pods? Just to imagine a couple of days with no television and I feel cabin fever."

"You should have been there," I smiled with memories. "Dad couldn't get to work and Mom couldn't either. We were out of school, so no homework."

"What did you do?"

"We were together. I know that sounds funny, but my brother and I were always hurrying off to either practice or play ball. My sisters had soccer and dance and friends. Dad worked hard and long. Mom was always busy each day teaching school. When she was home, she fixed supper, we ate, and she cleaned up. We helped a little but not much," I said with a bit of confession and sorrow. "Now, I wish I had done more. But those snow days became like magic. We played board games."

"Board? Do you mean bored?" Sonny asked.

"No, board games like Chinese Checkers, and Scrabble, and Clue. Then we all would pitch in and make pizza from scratch."

"From scratch? What was wrong with your Papa John's?"

"He hadn't been born yet," I laughed. "We made cakes and cookies. We popped corn and lit a fire in the fireplace. Dad would tell us hilarious stories of his antics when he was young. Mom would add stories of picking cotton and chopping weeds and walking five miles to church in the snow."

"Come, on now," Sonny interrupted, "nobody has done that since pioneer days."

I grinned. "There was a lot of poverty when my parents were young. During those snow days we kids would act out the stories of Adam and Eve. I was always Adam. Eve was portrayed by my sister who was ten years older than I. Age didn't matter. My other sister was a cow and my young brother was the serpent. It was hilarious. It was wonderful."

I calmed down in his memories. Off in the distance we could see God's lights blinking. We all assumed He was taking to the newly born original Gabriel.

Everything was quiet.

I finally broke the calm by quoting,

*"There was silence in Heaven for about half an hour.
(Revelation 8:1 NIV)"*

Sonny began to snicker then to laugh. Like a church bell ringing in the night, his laughter was so contagious until one by one we all joined in. Gasping for air, Sonny buckled over as if in pain from the hilarity.

"What is so funny about 'silence in Heaven for about half an hour?'" Sandra finally was able to calm down enough to ask.

"Brother Chris," Sonny began laughing again until tears flowed and his stomach hurt. "Brother Chris, do you remember that sermon? Ha, ha, ha, ha, ha." he snorted and we all burst out cackling again. He tried to continue, "You were preaching on the book of Revelation on Sunday nights, and you came to Revelation eight. Your message was good, but I was sleepy and just about ready to doze off when you read that verse about silence in Heaven for half an hour. You paused, then announced, 'Sorry ladies, but if there is going to be silence in Heaven for thirty minutes, it means none of you will be there!'"

"We all laughed that night. Here we are staring at eternity in some kind of vision or Heavenly journey. The lack of noise made me remember that sermon that night."

All laughed for a while then calmed down. Sonny stood motionless for a while then cried out like an overzealous cheerleader, "This is CRAZY! This can't be happening! Sandra, are we dreaming? Or is this just my delusion? If so, what are you and Brother Chris doing in my dreams?"

He slammed his fist against his chest like a one armed King Kong and said, "There is no way in the world this can be happening. Gabriel, or whoever you are or whatever you are, we cannot be going back billions of years in time. It is impossible to stand and watch the universe explode, then watch God make an angel like He's knitting a baby blanket."

With a pleading tone he turned to the mild mannered angel, "Where are we? What in the world is happening?"

A twinkle appeared in the old angel's eyes that radiated out like ripples from a stone thrown in a pond. A compassionate smile revealed teeth as white as the pearly gates, as he answered, "You are correct, 'There is no way in the world this could happen.' But remember we are not 'in the world.' Through a process Jesus used himself on the mountain, you are transfigured and you have stepped into eternity. Simply put, you are in another dimension."

+ + +

CHAPTER 15
HISTORY IS HIS STORY

Pausing for effect, he continued, "In this dimension we are not controlled by time nor space. Remember you are in First Heaven which is a recorded history of all that has ever transpired. Let me illustrate, suppose you turned on your television and watched the history channel. You might watch man landing on the moon. In earth time, you are not on the moon and you have not traveled back to 1969. You are watching a recording, but you are still in your living room. Here you watch recorded history. In First Heaven you see and hear what happened previously and you experience it."

"Oh," Sonny quieted down. "So it's like an instant replay in a football game? You get to go back and watch the touchdown or the fumble or the tackle and still feel the agony or the ecstasy."

"Close. All of history is recorded in this first part of Heaven. As your pastor has told you in church many times, 'History is His Story.'"

"I thought Brother Chris was just talking about what has happened since the birth of Jesus, the *Anno Domino* thing," Sonny replied.

We all laughed and Sonny joined in. Sandra floated over to him, put her kind hand on his shoulder and said, "That's pretty close. A better pronunciation is *Anno Domini*..."

"I thought *A.D.* means *After his Death*, and B.C. means *Before Christ*."

Sandra gave him a peck on the cheek and whispered a little too loudly, "That's very good, Sonny Miller. You nailed the *B.C.* part and many people believe *A.D.* stands for *After Death*. But think a minute, if time is divided into two parts, Before His Birth and After His Death, how do you count the time he was alive?"

"Houston, we got a problem," Sonny quipped. "So explain it to me."

"*Anno Domini* is Latin, *Anno* for *year*; *Domini* means *of our Lord*. We count our calendar from the year he was born," Sandra explained.

"O.K.. thanks, but let me get this straight," Sonny quizzed all of them. "We have not gone back billions of years in time, we are only watching the recording?"

I was glad to have a chance to get a word in edgewise, "Correct, give the young football player a gold star. No, give him another trophy."

Sonny did a comic bow. "And the reason you are showing Sandra and me all of this is because we have been chosen to share it with the world when we return?"

"Good Heavens, no," Gabriel said. "The world would never believe you. They would lock you up in the, uh, what do you call it?"

"The Looney Bin," Sonny answered.

"What you are seeing now is like a James Bond movie, *For Your Eyes Only.* You will have opportunity to share your knowledge of the Triune God at the right time. Also you will be able to explain that Angels were not born of some goddess, or some God Mother. We were created. Your main job will be to help them understand how God can take a long time to create an angel or a world. Then you will be able to explain how Adam appeared in 4004 B.C."

Sandra stopped him, "But we don't know how or if Adam was born in 4004 B.C."

"You are not listening carefully," Gabriel answered. "First, Adam was no more born than I was born. I was created and he was created. Plus, I did not say he was created in 4004 B.C., I said he appeared in that year."

It was Sonny's turn with the question. "What do you mean he wasn't created in 4004 B.C? Do you mean he existed before he appeared?"

"Yes."

"Oh, you mean he and Eve were in Heaven before he appeared on the earth? Were the Mormons right? They believe we are birthed in Heaven by God and one of his many, many wives, then we are delivered to earth," Sandra asked.

"No, the Bible plainly states that Adam was made of the dust of the ground. He was not manufactured in Heaven- then sent down here for assembly," Gabriel answered.

"How can we tell people about Adam if we don't understand?" Sonny asked.

"Patience," Gabriel smiled. "Patience is a quality of which man has very little and of which God is over stocked . Just bear with me. You need to know about the Triune God and you need to know how angels came about. I was the prototype and the result of billions of earth years of Heavenly engineering. But God is in no hurry. The Son, created all of the other billions of angels one by one."

"Each one different?" Sonny asked.

"Each one unique, just like one day He would create humans. Why do evolutionists insist we are all the product of accidental events and mutations and survival of the fittest and deal with the fact we are each completely unique?" Gabriel thought, then added, "If evolution were true, wouldn't all humans look alike? Don't rabbits and squirrels and fish and birds look almost identical?"

"I don't think the evolutionists deal with that question," Sandra answered.

"I think they are afraid of the answer," I mumbled.

"So each angel was the only one of its kind?" Sonny asked. "Did you have any similarities?"

"Of course, didn't you notice?" Gabriel asked. "When the Son finished creating me, when the Godhead breathed life into me, what or whom did I resemble?"

"You were in the image of God," Sonny answered. "So all Angels are little images of God. Hey, since we humans are in the image of God- does that mean we are to be little Gods?"

I said, "No, we are to be like Jesus. Remember your WWJC bracelets? *What Would Jesus Do?*"

Gabriel smiled, "In the creation process there was a time when Pre-man didn't look like either Father, Son or Spirit."

"Just like the unborn baby doesn't look like the father or mother or any human being at first," Sandra exclaimed. "The nine months of pregnancy is like a picture of the years it took to create Pre-man, whatever that means."

"Right," Gabriel answered.

"But it's not the process God used to create Adam," Sandra smiled.

"Whoa!" Sonny said. "Stop right there. You are losing me. You are trying to tell me that God had two creation processes? One for the earth and all living things and another for Adam?"

"Patience, Sonny," Gabe was delighted the young athlete was catching on. "There are some other things you must understand before you can understand Adam. It is amazing how theologians and scientists have knocked their brains out trying to understand how man began. But nobody seems to care about the beginning of Angels."

Sandra winked at Sonny then floated over to Gabriel, placed her hand on his shoulder and said, "I care. Please, Uncle Gabriel, tell me about how angels were created."

"I'm so glad you asked," he replied. "You already know we were made from energy. God not only emits light, He produces energy, far more than you can imagine. As you witnessed, God molded energy into Heavenly matter and I was formed. He did the same thing billions of times. But here is the part where you must pay attention."

"I'm all ears," Sonny said.

"God only gave us the knowledge of good," Gabriel said, then stopped.

No one said anything for a few earthy moments. We three humans looked at each other as if we had been presented a puzzle, and we were supposed to solve it. Sandra asked, "What do you mean God only gave you the knowledge of good?"

With a melancholy look the angel seemed to walk down memory's lane. A smile would appear, then a laugh, then another grin. "When we angels were created, there was nothing but good. There was no evil for us to know. Heaven was greater than it had ever been. The Triune God shared his love, joy and peace with all of us. Then we simply shared with one another."

"In other words," I added, "you loved God and loved each other."

"So that's what Jesus was talking about in his commandments to love God with everything we've got and to love our neighbors as ourselves," Sonny concluded. "Hey, that would be Heaven on earth."

"That's why He came," Gabe stated. "He came to establish a Kingdom of Heaven on earth. He gave humans the recipe, provided all the ingredients through his life and death on the cross. He even taught you to pray, 'Thy kingdom come, thy will be done, on earth as it is in Heaven.'"

"But He failed," Sonny said sadly.

"No, no, no! He didn't fail," Gabe replied. "Human beings failed. The first Adam failed, but not the last Adam."

"Oh, oh, oh," Sandra said. "I think I'm beginning to see the light. Jesus came to bring the Kingdom of Heaven to earth. He was rejected, but through His death, we can be cleansed, forgiven, saved and someday enter eternal Heaven. Is that the same reason the first Adam came?"

"Close. but no blue ribbon," Gabe said. "You are correct about the first Adam's being placed here to bring Heaven on earth, but salvation was always reserved for the last Adam, the Son."

Sonny raised his hand, "Confused! Thoroughly! You are over my head."

"Sorry," the angel apologized, "Let's fast forward through eternity and look at Heaven after the first set of angels appeared."

"First set?" Sonny asked.

"First set!" Gabe answered and we joined hands and were pushed forward through time.

We thought we were back on the edge of the universe watching stars and galaxies glitter. It only took a half second to realize the stars were glittering but not against a black sky. They were shining and twinkling in a bright, brilliant heaven.

+ + +

CHAPTER 16
THE SMELL, TASTE, SOUND AND FEEL OF HEAVEN

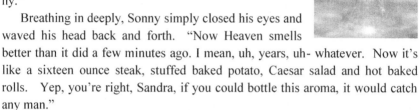

S andra sniffed, smiled and sniffed again. "Oh, if I could only find perfume like that," she said to Sonny."

Breathing in deeply, Sonny simply closed his eyes and waved his head back and forth. "Now Heaven smells better than it did a few minutes ago. I mean, uh, years, uh- whatever. Now it's like a sixteen ounce steak, stuffed baked potato, Caesar salad and hot baked rolls. Yep, you're right, Sandra, if you could bottle this aroma, it would catch any man."

"I can smell both," I said. "But add to it that special scent from your first born son, just after he's bathed and dusted, and you're holding him close to your face."

"Never thought of smells in Heaven until this trip," Sonny said. Curiously he held out both hands, made an imaginary ball with them, packed it close together. Then he lifted a small sphere of light toward his mouth, opened, swallowed, smiled. "That was delicious. Better than a Diary Queen banana split. What is this?" he asked as he made another ball and tossed it in his mouth.

"Believe it or not, it's the same stuff that was used to make manna?"

"Manna? Like mama taught me good mannas?" Sonny teased.

Sandra giggled, "Manna like God provided the Israelites in the desert."

"Oh, yea. That kind of manna," Sonny answered. "My second helping was better than the first, a bit like lobster tails soaked in butter. Why would they complain?"

"They would have complained had it been steak and lobster and banana splits over and over again," I answered this time. "We all have a tendency to grow tired of the same old, same old. That's the way of earthly beings."

Sandra quickly added, "But not the way of Heaven. In eternity we'll never be tired of foods and smells and experiences. Oh, I'm going to love it."

Sonny held her hand, looked deep into her blue eyes and said, "If God allows me to spend eternity with you, I'll never get tired."

"Thanks for the compliment," she teased. "And I promise I'll never be tired of you. You're so funny. And you're so good. No matter what happens, you'll always have me to be there with you."

"Enough love stuff," Gabriel said with a smile. "Do you notice all the lights shining?"

"Are those stars?" Sonny asked, then answered his own question. "No, I can see some up close now- they are angels! Beautiful, gorgeous angels. But they don't have any wings. I thought all angels had wings. I imagined yours were inside your gown."

"You must understand we were created in the image of God, just as humans would be. God has no wings- we have no wings. We don't flutter around like butterflies: we move faster than the speed of light through Heavenly energy."

I said, "But the Bible states that some angels are winged..."

Gabriel replied, "I forgot, we didn't go deep into angelology on our first trip here, did we? Don't let me forget to tell you about the second batch of angels. They had wings."

Colors began to explode around us. It was like the Fourth of July with the Boston Pops orchestra playing in the background. Fireworks of every color erupted.

Sandra said, "I'm sure I hear *Handel's Messiah* being sung."

Sonny groaned, "Once I had to suffer through all of *The Messiah*. It was like 'Ninety-nine bottles of beer on the wall-' I didn't think it would ever end. Boring!" He turned and listened, squinted his eyes, swayed, then said, " But this is the most beautiful music I have ever heard in my life. What is it, Gabriel, did they let the Mormon Tabernacle Choir in just so we could hear them sing?"

All laughed. Gabriel said, "Sonny, we are looking at time a billion years before Joseph Smith had his so-called visions and the Mormons were birthed. You are hearing the angels sing, as they sang the night Jesus was born."

A kaleidoscope of shades tumbled before us causing Sandra to ask, "What are those gorgeous colors?"

"Just angels. Made of energy they can reflect all kinds of lights."

Most of them were pastels with shades of mint green, and peppermint pink, and soft lemon yellows. One angel came close by in a stunning array of robin-egg blue and burgundy. Another flew past radiating all the colors of the prism. There were tints and hues and colors we had never seen before.

Sandra reached out to gather some of the colors floating in the air. She stopped and said, "Wait a minute, if we are just watching this like a video tape, how can we smell and hear? Sonny even grabbed something and ate it. How is this possible?"

Gabriel's eyes twinkled again. "You have heard of television? Welcome to smell-a-vision and taste-a-vision. Soon the Japanese will figure out how to do this with your television sets and everybody will rush out and buy one."

"Hey, you need to add another feature to your electronic equipment," I said as I rubbed a circular motion over my heart. "Feel-a-vision. I feel something here. There is a peace that passeth all understanding. Suddenly, I'm not worried about paying bills, or having car wrecks, or my children swallowing some poison or being run over in the street. Funny, the stress of getting a sermon ready for Sunday is gone. I sense a calm night beside a still pond. The moon hangs heavy overhead. My children and wife are safe asleep and all is well with the world. How can I put into words what I feel and what Heaven will be like for me permanently one day? Tranquility, serenity, harmony, stillness. All of those added up together can only be a part of what I now feel."

Sandra nodded her head in agreement. "Love. That's what I am experiencing from Heaven. Sweet memories of emotion are settling in my heart. I can feel Mama holding me safe in her arms and smothering me with kisses. Now it's Daddy walking me to Sunday School. I'm dressed in a white dress, with white shoes, purse, and even a little white hat. As people shower me with compliments, my dad picks me up, hugs me close to him and whispers, 'You are my little girl and I will always love you.'"

Dreamingly she closed her eyes and whispered to Sonny, "Now I remember the first time ever I saw your face. I recall the first Sunday you sat next to me in church. In the middle of Brother Chris's sermon you reached over and held my hand. Oh, I still get goose bumps. My mind is a scrapbook of love-soaked memories: our first date, the first time you kissed me, the night you told me you loved me, the day you finally were able to pay for your senior class ring and you immediately brought it and gave it to me. I don't think you ever even put it on your finger. If we think love makes the world go round, then it is obvious all of Heaven spins around love. I feel it."

Sonny wiped a tiny tear from his eye as he took Sandra's hand. "I feel all of that: the peace, the love, but also I am experiencing joy. I can see there is a great deal of difference between pleasure and joy, there's even a difference between happiness and joy. I can remember how I felt when I won the state track meet for the mile. But that's only a smidgen of how I feel now. When we were state champions in football I yelled until my throat was sore. Now those emotions are like comparing a little league trophy to winning the Heisman. Joy up to now was winning a tag football game in the backyard. What I experience now is winning the Super Bowl."

We all looked at Gabriel, who grinned back at us. Sonny finally said, "To be honest, Mr. Angel, I thought Heaven would be pretty dull. No video games, no cell phones, no text messages. But now I see and feel that Heaven is a whole lot more."

Sonny whirled in space in ecstasy. He stopped, looked at the angel and asked, "Will there be football in Heaven?"

I knew the answer to that one so I quickly answered, "Of course."

"But, but..." Sonny stammered. "How is that going to work? I was told that in Heaven, every golf shot is a hole in one, every basketball shot is a ringer, and every run with the football is a touchdown."

"I don't know who told you that," I said. "I sure didn't preach that."

"Well, maybe it was my redneck preacher at Tuscaloosa," Sonny guessed. "Hmm, then I could have picked that up at a meeting of Fellowship of Christian Athletes. Somebody has to win, or what's the use of playing?"

"Men's games are made to win and lose, women's games are different," I answered. "For example, boys will play football in the backyard and risk permanent injuries just to win."

Sonny thought, "So it's more like not whether your win or lose, but how you play the game?"

"More than that," I explained. "Girls play house- and there is no winner or loser. They just enjoy playing."

"Oh," Sonny said as the light blinked on in his head. "In Heaven, we will just play football to play, not to win! Then I'll get a chance to play with all the football heroes."

"Well, not all of them," I answered. "Not everybody is going to make it to Heaven,"

Again Sonny thought for a moment, then asked, "Will there be football in Hell?"

I laughed and told him, "I don't know about that. I do know Heaven will take care of all your needs and most of your wishes. As you can see, it's beyond beautiful."

Gabriel said, "As Randy Bachman put it in his 1974 song, '*You Ain't Seen Nothing Yet!*' There is far more to Heaven than you have experienced."

"I realize the stars we see twinkling and changing colors are angels. But what are those galaxies we see scattered around?" Sandra asked.

"Celestial cities. You don't think we all just float around in space like puffs of clouds and helium balloons that have escaped the fingers of a small child?" Gabriel then pointed toward the center of the lights and said, "There is the Holy City."

"Jerusalem?" Sandra asked.

"Let's say, it's the New Jerusalem. Would you like to take a quick peek?"

"I thought you would never ask," Sonny quipped.

+ + +

CHAPTER 17
A TOUR OF THE HOLY CITY

Gabriel led us and the golden glow zoomed larger and larger. As the city came into view, we sighed. Gabriel instructed us, "Since you are still human, you can't see fully all the beauty of Heaven. Remember the Bible forewarned you:

> *'No eye has seen, no ear has heard,*
> *no mind has conceived what*
> *God has prepared for those who love him'"*
> *(1 Corinthians 2: 9: NIV)*

"Wowee!" Sonny yelled as the city drew nearer, "It's neater than Disney World. Look at the walls, they are really glittering jewels. And the gates, just as promised, are made of pearl. Sandra, look, the streets are gold. Not dull, un-polished, but bright shining gold like the wedding ring I'm going to give you some day."

"These streets are going to have to go some to beat the beauty of my wedding ring," she replied. "The buildings are luminous- they are like neon signs. Multicolored angels are scurrying around as if they doing some kind of work."

Gabriel said, "Of course we work. Don't you remember after God made Adam in his image, he placed him in the Garden and put him to work? It was tough keeping the Garden up, the fruit picked, the trees pruned, the animals fed. We angels have our tasks. As I told you, my job is to be a messenger. Hmm, let's say, I'm like the postman and neither rain, snow nor hail can keep me from my job. Bear in mind I told you Michael is a warrior angel. However, the Heaven you see below you is pre-Lucifer. We were at peace then."

"Is Lucifer, Satan, the Devil, uh, is he in the Holy City? Can we see him?" Sandra asked.

"No, no. Satan has not been created yet- he was in the second litter," Gabriel chuckled. "Where we are looking is back before he and the others came into being. Just be patient. You have to understand all of this to understand Adam."

"There's the river," Sonny shouted. "Just like I promised Dad and Curtis. They both love to fish. I'll bet they catch a bunch and then throw them all back. The water shimmers blue-green, and light sparkles on it like birthday candles. Fruit trees! Just as the Bible promised on each side. What is that huge tree on the island in the river? Is that the Tree of Knowledge of Good and Evil?"

"No, that is yet to be created. It will be part of the Garden of Eden," Gabriel answered. "As I told you, the first angels were created with a knowledge of good. We were not aware of evil, because there was no evil. Only goodness bloomed and grew and flowed in Heaven. That tree in the center is the Tree of Life. To eat of it is to live forever."

"It has such a funny shape, Usually trees are rounded like oaks, or fairly straight like some firs. This Tree of Life is most unusual. If I didn't know better, I would say it is shaped somewhat like a, a, cross."

"How perceptual!" I exclaimed. "If you eat of the Tree of Life, you live forever. And if you come to know the one who was crucified on a cross of death..."

"You live forever," Sonny finished the sentence. "But this is before Lucifer, before the world was created, and pre-Adam. How could God know....?" He stopped his question and answered it himself. "God knew the cross would be needed someday."

"Right," Gabriel explained. "I told you we would only take a peek. We are not going to look at every tree, every mountain, every canyon."

"There are mountains and canyons?" Sandra asked.

"Of course." Gabe answered. "After visiting Yosemite Park, Mark Twain stated that after God finished making America, he had a lot of beauty left over, so he dumped it in Yosemite. Just imagine God took a small sampling of all the beauty of Heaven and sprinkled it lightly on the earth to give us a sneak preview of how gorgeous eternity is and will be. Instead of Yosemite he placed the beauty in the Garden of Eden."

I issued a great sigh and we all looked ahead. I said, "The thrones, I didn't have a chance to see them last time you brought me here. They are exquisite, solid white and encrusted with diamonds. Wow, I don't think I can take all of this in. Now we are closer. I can see God seated on the center throne. He is more brilliant than the noon day sun- we still can't see His face clearly."

I wiped my eyes, blinked and said, "Now I see three thrones and there is a red tinted figure on the right hand. The red is fading into flesh color. The robe is white with a deep red sash. I've just seen Jesus! All of you excuse me, I just have to bow down and worship him, I can't help myself." With that, I fell down on my face and wept saying, "Lord, Lord, thank you, thank you for saving me."

Automatically Sonny and Sandra went to their knees and each wept and worshipped and praised God and Jesus. Finally the angel nudged us and reminded us this was just watching history. But he assured us God would be in our future. As we rose, Sandra spoke out, "Now I see three figures on three thrones. The one on the right is the Son with a red sash. The figure in blue in the center must be the Father. His hair and long beard are turning gray, But I can't see his face- it is too bright. Somehow he reminds me of my grandfather. Now his robe has turned sparkling white with a blue cloak over his shoulder." She paused trying to take all of this in. "I like the yellow form on the left. He must be the Spirit. He is changing as the other two. His robe is transforming to white and a lemon sash hangs freely to his waist."

As we watched, the three were talking with all colors of lights flowing between them. Suddenly the red and yellow figures disappeared, and God on his throne was glittering white again.

"Don't think I will ever figure that one out," Sonny said.

Gabriel replied, "Don't try to figure it out. Just accept it. God is God and we are not. God knows what He is doing and we don't. We just have to trust Him."

Gabriel reached out and we zoomed away from the Holy City. In the distance we could now see other cities like villages on the Rhine River in Germany. When we were a good distance out, the Archangel told us, "God is very pleased with Heaven and His angels. However, real love keeps wanting to reach out and share with others. True peace is never satisfied by keeping it to oneself. Joy by its very nature desires to distribute what it has with as many as it can."

I guessed, "So, I imagine God was considering creating some more angels. The first had given him so much pleasure He wanted to create more."

"True," Gabe answered, "but you notice He had the triune Gods discuss this. The Father, the Son and the Spirit manifested themselves to determine guidelines for the new angels."

"Why didn't they just stick with the old pattern? If it's not broke, don't fix it," Sonny blurted in.

Gabriel nodded but added, "We first angels were a delight. But since we only had a knowledge of good, we could not be otherwise. God realized we were wonderful friends and company. But to be honest, we had little choice. So the three decided to create more angels, only this time they would be given the knowledge of good and evil."

"So, you and the first group of angels only had the knowledge of good?" I asked. "But now the Godhead is considering creating some angels with the knowledge of good and evil. I think I see where this is leading- the trouble with the second group is they were made too quickly and turned out badly.

"No, they were created in Heaven, like us. You need to remember God doesn't make cheap stuff," Gabriel answered. "Didn't you get a good look at the Holy City? What did you experience with your senses? Cheap perfume? Canned manna? With all due respect, Heaven was not made in China nor is it available at your local dollar store. The new batch of angels would be called Cherubim. They would be different because they would have wings, and they would have the knowledge of good and evil."

"And the first one God would create," Sonny asked, "would his name by any chance be Lucifer?"

"How did you guess?" Gabriel answered and his smile disappeared. Slowly, he turned away from the joyful scene of Heaven. He sniffed, then raised his arm to his face to wipe away some tears. We other three were dumbfounded. We had never thought of angels as having emotions. To be honest, we had not thought of angels of being anything other than cardboard characters in the Bible or stained glass figures in a church window. Sure there were memories of the pre-school children donning white gowns with tinsel covered wings and haloes a bit askew for Christmas. Angels were in the realm of Mother Goose and Santa Claus and Jack Frost. It was difficult to imagine an angel shedding tears at a funeral for one of their loved ones. It was equally hard to hear them laugh with others when there was sunshine and bluebirds.

"You lost Paradise, too, didn't you?" I asked. I tried to put my hands in my pockets, but gowns don't have places to park your hands so you don't know what to do with them. I badly wanted to go over and give Gabriel a hug and tell him everything would be all right as I do with his church members when they experienced a great loss. However, I nor human beings ever had a clear picture of how breathtakingly beautiful Heaven was before Lucifer tore it apart. I knew of churches where all was well with their soul before some preacher became hooked on a goofy doctrine. Church members became angry for large and small reasons- and church-going became more like Hell on earth than Heaven. Hundreds of churches were being ripped into shreds because someone or some group didn't like the music or the sermon or the secretary or the pastor's wife or the youth director's programs.

"Eureka!" I shouted. "I understand it better now. All church problems and most family difficulties can be traced back to Paradise Lost. I don't mean John Milton's great book and I'm not even referring to Adam and Eve being booted out of the Garden. The first Paradise that was splintered took place in Heaven. It was not attitudes nor preferences nor the type of music the angels sang. It was the Devil. He is still tearing up every available kingdom of Heaven."

Gabriel raised his teary eyes and blinked at me. "If you could only imagine how wonderful every thing was before ..." He stopped and bowed his head in memories.

I said, "No, I can not dream of how fantastic Heaven was *B.L.*"

"*B.L.?*" Sonny asked.

"*Before Lucifer,*" I answered. "although thanks to our tour of Eternity, we have a pretty good picture of what Heaven is going to be like *A.D.*"

"*A.D.?*" Sonny puzzled. "*Anno domino,* I mean, *domini?* The year of our Lord?"

"No, *A.D. After the Devil.* The Bible promises he will be tossed into the pit. Then Heaven will be returned to its full glory. Good news, we will be permanent residents and not just fly-by-night visitors."

Gabriel nodded in agreement. "Wonderfully worded. I have to be careful that I do not dwell on history nor become too infatuated with the outlook. As one of your preachers put it, 'The past is a cashed check, the future only a promissory note. The present is ready cash.' There is a great battle that has been raging down through the ages. It began in Heaven, spread to earth and envelops the world today. We do have hope, real Hope in Him, the Son."

"May we take a look at the Great Exorcism?" Sonny asked.

"The Great Exorcism?" Gabriel finally laughed. "The Greatest Exorcism! The most devils ever cast out at one time. Yes, you must see that part of Heavenly History to understand what happened on earth. However, we must make a few stops along the way so you can best understand."

+ + +

50 Billion B.C.

CHAPTER 18
LUCIFER ARRIVES

Gabriel talked as the scene of the Happy Heaven faded. We were propelling forward at speeds far beyond that of slow-poke light. Like a tour guide, he explained to us, "At the next stop we will see the creation of Lucifer."

It was not clear whether our traveling was like an elevator, an escalator or a moving sidewalk. We knew we were moving only because the scenes blurred before us. There was no whistle of air as you have on even the best of airplanes. Nor was there the bumpity bump bump bump of the elevator. One scene would fade away and a smudge of scenery would flash by. There was no way of our knowing if we had traveled an earth year or an earth light year. Or if we had even moved.

This time the scene materialized of a more beautiful Heaven than before. Gold glittered in the atmosphere like snowflakes. Northern lights shimmered in the sky. But they were not of blue and green and red. Silver and crystal and gold spun back and forth above us. Obviously this was a special day. Angels gathered around like relatives at the birth of the first grandson.

The Son was finishing up the angel form. This one was different from those of Gabriel. Wings had been added. Not just bird wings, not even butterfly wings. They were translucent and shone with the brilliance of every jewel imaginable.

Gabriel reassumed his role as the tour guide. "The new angel model is the Cherub. Soon billions will be created and you will know them by their plural name, Cherubim."

"But I always thought Cherubim were tiny angel babies. Cute and cuddly," Sandra said. "Mama put some pictures of them in my nursery room when I was young. Dad often called me his little angel, his little Cherub."

"A lot of things get mixed up by you human beings," Gabe the professor now declared. "You prefer to think of Lucifer as an comical character in red underwear, two black horns, a long tail and a pitchfork. As you can plainly see, you could never identify him from that picture."

The Son dressed in a white gown with red sash beckoned to GOD. They faded into each other, then breathed into Lucifer's nose. His eyes opened and Sandra gasped. "Those are the most beautiful eyes I've ever seen, uh, except for yours, Sonny."

Sonny said. "Never have I seen such an ice-blue color in eyes- they are almost seductive."

"Well worded," Gabriel said. "God made him much more handsome than I. Had I been endowed with the knowledge of good and evil, I would have been jealous. Instead, he was the new baby brother and all of us angels loved him from the very first. We were fascinated with his wings, his good looks, his charm."

Angels rushed forward to hug the new Cherub. His eyes danced with glee, his smile reflected teeth as white as the throne of God. He stood a bit taller than the other angels and his golden hair was longer. Sonny was tempted to see if he had a tattoo or an earring, but realized that was not sane thinking.

Lucifer curtsied before God as a visiting prince might. We could see the Original Gabriel in the front row. Even though he was smiling, one could tell he had some thoughts about this new kid on the block. When Lucifer lifted his head, the smile had a touch of a smirk about it. His back stiffened as if he wanted everyone to bow down to him. Oddly enough, that's exactly what happened. Millions and billions of angels bowed down to him. The Original Gabriel was the last to bow. But God did not bow to this newly created Cherub.

As Lucifer scanned the audience, his eye fell on the Great Throne. The human spectators noticed his stare, as a longing for power. His head continued to turn, taking in the River of Life, the trees. When he saw the Tree of Life, he turned to God and asked in a honey voice, "What is that gorgeous tree in the middle of your Garden?"

"That is the Tree of Life- the food supply for all of Heaven," came the answer. "Eat this and you shall never die."

The rich baritone voice of the Cherub said, "So, I'm not eternal like the other angels?"

A Red Light blinked, the Son emerged and a soothing voice said, "Of course you are eternal. But you still have to eat. Angels eat the food of Heaven and the fruit of the Tree of Life. If you could not eat from the tree, you would become very, very hungry and very, very weak."

"Why do I feel different from the others?" Lucifer asked. "Is it because of my attractive wings? Or my good looks?"

Sonny whispered to Sandra, "That guy could get a job in Hollywood without a screen test. Look at that perfect face and nose. And take a gander at his physique. Whew! He looks like the cover boy for some of these muscle men magazines."

"And that tan, have you ever seen anything so smooth?" Sandra asked. "I had not noticed until now all of the angels are pale. I doubt if they were aware of their pallor until the new Hercules arrived."

Angels didn't seem to notice Lucifer's behavior, for they flowed forth to shake his hand, hug his neck, welcome him into their Heaven and homes and hearts.

Gabriel sighed, "Lucifer probably didn't know he had a knowledge of Good and Evil. Now when I look back at his beginning, I can see tiny traces of evil from the start. God the Father loved all of us as His children. The Son loved us like brothers. The Spirit has the ability to love others and fill them with the love of God so they may love God in return."

"I'm not sure I followed all of that sentence," Sonny said. "The Spirit loves us and imparts God's love in us so we can love God back."

"Oh yes," Gabriel smiled. "He helps you develop the love of God within you so you can then love those about you. Probably the biggest problem of your world is that you simply don't know how to love anyone other than yourself. Think about it- why do you guys put on cool clothes, fix your hair, take a breath mint, put on the charm around other people?"

"Simple, so girls will like us," Sonny answered.

"True," Gabe answered, "so others will like or love you. However, what do you put on, spray on, paint on, to help you love them?"

"Un," Sonny sputtered, "Nothing, I guess. But is that why girls spend so much time on their makeup, and hairdos, and jewelry, and clothes, and make those silly giggles every time a guy makes any kind of remark?"

Gabriel nodded, "Right. Has it ever occurred to you humans that you spend a lot of money on yourself, your food, your games, because you love yourself? You also pour out a lot of cash for things to make others love you by the way you smell, look, or sound."

Sandra blushed, "Guess I never thought of it that way. But I know this, I love God, and I love Sonny, and I love my parents and my preacher and..."

"Sandra Hall, you are the exception, not the rule of human beings," I said. "Gabriel is right. One of our biggest sin problems comes from the fact we love ourselves. Even our prayers are something like:

'God bless me and my wife,
My son John and his wife,
Us four and no more.'"

Sonny laughed, "Preach, you hit it right on the head. Playing football, you would think all of those guys are real gentlemen, who really love their schools, their coaches, the fans, the game. I found out real quick most of them, well, most of us, really love old number one- ourselves."

"You don't have to play football to discovery vanity," Sandra said. "Try being in a beauty pageant sometimes."

"I'll pass on that, but I can imagine how some girls can become prima donnas," Sonny said as he squeezed her hand. "I'm glad you're not like that."

Gabriel interrupted them. "Since you know the outcome of Satan, you easily caught all of his little quirks from the beginning. The way he strutted, his used-car-salesman smile, his interaction with others. Back then we could not see all of his craftiness, just as you don't notice the selfishness in a new-born baby. Junior does something clever such as snatching another baby's pacifier and you double over with laughter. Then you coo, 'That's so cute. Do you have a camera? That would look good on America's Funniest Videos.'"

I confessed, "We come into this world self-centered then we don't move very far from that center of our gravity. I can identify more with Lucifer at times than I can with Gabriel. Seriously, we have the knowledge of good and evil, and most of the time we just prefer the evil. It's not that we don't know what's good and right. We just don't do it. Evil is often more attractive, more fun, and all the rest of the world is doing it."

"Evil probably tastes pretty good, too," Sandra added. "That apple sure lured Eve in."

Sonny thought then said, "It was probably more the Serpent who lured Eve than the apple, or whatever fruit it was."

"It was forbidden fruit," Gabriel snapped. "It hung on the Tree of Knowledge of Good and Evil. I'll tell you more when we come to the creation of Eden."

Sonny asked, "If Heaven had a Tree of Life, why didn't it also have a Tree of Knowledge of Good and Evil?"

Gabriel smiled sadly, rubbed his chin, cut his eyes over to the newly created Lucifer and said, "I think Heaven just added that tree."

We watched Lucifer strut away. Flowers of every color and hue fell down upon him like a victory ride through New York City after World War II. The handsome Cherub waved at his audience, threw them kisses, beamed as triumphantly as a Roman general returning after a great conquest.

+ + +

"Heaven was never the same after that day," Gabriel lamented. "The sounds, the smells, the tastes, they never changed. But the atmospheric layer of love seemed to diminish. You could never quite put your finger on it. After God created a billion more Cherubim, we all thought we would return to the good old days. I was happy, peaceful, joyful. My love for God grew stronger, or as you humans sing it, 'Every day with Jesus is Sweeter Than the Day Before.'"

"A billion or more earth years swept by, and we figured soon Lucifer would be so overwhelmed with our love, he would become like us. I suppose this is how parents feel about a bad kid. I am aware you think witnessing is being pleasant to your lost neighbors. Preachers tell church members if they just love their neighbors, they will respond to our love and be saved?"

"Isn't that true?" Sandra asked.

"Not all the time," Gabriel answered. "Sure you and I are to love others. I have case files of zillions of good Christian parents who loved their children to pieces, only to have their offspring turn out bad. Church folks will often take in a bum or homeless couple, love them, provide for them, only to discover they have been used. Love can be manipulated. You see, the problem with the bad child or bad adult is not the lack of love but the presence of evil."

"Whoa," Sonny said. "We've been taught there is no sin in Heaven. Angels can't sin, can they?"

"Brother Chris, have you taught this to your members?" Gabriel asked.

"Uh, not exactly," I mumbled. "I do tell them of the promises in Revelation there will be no sinners in Heaven."

Gabriel sighed, "It's so difficult for you humans to understand. If there will be no sinners in Heaven, how do you three expect to enter?"

Sonny thought a moment and answered, "Good question. Is the answer something about Jesus and His death?"

"Yes. Once sin entered Heaven, it had to be cleansed."

"When God cast Lucifer and his Cherubim out, wasn't that the cleansing?" Sandra asked.

"It got rid of the rats and fleas, but the disease of sin had broken out like the Black Plague," Gabriel remarked.

"Couldn't the Son just have died in Heaven to forgive all the sin?" Sonny asked.

"You have asked a deep theological question,' Gabriel smiled. "No, The Son could not die in Heaven. He was eternal as was Lucifer and the angels. Think very hard and you might can see why God created the Heavens and the Earth."

Sonny pondered a moment. "If God the Father, Son and Spirit can't die, and if angels can't die, then humans had to be created to make a sacrifice."

"Right!" Gabriel snapped his fingers and we fast forwarded. The scene blurred. Now before us stretched white clouds and a zillion lights. More Celestial cities glittered with blue and white beams in the distance. However, many of them were not as bright as others- countless cities were off white, even gray.

"In the past scene you witnessed the creation of Lucifer. Soon billions of Cherubim were inhabitants of Heaven. They grouped themselves into cities. At first, we didn't even notice their towns were dimmer than ours. It was obvious all of the Cherubim were made similar to Lucifer. This was made possible by *A.N.A.*"

"*A.N.A.*," Sandra asked. "Do you mean *D.N.A.*, DeoxyriboNucleic Acid?

"No," Gabriel answered, "I mean *A.N.A.*, AngelicNucleic Acid. It took mankind millions of years to discover the building block of information of creation. What they have not discovered yet is that D.N.A. is a human replica for *A.N.A.*"

"That doesn't make any sense," Sandra argued. "Why do angels need *D.N.A.* or *A.N.A.* or whatever *N.A.*?"

"I thought I had taught you God created us angels over a long, long period of time. We are not made of the same kind of atoms you have which are controlled by chemicals and electricity. We are energy that has been molded into matter, but not the same matter you know. Our atoms are controlled by Heavenly energy. Chemicals can die and electricity can be used up or the power turned off. Heavenly energy is eternal."

"So we were made just like angels," Sonny asked.

"A little lower than the angels," Gabriel smiled, "and quoted:

> *"What is man that you are mindful of him,*
> *the son of man that you care for him?*
> *You made him a little lower than the angels;*
> *you crowned him with glory and honor*
> *and put everything under his feet."*
> *In putting everything under him,*
> *God left nothing that is not subject to him.*
> *Yet at present we do not see everything subject to him.*
> *But we see Jesus, who was made a little lower than the angels,*
> *now crowned with glory and honor because he suffered death,*
> *so that by the grace of God he might taste death for everyone."*
> *(Hebrews 2:6-9 NIV)*

"Is this Scripture talking about man or Jesus?" I asked.

"Both. Man was made lower than the angels but He, Jesus, was crowned with glory, and you recall that He put everything under Adam's feet- or under his authority. But now with Paradise lost, it's quite obvious that not everything is under man's control. There are hurricanes and famines and earthquakes. There is crime and suffering."

"But isn't all of that due to the fall of Adam?" I asked.

"Yes, when Adam fell, all of creation fell- all of nature," Gabriel thought for a long moment and said, "We will get there eventually. Let me give you a progress report on Lucifer and his followers. Then you will better understand the Creator, the creation and the creature."

+ + +

CHAPTER 19
LUCIFER BEGINS THE UPRISING

Lucifer

Much like Google World Search, we zoomed into one of the dimmer cities. We could see great clusters of Cherubim standing at attention as Lucifer was speaking. Now he was more handsome than at his creation. All were spellbound by his speech. When Lucifer raised his hand into the air, millions of other hands shot up as in salute to him.

"This looks like an old war movie where the Nazis are saluting Hitler," Sonny whispered loudly. "The angels are mesmerized by him. Can we get in a little closer to hear what he is saying?"

"Sure," Gabriel replied.

Lucifer spat out his words, "We are the superior angels. Look at our beautiful wings, our handsome faces, our physiques. God made us greater than his so-called angels. They are nothing but messengers. We Cherubim are the guardians of light. We are the guards to make sure the light is defended, held high."

A great roar of approval erupted, "Hail Lucifer, the Bearer of Light!"

Tossing his golden hair, Lucifer continued, "We are made better and bigger than all the other angels. We are much brighter!"

"That's not true," Sonny said loudly. "That's a lie. We can tell this city is dimmer that others. This whole bunch are darker than the other angels."

Sandra said, "People who walk in darkness usually think they are brighter than the rest of us."

"All other angels have outlived their usefulness," Lucifer ranted. "They were only created as a working model so God could create us. The old have to go. When they are defeated, then we will take control of the thrones. Their three in one God must go. Instead we three will take over the power. I will be the King, and sit on the highest and middle throne. My good friend and your good friend, Beelzebub, will sit at my right."

A tall handsome Cherub stepped forward. The human group did not recognize him until he stumped his toe on the step and swore what must have been an angelic profanity. Also we could see his darker hair was tied in a pony tail.

"That's our old buddy from the Cross Garden," Sonny said. "Whew, he was pretty high in rank. We must be somebody special if Satan sent him after us."

"You are somebody special," Gabriel said, "All God's children are special."

"If he's on second, who's on third?" Sonny asked.

"Leviathan was third in command," Gabriel answered as another Cherub stepped forward to stand by Lucifer and Beelzebub.

"Leviathan?" Sandra asked. "I thought he was some kind of sea monster."

"Monster? Yes," Gabriel said. "But he was not confined to the sea."

"They look like the three top medalists in the Olympics," Sonny whistled.

"They are the three worst in Heaven," Gabriel said sadly. "We did not know this coup was developing. When we would see the Cherubim, we would always hug them and greet them. In turn they would give us bear hugs and special greetings. They would even give us a kiss…"

"Just like Judas kissed Jesus?" Sonny asked.

"Perceptive little rascal, aren't you?" Gabriel beamed at God's chosen one.

"Cherubim would then compliment us on how good we looked- they would even tell us how much they loved us. Such hypocrites!" the old angel snorted.

"Were all the Cherubim involved in the revolt?" Sonny asked.

"Of course not," Gabriel snapped, "Not all of the Germans were Nazis, nor all the Russians Communists, nor are all the Muslims terrorists. There were good Cherubim, in fact you may remember the high honor given two of them."

Sonny and Sandra looked at each other like two children struggling to remember the answer to a Sunday School question. "Didn't Isaiah see Cherubim in the Temple?" Sandra finally answered.

I said, "Close but no cigar. He saw Seraphim. You may remember from one of my most memorable sermons, I tell the story how Isaiah saw the Lord high and lifted up. There were the special angels, Seraphim, flying around with two of their six wings. With two they flew, with two they covered their faces and for some reason they used two to cover their feet."

"Yuk," Sonny said, "I don't blame them. The foot is the ugliest part of the body- I don't think God designed it. Who wants anybody to see their feet?"

I grinned and continued, "As the Seraphim flew they called to one another, 'Holy, holy, holy is the LORD Almighty; the whole earth is full of his glory.' The reason for this is simple. The angels were messengers, the Cherubim were guards, but the Seraphim were the Praise Team that God created after the Cherubim.

When Isaiah heard all of this, he was made aware of his sin and uncleanness. He yelled out 'Woe is me.' A Seraph is a singular Seraphim as a Cherub is a singular Cherubim. A Seraph flew down to Isaiah with a burning coal from the altar with some tongs and said, 'See, this has touched your lips; your guilt is taken away and your sin atoned for.' Then Isaiah heard the voice of the Lord saying, 'Whom shall I send? And who will go for us?'"

"I know that answer, 'Here am I. Send me!'" Sonny finished the Scripture. He looked back at the raving Adolph Hitler Lucifer and the roaring crowds of Cherubim. "Where did the Seraphim come from? Are they good guys or bad guys?"

"Seraphim are are good guys. God created them after the fall of Lucifer for the sole purpose of praise. They were the forerunners of music directors and choir leaders. But you still didn't figure out how the most Cherubim were used. A hint: the Cherubim were made to guard the light."

"I remember now," Sandra smiled. "When Adam and Eve were driven out of the Garden, God put Cherubim to guard the entrance with a flaming sword."

Sonny raised his hand, "Wait a minute- if God just drove Adam and Eve out of the Garden, what happened to the animals?"

Gabriel applauded, "Very clever question. In fact, I don't remember any preacher ever even thinking about the animals before."

I sighed, "We have some preachers and churches now more interested in ecology than theology. Save the whale! Save the mustang1 I think we need to get back to Save the Sinners."

Gabriel nodded his agreement to my short sermon. He asked, "What happened to the animals in the Garden? Of course, most of them were cast out of the Garden into the Land of Eden."

"The Land of Eden?" Sonny asked. "I thought it was the Garden of Eden."

"The Garden was located in the east of Eden, or as it was known then- the Land of Eden," Gabriel told them. "As for the animals, you will discover the answer to that..."

"In due time," Sonny added. "Why can't you just go ahead and tell us all of it?"

Gabriel rubbed his hair back from his eyes, looked at Lucifer raising the Cherubim to a frenzy, then turned his gaze back to the young man and woman God had chosen. He was amazed how closely they resembled the two in the Garden. Finally he answered, "In due time. It will make much more sense to you if you see how the characters develop as the plot thickens."

"Why didn't God just throw that bunch of bums out when all of this was happening?" Sonny asked.

Gabriel sniffed then said, "First of all, don't call any of God's creatures 'bums.' We angels are not allowed to criticize them. Second, you cannot imagine how much God loves each and every one of his creatures. The closest you can get to experiencing the special agape love is when you see some perverted criminal executed for his sins and in the background you see a mother weeping. Why does she cry? Because she loves her children."

"Thirdly, you have to try to understand our God believes in giving people second and third and fourth chances, etc. Classic example: Why didn't Jesus boot Judas out of the camp when He knew what Judas would do? There are many answers by many different people, but one which stands out is, 'It is the nature of God to love his children and to give them opportunities to love Him.'"

Behind us the crowd shouted,
"Hail Lucifer, Bearer of the Light. He will deliver us."

+ + +

As a young preacher I watched the scene, meditated, then asked, "Gabriel, what was Lucifer's sin? I thought angels were unable to sin."

Gabriel said, "Well, have a seat and I'll try to explain it to you." Three student desks appeared as he spoke. We three sat down while the teacher delivered his message. "We angels can't commit a lot of sins. We can't commit adultery nor lust for obvious reasons. We lack the tools. All of us angels with the knowledge of Good cannot break the other commandments, 'No other Gods, no idols, no blasphemy.' Since we are the product of a single parent, we can honor our father but we have no mother. I assure you we do not venerate 'Mother Earth,' as the New Age does. Since we are immortal we can't murder and it's obvious when you have everything in Heaven, there is no need to steal, nor covet, nor lie."

"Therefore, angels were pretty well exempt from breaking any of the Ten Commandments you humans have to obey," Professor Gabriel continued as he walked back and forth. "But there were two sins which came with the knowledge of good and evil. They weren't built in but they developed quickly. We discovered outcroppings of these two evils very promptly in Lucifer. He began to sin and drag millions of Cherubim with him."

"Just like Adam," Sandra said.

"What are the two sins?" Sonny asked after a moment of silence.

Gabriel answered slowly. "The first is pride. Pride is arrogance- an overgrown sense of importance. It can easily be the beginning of almost every sin.

To put it bluntly, Lucifer had an overdose of conceit- he wanted to be as important as God."

Sonny said, "Isn't that exactly what happened to Hitler and Napoleon and Stalin and all the other dictators?"

"Yep, you didn't have to dig deep under their skin until you discovered vast amounts of Pride," Gabriel said.

Pride was the First Sin

Sandra added the woman's touch. "It's easy to see how Satan tempted Eve now. What he had was contagious- conceit. And he wanted to share it. So he told simple-minded Eve she could be as good as the gods and could be just like them, if she would only eat the apple."

"Forbidden fruit," Gabriel corrected. "Wherever you humans came up with the apple I'll never know. It's a wonder you didn't say it was a pineapple, or an orange, or a peach, or some kind of blackberry. But you are correct He temped the then innocent Eve with Pride. Then not-so-smart Adam joined right in. Uh, I still can't understand why Lucifer and his gang would be unhappy in Heaven, nor why Adam and Eve lost paradise for a bite of forbidden fruit."

I added, "Every religion has stories of the results of pride. Even mythology tells the story of Narcissus, who was so proud of himself, who loved himself so much, he would sit beside a reflecting pool for hours admiring old number one. Finally he fell into the lake and drowned. Just like a lot of people puffed up with pride are going to fall into the lake of fire and drown in their suffering."

Sandra said, "Brother Chris, I don't want to hurt your feelings, but it is rather obvious that Pride has joined the church, sings in the choir and often stands in the pulpit. Not you of course, but …"

"You are correct. Conceit sets up its shop in churches. We saw it in the middle ages when the pope was one of the richest men on earth. Martin Luther renounced the pope and pride and we had the Protestant Reformation. However, I am sad to report pride is more rampart now than ever. So many of us preachers want the biggest church, the best congregation, the most perks," I confessed, "I have to get down on my knees often like Isaiah and ask God to forgive me for being so puffed up."

The Second Sin Was Envy

Gabriel listened quietly then added, "Lucifer's second sin was Envy. Pride and Envy are Siamese twins in the garden of evil. Pride is the feeling of being overly important, and Envy craves what it thinks is of greater value."

I wiped a tear or two away as I said. "Tell me about it. Remember when I wanted to go to the big church in Birmingham? I recall when I wanted to be one of the big shots, the big dogs. We have been lured into the Devil's Den by thinking bigger churches are better churches. It's like thinking bigger families are better families- the man with twenty children is greater than some guy with only three. Preachers spend too much time counting nickels and noses. And I am guilty- a lot of the time. We forget we should be honored to pastor any of God's children. We are going to be judged not by our success- but by our faithfulness."

"Humility is a virtue," Sonny said as he patted his pastor on the shoulder. "You are not the least bit proud or puffed up, Preacher. You're just a plain old sinner like the rest of us."

We all laughed. Sonny then continued, "I did a study of some of the groups who stress humility to the point of absurdity. The Amish people are good folks, hard workers, but they are so dedicated to modesty they won't wear any clothes that look too fancy nor use any technology developed since the Sixteenth Century. Their ancestors were the Anabaptists. They were so meek they wore signs, 'Look How Humble I Am.'"

Gabriel grinned, "Christianity can go to either extreme. In the name of Christ we can flaunt ourselves over the world of sinners or we can hide in a cave like a monk. If we would just keep our eyes on the Son, we would see the way we are to live."

I said, "Amen. Pride has been transformed from one of the Seven Deadly Sins to One of the Highest Virtues today. We have 'movie stars' who are prettier, wealthier, and smarter than the rest of us. And they know it! Pride has always been around. The French loved Napoleon whom we consider evil. What you may not know that in 1799, he crowned himself as emperor, because no one else was worthy. But he met his Waterloo and all the rulers of this world will someday meet their Armageddon."

"Pride is disastrous but Envy is destructive," Gabriel said. We looked at him and waited for further explanation. He continued, "Because Lucifer was so handsome and popular, it never crossed my mind he would be envious of me."

"Uh, well, we think you're the greatest," Sonny said, "but why was he resentful of you? Was it because you are so smart, so wise, so knowledgeable?"

"That is flattery, young man," Gabriel said, "and it will get you a long way on earth but is easily discerned in Heaven. To answer your question, at first I had no idea he was even aware of my presence. From the beginning, he was the life of the party, the newest of God's creation. He was adored by all and I threw in my compliments and love for him. It took a couple of millennia for me to even notice how his light blue eyes would take on a shade of pale green when he looked at me or spoke to me. Plus, he despised the Seraphim- for they had six wings and he only had two!

"Since I was the Archangel, I was close to God and around Him much of the time. Often He would give me a message to take to another city and off I would fly. Other times, the message would be of less priority and I would assign it to someone else."

"Gee, it must have been tough not having cell phones and text messages," Sonny said. "But then I don't guess there were a lot of messages to send."

"Oh, quite contraire, my son," Gabriel answered, "God was in constant contact with his angels, sending them points of advice, instruction and often encouragement."

"Encouragement, do you mean angels get depressed?" Sandra asked.

"Not depressed as you humans," he answered, " It's more concern. Love always carries with it the capacity to be wounded. For example, Chris, do you recall the little red headed girl you thought you loved in the sixth grade?"

"Little red headed girl?" I laughed, "Good grief, I sound like Charlie Brown. Yes, I remember her. She was as cute as a button and all of us guys went wild over her. What I thought was deep passion was only puppy love. When I finally built up enough courage to ask her for a date to the Sunday School Valentine Party, she blinked those big blue eyes at me and said, 'Oh Chris, thank you, but I'm going with my boy friend, Foster Watson.'"

"I thought I would die." I put my hand over my heart and struck a Shakespearian pose, "Tis' better to have loved and lost, than never to have loved at all."

We all laughed and Gabriel said, "Then you see the weakness we angels had. This was our Achilles' heel. When you love, you leave yourself open to rejection. Lucifer like the cowboys of old, was rounding up his herd- his followers. Everyone tried to love him. But when they would disagree with his ravings, he would reject them, even spread gossip about them. God was aware of all this, so He was constantly sending messages to give confidence to the loyal angels. There were also regular instructions on how to keep the faith, to build up courage, to love even those who do not love you."

"Wow, that sounds like our weekly newsletter to church members," I said. "Somebody's always sick or hurt or down. They need a visit, a phone call, a card. Thank God for those saints who minister to the sick and the shut-ins."

Sonny turned his attention back to the Archangel and said, "You still haven't explained how Lucifer was driven by Envy. I thought envy was wanting what someone else has. I imagined angels were like monks in the monastery who didn't have anything but the robe on your backs. I sure didn't know you angels had anything to be desired."

"We had everything," Gabriel smiled in remembrance. "Someday all will be restored. Lucifer envied my relationship to God, he thought God loved me more than He loved him. I think he also wanted to be a messenger. It was his desire to stand before the multitudes and proclaim the message. Unfortunately pride has pushed many a preacher into preaching, just so he would have power over his listeners. There are only a minority who think that way, but those few, like Lucifer and his cohorts, can cause a lot of damage."

"Like terrorists," Sonny said, "A few terrorists with machine guns or suicide bombs can terrify an entire nation. As my dad, Smiling Sam, used to say, 'Sonny, a few skunks can stink up a whole house.' Hmm, maybe a few skunks can make Heaven reek."

Sandra said, "I know a good example of Envy and how destructive it can be. Remember the wicked queen in Snow White? She had double pneumonia of pride and envy. Sitting around her mirror, she would admire herself and ask,

> *'Mirror, mirror on the wall,*
> *who in this land is fairest of all?'*

Of course, the mirror knew that if it didn't want to end up cracked or broken or having seven years of bad luck, it had better say,

> *'You, my queen, are fairest of all.'*

But when Snow White was seven years old, she was so beautiful she surpassed the queen herself. Now when the queen asked her mirror:

Mirror, mirror, on the wall,
Who in this land is fairest of all?
The mirror said:
you, my queen, are fair; it is true.
But Little Snow-White is still
A thousand times fairer than you.
When the queen heard the mirror say this, she became
pale with envy.

"Good point," I said as we all applauded. "Pride and Envy, the twin sins, are both insatiable, like cancers eating away and always wanting more. It's easy to see how Lucifer was so puffed up with his set of wings and good looks he thought he was better than anyone else in Heaven. I am sure this led to the revolt against God himself."

"Right," Gabriel announced. "Next we see the final battle scene."

15 Billion B.C.

CHAPTER 20
WAR IN HEAVEN

The lights of Heaven began to fade as they do before a play begins. Darkness was not fully achieved- gray clouds settled over the Celestial Cities. Shouting erupted, bolts of lightning hundreds of miles long sizzled back and forth between the two armies. As far as the eye could see there were warriors on both sides. One side wore uniforms of solid white. The group being pushed back wore uniforms of different shades of gray and black. A cata-pult lofted a huge ball of fire against the darker forces. There was no blood, there were no casualties. Angels can't bleed and angels can't die. But they can lose their energy.

A bluish-gray haze hung over the battlefields. We could see the white forces had completely surrounded the Tree of Life. The dark force had tried to seize the Celestial City, take over the thrones and capture the Tree of Life.

"Oh, I think I understand," Sonny shouted over the noise of battle. "Lucifer's forces wanted to take the thrones so they could have all the power. Plus, it was necessary for them to eat of the Tree of Life to sustain their energy. They launched an attack on the very center of Heaven and God Himself. But now, I can tell they are not only being held back they are being forced back. Who is that ferocious angel leading the white forces?"

Gabriel shouted, "Michael, the Archangel, Go get'em, Mike!" Then he low-ered his eyes and said softly to the group, "That's not very angelic!"

"Yea, I know," Sandra said, "but them's me sentiments exactly! Who-ee, atta' boy Michael, put it to them! Knock'em down! Shove'em back!" Sandra turned to Gabriel and said, "I know that's not very lady like, but you remember I was once a cheerleader."

"Both of you are forgiven," I said. "I must confess, I was so carried away that I yelled, 'Roll Tide.'"

The panorama before us became silent. Lucifer waved a white flag, well, a dirty white flag, in surrender. Michael towered over him with his sword drawn.

"How do they have swords in Heaven?" Sonny asked, then remembered, "Oh, now I understand, Armor Check! 'The Sword of the Lord is the Word of God.' It is true in Heaven, just as it is on earth- God's Word is a Sword. We think of it just as the words of the Bible, but God spoke millions of years before the Bible was written down."

We were high enough to see the battlefield, the Tree of Life and the Thrones. The Father God rose from the center throne. His blue sash waved as he moved to the front line and stood between Michael and Lucifer, between His sons of light and His sons of darkness. He wavered a moment and love radiated from him as shafts of light through clouds in the afternoon sky. The group felt an emotion we had not encountered in Heaven until this time. The Father God trembled and His form changed from palest blue to darkest purple. Sonny and Sandra fell to the ground from the eruptions of pain coming from Father God. Sandra cried out and Sonny tried to hold her and hold back his screams at the same time. "What is happening?" he yelled.

+ + +

CHAPTER 21
THE WRATH OF GOD

Y ou are experiencing the Wrath of God," Gabriel stated. "Nobody desires His fury! Most do not even know it exists. You humans have painted a smiley face on God and refuse to accept the fact on Judgment Day sinners will fall into the hands of an angry, wrathful God. However, you two do not have be afraid. His rage is not directed toward you, it is aimed at Lucifer and his followers. Listen!"

Father God's voice boomed like thunder as He said, "Lucifer, I created you in my own image. You were made more blessed than the other angels. You converted this honor into pride. You craved the role of Gabriel and finally you wanted to overthrow the Godhead so you could be god yourself."

Lucifer lifted his head and flashed his artificial smile, "Father, I am sooo sorry, I did not mean to harm anyone..."

God roared, "Your damage was extensive and eternal. Not only did you harm yourself- you defiled Heaven. You drew billions of my Cherubim with you. Not all of them followed you as you desired. A few still remain my faithful guards."

"Father," Lucifer smiled again without no sense of repentance. "We seem to have a problem. What can you do to me? You made me eternal. All that exists is Heaven. Will you isolate me and my followers to some far corner?"

"No," God said. "Heaven is too good for you. You have damaged Heaven with your pride and envy. My followers now experience Fear. They never had this before. There are those who say they follow me but are simply mouthing words for fear of what I will do to them."

Lucifer smirked, "Since there's no place for us to go, I suppose all of you will just have to get used to us. Let's see," he said as he looked back at his troops, now weak and weary from war and lack of energy. "Hmm, why don't you just let us have those darker Celestial cities over there, and we'll just mind our own business."

"Lucifer, your knowledge has driven you insane," God roared. "You are

not welcome in Heaven any longer. You will not be allowed to spread your hate to my angels."

Lucifer sneered, "As I said, there is no place for us to go. We are eternal, you can't destroy us. So, really, Father God, you have no choice but to..."

"Do you think I am blind?" God asked. "I knew your schemes from the first day. But I loved you and offered you every opportunity to change, to be a loyal angel. You and all of your followers were created to share my Love, my Joy and my Peace. Instead you perverted my gifts into Lust and Misery and War."

Lucifer still refused to bow before God like a defiant young boy who has stolen the cookies from the cookie jar and will not say he is sorry and will not give back the cookies.

Blue bolts of lightning shot from the Father God, "I am a loving God but I am a just God. God the Son and God the Spirit have held court with me and we have decided you are guilty. You and yours will be cast into an eternal place of suffering I am preparing for you. It shall be called Hell."

We three humans shuttered as the word "Hell" was uttered. We felt a terrible pain shoot through our bodies. The putrid odor of decaying flesh swirled around us. The sounds of Heaven's music was replaced by the screams of millions suffering. Whatever Hell was- it was just the opposite of Heaven.

Still Lucifer smiled as if he had an ace card to play and God was only bluffing- trying to frighten them back into servitude. "So, is this 'Hell' ready now or do we wait for you to finish it?"

"It is not finished, but you can not stay in Heaven. I have prepared a temporary place for you and your disciples," said God.

"May I ask what my temporary arrangements are called?" Satan smiled as he winked at those defeated Cherubim who stood behind him.

God hesitated then said, "It is called Time and Space."

"Are there any restrooms there?" the dark angel laughed.

"There is nothing there now except time and space. It's only temporary while I finish preparing a place of eternity for you and for your supporters," God's voice turned raspy, almost tearful as he added, "And it will be the place of punishment for any who wish to come after you in the future."

"Is it in some corner of Heaven?"

"No, it is another dimension. We can go down to you, but you and those like you cannot enter Heaven again. Unless,..."

"Unless what? My Lord," the devil asked.

"It is not 'Unless', it is 'Until.' You nor your followers can enter Heaven until I have cleansed my creation from your corruption," God answered.

"Remember, God, you taught us Evil can only be cleansed by a sacrifice," Lucifer said. "You can't sacrifice anything in Heaven, nothing can be killed, nothing can be destroyed. You made up eternal. Tsk, tsk, too bad. You've got a problem."

"I also have a solution," God answered. "It will be a painful solution but it will be done."

"Now I will allow all of you to take a peek at my newest creation, Time and Space." As God said this, a huge hole began to open beneath them. Angels on both sides scurried back to keep from falling in. Then we scrambled back to the edges to look at what God had made. There was nothing there except darkness. Everything was as black as a cloudy midnight at the north pole. Our human group hovered over to see what was there and we were astounded at it's emptiness.

"There's nothing there," Lucifer stated. "Nothing at all."

"You are wrong again," the voice of God echoed down into the emptiness. There is time and there is space. From this day on you will be confined, limited, bound by minutes and hours and years. In Heaven, you were free to go wherever you desired whenever you desired. Now there will be boundaries, and you will be confined to one place at a time."

"Couldn't we work out a deal?" asked Lucifer for the first time showing a little fear. "I mean, we were just boys playing pranks. No one was killed nor really injured."

"You have caused more damage than you will ever know and the price to repair it is far greater than you can imagine. You and your followers have been judged and you have been found guilty. Your sentence is to suffer in Hell, whenever it is finished. Until then you will be kept in a restraining area of time and space."

You have caused more damage than you will ever know and the price to repair it is far greater than you can imagine.

God the Father grew to gigantic proportions towering over them by miles. Down came two hands that stretched farther than they could see. The huge hands fell upon Lucifer and his billions of disciples. Picking them up, they were then rolled into an enormous ball. Squeals and shrieks were heard like rats caught in a million traps. They were squeezed tighter and tighter together as is compressing all the air from them.

The gigantic ball was then lifted high into the heights of Heaven. There was a pause, then God hurled it through the hole into the bleak darkness. Then he shouted, "LET THERE BE LIGHT!"

What happened then surprised all of Heaven and all three of us humans who were watching. A enormous explosion ripped through the darkness below. Before the sound could reach us, Gabriel rushed over, punching buttons to cover our ears. Even then, there was the biggest bang we had ever heard.

+++

13.7 Billion B.C.

PART 3 THE BIG BANG

Chapter 22

WHAT IN THE WORLD WAS THAT?

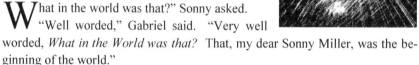

What in the world was that?" Sonny asked.
"Well worded," Gabriel said. "Very well worded, *What in the World was that?* That, my dear Sonny Miller, was the beginning of the world."

"You mean that explosion created the earth?"

"In time, yes," Gabriel explained. "However, as I remind you…"

"God is in no hurry. Yea, yea, yea." Sonny said.

"Was that the Big Bang?" Sandra asked.

"Give yourself a double A plus," Gabriel said.

"I'll take the grade but I don't understand," she answered.

I cleared my throat and began, "Plainly speaking, The Big Bang Theory believes the universe began when a hot and dense initial condition exploded at some finite time in the past. Since then the universe has expanded and continues to expand to this day."

"I know the theory- it's basic to most science today," Sandra said. "Georges Lemaître proposed what became known as the Big Bang theory of the origin of the Universe, although he called it his '*hypothesis of the primeval atom.*'"

"Yea, we had to study it in high school," Sonny said. "but our teacher, Mrs. Jordan, was a wonderful Christian. She stated this was one theory of how the world began. Without breaking any of the government rules in place today, she said there are many other hypotheses about creation including many religious views. Her statement was acceptable in high school, but now in college, many professors are proud of their atheism. They tell us there is no God; the world began with a big bang, and evolution has made us into what we are today. Hmm, wonder why they can state their disbelief in God and His Creation, but Christian professors are not allowed to state their beliefs?"

Sandra watched the explosion spread rapidly into space A thousand different questions were rattling around in her head. Finally she asked, "What caused the Big Bang? No scientist has answered the question fully. They don't have any idea where all that matter came from that led to our universe. It could have been energy or their primeval atom. They won't and can't explain where the source came from and they won't even discuss what was before the Big Bang. They do believe an enormous amount of energy was released which resulted in our universe."

Posing as a Billy Graham look-alike, I pointed to everything happening and said, "Again, according to my source, *Wikipedia*, the universe is defined as everything that physically exists: the entirety of space and time, all forms of matter, energy and momentum, and the physical laws and constants that govern them."

"Well, I'll be," said Sonny, "somehow I thought the universe was limited to the planets that orbit around our sun."

"People call our solar system the universe from time to time. But as I stated, the universe is everything: time, space, matter, energy, and all the laws that govern them."

Gabriel shook his head, "I never understood Lucifer, and I cannot understand how some of your scientists actually believe all the universe just, uh, happened. They hypothesize every law, including those of gravity, physics and science were just there waiting for something to happen so they could be put to use. Even harder to comprehend is the explanation of the human being; eyes, mouth, nose, ears, brain, heart, miles of nerves and blood vessels all just accidently worked their way into livelihood from a simple protein molecule which, fortunately, was able to come alive."

"You still haven't answered my question on the Big Bang." Sandra said, "We saw God cast Lucifer and all of his angels out of Heaven into time and space and then, ka-boom. What happened?"

Gabriel answered, "Really, Sandra, if you are going to teach students then you should be able to figure it all out. Over and over I have repeated that we angels are not matter, we are of a heavenly stuff. We are simply compressed energy. That was true of my creation and the formation of Lucifer and his gang. Now, can you see...?"

I put in my two cents worth. "First and foremost, we believe the universe came into being by the word of God. God said, 'Let there be light,' and there was light. Our main theology is based on the word of God- both His written word and His spoken word. But Gabriel helped me understand how other energy was generated in the Big Bang. Can you understand how Lucifer's exorcism from Heaven helped in that great explosion?

"I do see," Sandra responded. "Oh, yes, I see clearly. Einstein's Theory of Relativity was correct- $E=mc^2$. Energy is the result of Matter accelerated to the speed of light. In reverse- Matter is the result of Energy slowing down in time and space. So when heavenly energy met time and space- Ka-boom!"

Gabriel said, "Who knows? You may win the Nobel Prize for Physics one day as being the only person who figured out the real cause of the Big Bang- God's Word plus the Devil's entrance into the physical realm."

Sonny laughed, "I doubt if she'll receive it if she tells them it was the result of Lucifer's being thrown out of Heaven- plus a word from God."

"But that is exactly what happened," Sandra exclaimed. "Wow. It makes sense now. When Lucifer and his billions of followers were cast into the emptiness of time and space, the very laws of God went into effect. Their huge amount of energy simply exploded into materials stars are made of, and galaxies, and suns and moons, and the earth. How about that?"

Sonny placed his arm around her and said, "But nobody will believe you."

Smiling she pecked him on the check and said, "That won't stop it from being true. It lines up exactly with the Bible. God said, 'Let there be light' and there was light from the blast that rattled Heaven and began the Universe. This is so exciting!"

Sandra pondered for a moment, then asked, "When did this happen?"

"A few moments ago," Sonny teased.

"I mean how many years ago did this take place?" Sandra inquired.

"Thirteen point seven billion years ago is what your scientists say," Gabriel answered. "But every time they send up a new satellite they assure you humans they will find the origin of the universe- on the moon, on a comet, or Jupiter, or Mars. Each time the scientists find a rock they swear the earth is older than they had imagined."

Sandra said, "They did find some very old rocks. The Genesis Rock was found on the moon. It was retrieved from the moon by Apollo 15 astronauts- James Irwin and David Scott."

Sonny asked, "What was the Genesis Rock doing on the moon? Is the moon where the real Garden of Eden was?"

Sandra laughed, "No, it is the Genesis Rock for the moon, not for the earth. It is a sample of original lunar crust from around the time the moon was born."

"Did they ever find a rock down here that coincides with our Genesis, our Beginning?" Sonny asked.

I was quick to answer. "Glad you asked that question. You see there is a rock associated with our Genesis. Do you remember the song from children's church, 'The wise man built his house upon the rock.' Come on, Sonny, tell us who the rock is."

"The rock is Jesus," Sonny answered. "but is He the Genesis Rock also?"

Gabriel answered, "Oh yes, He is definitely the Genesis Rock. Take a look at what happens after the Big Bang."

JUST AFTER THE BIG BANG

Gazing down into the hole in Heaven, we watched the eruptions spewing out massive amounts of light and matter. There in the midst of all the cosmic beginning was a huge Red Form of the Son. Already He was directing traffic as chunks of energy and substance shot out into space."

"I thought God created the Heavens and the Earth," Sonny mumbled. "That sure looks like The Son down there engineering the whole thing."

Again, I had to sermonize, "Folks, if you will turn to Colossians 1:15-17, we find all of this about Jesus, the Son God:

> *He is the image of the invisible God, the firstborn over all creation.*
> <u>*For by him all things were created: things in Heaven and on earth,*</u>
> *visible and invisible, whether thrones or powers or rulers or authorities;*
> *all things were created by him and for him.*
> *He is before all things, <u>and in him all things hold together.</u>*
> (Colossians 1:15-17NIV)

"In other words," I continued as I gazed at the spectacle taking place below me. "The Son is the one who created all things in Heaven and on Earth. This includes us humans and the angels. Notice not only were we created *by Him* but we were created *for Him.* And the Scripture plainly says, 'In Him all things hold together.' I give you, Jesus, the Creator and the Super Glue of the Universe."

"Three cheers for Jesus!" Sandra shouted, "Rah! Rah! Rah!"

"What happened to Lucifer?" Sonny asked.

"Since he is eternal, he didn't disappear. He just lost a great, great deal of his energy as did his buddies," Gabriel answered.

Sonny glanced down at the Son amidst the blasts, "Now what is the Son God doing?"

"First he is making all the laws which will govern the Universe. He is the law maker. The Son will fashion all the laws of physics, chemistry, math, gravity, etc. These laws will then govern the formation of the cosmos. Secondly, he is changing energy into tiny bits of matter which will ultimately become atoms. This will take a long time. Then those atoms have to be fitted with a type of earthly energy to make electrons. Much, much later in your earth time, they will change into different kinds of atoms. Hydrogen will be the first atom, and it will take many, many millennia just to get it right," Gabriel explained.

"I get it," Sonny said. "First God made the atom, then He made Adam. Neato!"

Sandra shrugged and asked. "I know the atomic element chart. We were told that everything began with hydrogen and fused to make larger atoms. Is that true?"

"Basically, yes," Gabriel answered, "your teacher made it sound so simple and so, uh, natural. Honestly, it's much harder and takes much longer than you humans can realize."

"Why atoms?" Sonny asked.

"To show how meticulous God is in His planning," Gabriel answered. "Suppose he had put you together with Heaven-dust, scotch tape and safety pins? How long would you last?"

"Hmm, I see. The tiny parts all work together to make the whole?" Sonny replied. Then looking at the gaseous expanse below him, he asked, "But why galaxies? They are enormous!"

"What do they remind you of?"

"The Celestial cities," Sonny answered. "Why did everything have to be so big?"

"It's not just that the universe is big," Gabriel quipped. "Mankind has made God so small. Besides, The Son wanted the Universe to be beyond man's comprehension. It is a model of eternity and its greatness."

"Hmm, makes sense," Sonny said, then added, "I guess. Whew, this is pretty heavy stuff you're laying on us, Gabriel. We three human beings have been shown the answers to theological and scientific mysteries. The funny thing is, the way you have explained it to us, it all sounds so logical."

"God is a sensible, reasonable, practical God," Gabriel answered. "He even revealed much of Himself to you through creation. Just look around. Flowers, music, aromas of steaks sizzling on a patio, stars, sunsets. All of it says over and over there must be a God somewhere. Every good thing you see is a thumbprint of God. The picture is only blurred when man tries to become a god himself. He further muddies the picture when he rebels as Lucifer did."

"And like Adam and Eve rebelled?" said Sandra.

"Yes. Then all of mankind fell," Gabriel said sadly. "But we must move on. We have miles to go before we can sleep."

"One last question before we leave the Creation of the Universe," Sandra said. "We are now being told there is a Dark Energy which dominates and permeates all of space. Observations suggest 72% of the total energy density of today's universe is in this form. Does this have anything to do with Lucifer and his fallen angels?"

"Sandra, my dear, you have such a keen mind," Gabriel answered. "However, if you tell your professor at Samford this, he might give you an 'F.' Let me just say, there is a dark energy on planet earth, and it looks as if at least 72% of the world's energy is being directed by the Prince of Darkness."

Spellbound, our tiny group watched the great ball of fire continue to zoom outward in all directions. Titanic bursts of red erupted followed by orange and yellow explosions. Heaven seemed so comfortable, so homey, so safe compared to this chaos. Underneath us reverberated the commotion of creation. Gabriel was set to lead us down into this chaotic space. We looked around Heaven. The gray clouds of eternity were beginning to whiten again since Lucifer was gone. Still there was the smell of death in the air- the music was not so beautiful- and when we tried to take a taste of manna, it was as if someone had poured in too much vinegar.

Gabriel read our minds. "Don't worry, God is God. He will have everything cleaned up and made right. Someday all of Heaven will be restored, and we will take part in the Grand Reopening."

We joined hands and the angel informed us, "We are now leaving the historical review of Heaven. Now we will zoom forward to the birthday of the earth and the beginning of life."

+ + +

6.5 Billion B.C.

CHAPTER 23
PLANET EARTH IS BORN

Time zoomed past with great flashes of light; comets sped by; suns slammed into each other like sumo wrestlers. Galaxies unfurled like rattle snakes on a lazy summer afternoon. Fluorescent gases of crimson and of pink billowed and detonated, only to collapse into themselves. Stars shot forth like Roman candles on the Fourth of July.

As we slowed down we saw a yellow sun burning away at the darkness. Before us was a giant red molten rock bubbling with volcanic blasts. "Recognize that?" Gabriel asked. "That's home sweet home before it became so sweet."

I recited, "In the beginning God created the Heavens and the earth. And the earth was without form and void."

Sonny looked at the fiery planet. "Preacher, if you and Gabriel weren't here I would say that doesn't look much like the earth- it looks more like Hell. Wow! Look at that!"

A meteorite the size of Alabama slammed into the molten mass sending lava splattering into the dark sky. Bright red tsunamis of red hot rock splashed out and around the world, only to crash into each other on the far side.

"Where are we now in time?" Sonny asked. "I mean, earth time."

"I know the answer," Sandra replied. "The Big Bang took place approximately 13.7 billion years ago. Now we are at the birth of the earth. We have traveled forward in time a whopping 9 billion years. Below us is what the world was like 4.5 billion years ago, give or take a few million years."

"I don't see the moon," Sonny stated.

"Next up," Gabriel said, "prepare yourself for Mr. Moon to make his debut." In fast forward the scene sped along. Other asteroids collided, volcanic bursts spewed lava and smoke over thousands of miles. Now we watched a planet creeping nearer and nearer to the red hot earth.

"Watch out, they're going to crash!" Sonny shouted.

Another bang filled the Heavens. The planet crashed into earth on an angle causing the world to shake and wiggle. A portion of the planet skimmed off in a murky mess. Instead of tearing off into space, it slowly began an elliptical orbit around the earth. Fast-forwarding, we saw the mass form into a ball then into a regular circular trajectory.

"So that's where the moon came from!" Sandra said. "You know this is one of the theories we have been studying. Some astronomers believe there were two planets circling the sun at 150 million kilometers: earth and a small planet about the size of Mars. 'Theia' was its name."

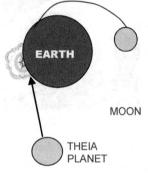

"Theia?" Sonny asked. "Sounds like a name some hippy parents would give their daughter."

"Theia, the second planet became unstable in its orbit and crashed into the Earth. Part of it ricocheted off and became the moon- *Reader's Digest Condensed Version*," Sandra said with a bow.

"Wait a minute, wait a minute!" Sonny shouted. "We are out of sync, way out. I know the Bible says Creation took six days. Big problem, now you have the moon emerging before the first day. Uh, when was the first day? It's not working out correctly. My atheist professor loves to point out the Bible has God creating light on the first day and the sun and moon on the fourth day. Then after it's all over and God rests on the seventh, Adam pops up. Can anyone explain that to me?"

Gabriel gazed at his young students fondly. It was easy to see why God had chosen the two of them for his special task of revelation. "Let me make us a place to rest while I explain this to you. Would you like to sit on a U.F.O.?"

"Don't tell me God made flying saucers!" Sonny said.

"I was only kidding, but we do need a place to sit down," Gabriel grinned. "I'll just construct a patio here in space where we can watch the world grow and see life emerge. This is going to take some time, so have a seat."

A picnic table appeared along with four easy chairs. Glasses of Diet Coke materialized with some sandwiches and cookies. We three humans didn't realize how hungry and thirsty we were. Then Sandra giggled, "I'm famished, I haven't had a bite for zillions of years."

Gabriel took a drink, wiped his mouth with a solid white napkin, then continued. "First, we must understand the Bible is God's Word. It is our sole source of reference about Him; it tells all we need to know about Him, and it contains all the information necessary for salvation and living a righteous life. Also it is the only book that has the correct map to Heaven. Do we agree on that before we start?"

All agreed as we sipped on our drinks and ate our food. Gabriel smiled approval. "Listen to what I told you: *In the Bible, God gave us all the information we need to know*, right?"

Again we said, "Yes, sure, OK."

"But God did not give us all *the information that exists*. There was much, much more God did not disclose in the Scriptures. We have all we need to know about Salvation, but not all there is to know about history, geography, languages, math, social studies nor science. God left much to be discovered. Let's say God loves to play 'Hide and Seek.' He hides diamonds, gold, jewels, oil in the earth- and man has to seek them out. God also hides His scientific achievements, man has to find them. Einstein discovered the Theory of Relativity. Listen, Einstein did not *CREATE* the Theory of Relativity- he *DISCOVERED* it. Sir Isaac Newton did not take out a patent on the Law of Gravity as if it were something he made in a laboratory- he discovered it. Do you understand what I am trying to tell you?"

God made all the laws, we only discover them.

Sandra and I nodded our heads. Sonny had a dazed look as if he didn't understand which play the quarterback had called and what he was supposed to do. He said, "You are saying God made all the laws of physics, chemistry, etc. We only discover them?"

"Exactly," Gabriel beamed. "You must understand this fact before I explain to you the mystery of creation." He waved his hand and a computer and projector appeared on the table and a screen rose up. "Since Sesame Street, you humans learn best with show and tell. So I will show and tell you about the Genesis account of Creation. You will find science and religion agree on many points about the beginning. Moses did the final editing of the story 3500 years ago when he wrote down the book of Genesis. Today, scientists are just discovering the deep, deep truths of creation."

+ + +

CHAPTER 24
THE SIX PHASES
OF CREATION

SIX PHASES OF CREATION	
1- Light	4- Sun & Moon
2- Waters	5- Fish
3- Earth	6- Animals Man

L ike 'The Sound of Music,' we'll start at the very beginning," Gabriel announced as he flipped on the computer and adjusted the projector. "Let's start with Genesis 1:1,2. King James Version." A slide appeared on the screen.

INTRODUCTION TO CREATION

Genesis 1 (KJV)

1- -In the beginning God created the Heavens and the earth.
2- And the earth was without form, and void;
and darkness was upon the face of the deep.
And the Spirit of God moved upon the face of the waters.

Gabriel allowed us time to read the words, then explained, " You will notice this is 'The Introduction to Creation.' Sonny, if you wrote a book about football, you might have an opening spot of introduction in which you would say, 'In the beginning of sports, football was played by ancient Greeks. It reappeared in the Middle Ages and became Rugby in Europe. We now play American football. There was a time when the University of Alabama football team was without form and void; they had lost a lot of games and darkness covered the alumni. But a new spirit of enthusiasm arrived with Coach Saban. I was fortunate enough to win a scholarship and play on the team.'"

"Now you have not told me how the game of football began nor how it is played. You haven't given me many of the facts nor have you told me what position you play nor even who Coach Saban really is. This is just the Introduction. Get it?"

"Got it!" Sonny grinned. He leaned forward, for he knew this was a learning lesson, and some where down the line he had to get this part straight.

"O.K., Slide Two- Phase One," Gabriel announced.

PHASE ONE

Genesis 1:3-5
And God said, Let there be light:
and there was light.
And God saw the light, that it was good:
and God divided the light from the darkness.
And God called the light Day,
and the darkness he called Night.
And the evening and the morning were the first day.
(KJV)

"Now we begin the story of Creation, the *How*," Gabriel lectured. "You saw the Big Bang and you heard God shout, 'Let there be light!' When eternal objects, even fallen angels, smack into time and space they release energy- which causes light. Before- there was nothing but darkness. Now light began to expand into the darkness. God divided them in two and called the light 'Day,' and the darkness he named, 'Night.'

"No difficulty so far with our scientific friends, except they call it the Big Bang. As I have informed you, the real name is *Creation*." Gabriel paused for us to take this in. "Now it seems there is a problem with 'The evening and the morning were the first day.' At first look, God started on a Sunday and finished on Friday and took Saturday off to rest. A closer examination of the word '*evening*' reveals it means '*dusk*' or as the light begins to fade- the *ending* of a day or the end of a phase. '*Morning*' means '*dawn*' as the *beginning* of a new day- or a new phase.

"yowm"

a day

or

a space of time

Strong's Definition

"Stay with me now, 'Day' often means a 24 hour day. But since there is no sun or moon yet, here it must mean something else. The word 'yowm,' means a day- but it can also be used figuratively, meaning 'A space of time defined by an associated term.' So you see in Slide Three."

And God called the light Day, and the darkness he called Night.

God called the   Light   Day

God called the   Darkness   Night

And the evening and the morning were the first day.

Evening `ereb   evening, night
Morning *boqer*   point of time when night changes to day

Word for Evening and Morning used together means
a long space of time in Daniel 8:14 (2400 days)

Day (*YOWM*)   Day, Light or A Space of Time

Gabriel continued, "Therefore, what you have been taught all your life about the *Six Days of Creation* were really the *Six Yowms, or Phases, of Creation.* The amazing part is how similar the process of Genesis coincides with that of science. We don't have to stop and say, 'Oh Great Infallible Scientist, we will bend our beliefs to whatever you discover.' We say proudly, 'Your discoveries are bending to our beliefs.'"

Another slide illuminated the screen. "Phase Two," Gabriel said. "I'm going to use one of your newer translations, the New International Version. The word '*firmament*' in King James is rather difficult to understand or explain."

PHASE TWO

Gen 1:6-8

*And God said, "Let there be an expanse between the waters
to separate water from water."
So God made the expanse and separated the water under the expanse
from the water above it. And it was so.
God called the expanse "sky."
And there was evening, and there was morning-- the second day.
(NIV)*

"Oh, I know this one," Sandra exclaimed. "We have been studying the *Hadean Eon* at school. It was funny to me because it refers to the hot period, and it sounds like *Hades Eon*. The early earth had no oceans and no oxygen. Heavier elements like iron sank to the center of the earth producing the magnetic field. Lighter gases such as hydrogen and helium rose above the earth. Soon an atmosphere developed which included water from the surface of the earth. This water also extended up into what we would call the atmosphere. It was one big muggy mess until God separated the water in the atmosphere from that on the earth. We thought it was funny when our professor told us it must have rained for hundreds of years when the earth began to cool."

"Simply put," Gabriel congratulated her. "Now I see why God will use you along with Sonny to explain scientific achievements in a language people can understand."

The next slide replaced the former. We all took a look excitedly as to what was going to happen next.

PHASE THREE A

Gen 1:9-10
*And God said, "Let the water under the sky be gathered to one place,
and let dry ground appear."
And it was so.
God called the dry ground "land,"
and the gathered waters he called "seas."
And God saw that it was good.
(NIV)*

"Now you notice I call this slide, *Phase Three A*." Gabriel stated. "You will understand why in a moment. So let's take a look at the next phase of the creation of Mother Earth. The waters gathered into one place, the oceans. Then, lo and behold, dry ground appeared. It was so and it was good."

Sandra raised her hand and continued. "Again this is right in line with recent discoveries. They say the ocean appeared around 4 billion years ago and separated itself from the dry ground or land. You're right on target, Professor Gabe."

"Thank you," the angel said as he sipped his Coke and prepared the next slide. "Now here is where we have difficulty with some of our brothers. But take a look, see what it says in Phrase Three B, and I'll try to explain it."

PHASE THREE B

Gen 1:11-13
Then God said, "Let the land produce vegetation:
seed-bearing plants and trees on the land that bear fruit with seed in it,
according to their various kinds."
And it was so.
The land produced vegetation:
plants bearing seed according to their kinds
and trees bearing fruit with seed in it according to their kinds.
And God saw that it was good.
And there was evening, and there was morning-- the third day.
(NIV)

"I don't see any problem," Sonny said as he read over it the second time. "You have dry land in the first part of Day Three, I mean Phase Three A. Once you have land and water, you can have plants that grow in the ground- which appear on schedule in Phrase Three B."

Sandra exclained, :Whoops, we do have a problem. We have vegetation growing before there is sunlight- the sun doesn't appear until Day Four or Phase Four."

"O.K., science teacher, if you are all right with it, let me throw out the bugger bear and be done with it," Gabriel remarked. "Now we come to Phase Four."

PHASE FOUR

Gen 1:14-19

And God said, "Let there be lights in the expanse of the sky
to separate the day from the night,
and let them serve as signs to mark seasons and days and years,
and let them be lights in the expanse of the sky
to give light on the earth."
And it was so.
God made two great lights-- the greater light to govern the day
and the lesser light to govern the night.
He also made the stars.
God set them in the expanse of the sky to give light on the earth,
to govern the day and the night, and to separate light from darkness.
And God saw that it was good.
And there was evening, and there was morning-- the fourth day.
(NIV)

Sonny was quiet as he read over the scripture of the creation of the sun, the moon and the stars. "Wait a minute," Sonny cautioned as he read it again. "On the fourth day God made the sun and the moon and the stars? Houston, we've got two problems.

1- We have light in Phase One but no sun until Phase Four.

2- We have plants growing on earth on the third day
    before the sun and stars arrive on day four."

"I'm glad you noticed that, Sonny Miller," Gabriel answered. "I must admit it is confusing at first. It needs some clarification. Let's use your football book again, do you remember it?"

"Sure, I've already got the introduction written," Sonny smiled.

FOOTBALL
CHAPTER ONE- "So how much do you know about ancient football in Greece?" Gabriel asked.

"Uh, nothing," Sonny admitted.

"But to make your football history correct, you will have to go back and research the ancient origin of sports that used balls. Are you with me?"

"Yeah, I guess. Is this a trick question?" Sonny asked.

CHAPTER TWO - of your book, you tell of 'Football in the Middle Ages up through Modern Rugby.' You don't give a lot of details, just brush in enough information to let us know that football and baseball are different. Are you with me?"

"I'm trying to keep up," Sonny answered. "But go on to Phase Three and maybe I will understand."

CHAPTER THREE – "Phase Three of Sonny Miller's best selling book is entitled 'Modern Football.' This will include the origin of the game you play and its rise all the way up to the Super Bowl. Then you inform your reader you have shown them the historical scope of football.

CHAPTER FOUR- expands Chapter one, Itis filled with interesting stories of its ancient origin- one by Cicero would be a good one. The Roman politician writing about fifty years before Christ describes the case of a man who was killed while having a shave when a ball was kicked into a barber's shop."

"Really?" Sonny asked. "Wow, it started as a dangerous sport."

CHAPTER FIVE- would elaborate on Chapter Two, Football in the Middle Ages. You would tell how football progressed or digressed in the Middle Ages." Gabriel enjoyed watching the young athlete's rapture with the game he played so well but understood so little of its history. "You would throw in stories of how whole towns would have football teams. The town teams would play each other. Oh, teams were not limited to eleven players. Everyone could join in the game. You would tell them it was 'Mob Football,' and hazardous. Your reader would want to know details of how King Edward II of England issued a proclamation banning handball, football or hockey in 1363. The Parliament of Scotland passed a decree making 'fut ball' illegal and punishable by a fine of four pence."

"I didn't know all that," Sonny confessed. "I thought there were always eleven players on each team and the rules were set."

CHAPTER SIX – OR PHASE SIX - This last part would be Phase Six, 'Modern Football.' There you would bring them up to date on rules, uniforms, great teams, great coaches, and finally, you would introduce Coach Saban and a future Heisman Trophy Winner, Sonny Miller."

"What? I can't put that in the book because it's not true," Sonny replied.

"It's not true YET," Sandra added. "The story is not complete. Gabriel, I see what you are saying.. The football book would outline the history in chapters 1, 2 and 3. Then chapter 4 would elaborate on chapter 1; chapter 5 would give deeper details of chapter 2. Then chapter six would complete what chapter three had begun."

"Exactly, I just happen to have a slide prepared to display this:

FOOTBALL	
By Sonny Miller	
1st Chapter Ancient Football	4th Chapter Ancient Football in Detail
2nd Chapter Medieval Football	5th Chapter Medieval Football in Detail
3rd Chapter Modern Football	6th Chapter Modern Football in Detail

"Sonny, does that seem to be one way you could write your book and turn it into a bestseller?"

"It looks great," answered Sonny, "especially since I've never written a book, don't know how to write a book; and if I did write one, Sandra would have to correct every other word."

"Sandra, you are to become a science teacher, not only in high school, but also in college," Gabriel said. "Sonny will win the Heisman, you will win the Nobel Prize for your understanding of the Big Bang and Life on Earth. You will win another Nobel for a discovery you will make when you return home."

"Surely you're kidding," Sandra blushed.

"I keep reminding you two that God chose you and has prepared you for a great spiritual and scientific break through," the angel said. "However, that's in the future. My question is, 'Do you see the correlation between Phase One and Phase Four of Creation? Does it seem possible to you that Phase Four was to complete and explain Phase One?'"

A new slide appeared on the screen.

CREATION	
1st Phase Light	4th Phase (expansion of 1st Phase) Sun, Moon and Stars

"Sure, as my daddy would say, 'That's as plain as the nose on your face.' Sonny answered. "Phase One is the general appearance of light. Phase Four then elaborates and gives the details on how light appeared and even tells us God made the stars also. Phase Four is the completion of Phase One."

"Good, keep that in mind now as we quickly look at the next two slides."

PHASE FIVE
Gen 1:20-23
And God said, "Let the water teem with living creatures,
and let birds fly above the earth across the expanse of the sky."
So God created the great creatures of the sea
and every living and moving thing with which the water teems,
according to their kinds,
and every winged bird according to its kind.
And God saw that it was good.
God blessed them and said,
"Be fruitful and increase in number and fill the water in the seas,
and let the birds increase on the earth."
And there was evening, and there was morning-- the fifth day.
(NIV)

"You don't have to be an Einstein to understand the creation of fish and birds," Gabriel explained. "You will notice all of them were to reproduce 'after their kind.' That is a remarkable statement to be written so long ago. In other words, catfish don't produce sharks nor do buzzards give birth to eagles."

Fifth Day- God Creates Creatures of Sea and Air

"Let's move on to the Sixth Phase," Gabriel said as he clicked the computer.

> **PHASE SIX – Part A**
> Gen 1:24-31
> *And God said,*
> *"Let the land produce living creatures according to their kinds:*
> *livestock, creatures that move along the ground,*
> *and wild animals, each according to its kind."*
> *And it was so.*
> *God made the wild animals according to their kinds,*
> *the livestock according to their kinds,*
> *and all the creatures that move along the ground according to their*
> *kinds.*
> *And God saw that it was good.*

"Bear with me, young people," Gabe apologized, "I haven't done this much teaching since I had to train the Seraphim in Angelology 101. Read this slide very closely as there are some things most people overlook."

Sonny said, "Livestock, wild animals, all creatures that move on the ground. He *made* them after *their* kind. Now take a close look at Phase 6 B. He didn't *make* man, he created man - not after *their* kind, but *in our image*.

> **PHRASE 6- PART B**
> *Then God said,*
> *"Let us make man in our image, in our likeness,*
> *and let them rule over the fish of the sea and the birds of the air,*
> *over the livestock, over all the earth,*
> *and over all the creatures that move along the ground."*
> *So God created man in his own image,*
> *in the image of God he created him;*
> *male and female he created them.*

Sonny studied the words as if preparing for a final exam. "Wait a minute, if Jesus, uh the Son God created all of this, He said animals were made *according to their kinds.* Yet why does He create man *in His own image?*"

"Good question," Gabriel answered. "As you have noticed, God is not some big blob of energy off in the far recesses of space. He is humanoid in His form. So are each of the three persons of God, the Father, the Son and the Spirit. Man was made to look like them, just as He made us angels to resemble Him."

I chimed in, "We learned in the seminary we are made in His image as W.I.M.E."

Sonny looked at Sandra for some clue; she shrugged him off. He asked, "O.K., Preach, we give up, what does W.I.M.E. stand for?"

"Will, Intellect, Morals and Emotion," I grinned. "Just as God has Will, Intellect, Morals and Emotion, so do we. Animals have some will, but they cannot discern the Will of God. They have intellect and though some are trying to say pigs and monkeys are as smart as we are, I don't see any pig cities only pig pens. Monkeys can be taught to recognize sign language, but they have yet to write a book or send a rocket to the moon. Morals? Sad to say, much of Hollywood and a great percentage of people seem to act more like animals than children of God. But the one I love is the fact that we humans have emotions. Because of them we can love."

Sonny snuggled closer to Sandra and said, "Amen, thank you Lord."

"All of those are true," Gabriel answered, 'but don't forget the main one. Since mankind is made in the image of God, there is something heavenly, something eternal inside every person. This something is the soul, and it longs for its maker. The soul becomes homesick for the homeland of Heaven."

Gabriel gazed down at the Red Planet Earth and its lopsided moon swinging around it. "I'm still amazed God went to all this trouble to make mankind. But then I remember, to God it was no trouble at all. All right, are you ready for another slide? I need to show you what else took place in Phase Six."

**Day 6
God
Creates
Man
In His
Image**

PHRASE 6- PART C

God blessed them and said to them,
"Be fruitful and increase in number; fill the earth and subdue it.
Rule over the fish of the sea and the birds of the air
and over every living creature that moves on the ground."
Then God said, "I give you every seed-bearing plant
on the face of the whole earth and every tree that has fruit with seed in it.
They will be yours for food.
And to all the beasts of the earth and all the birds of the air
and all the creatures that move on the ground—
everything that has the breath of life in it—
I give every green plant for food." And it was so.
God saw all that he had made, and it was very good.
And there was evening, and there was morning-- the sixth day.
(NIV)

Sandra stared at the words, then said, "The sixth day was pretty busy. I guess God wanted to get in everything before the weekend."

Gabriel smiled. "Now let's see if we can put all of this together in the way it happened. You will find this is exactly the same order of creation which scientists have finally gotten around to discover in the last one hundred years. Are you ready for another slide?"

We all cheered "Yes," as the screen glowed.

CREATION	
Beginning	**Completion**
1st Phase	4th Phase *(expansion of 1st Phase)*
Light	Sun, Moon and Stars
2nd Phase	5th Phase *(expansion of 2nd Phase)*
Water and Sky	Fish and Birds
3rd Phase	6th Phase *(expansions of 3rd Phase)*
A- Dry Land,	A- Animals Made
B- Land Vegetation	B- Creation of Man:
	Male & Female- In His Image

All three of us humans studied it for a while. I cleared my throat and said, "I need to apologize to both of you for not sharing this sooner. It's just, uh, I'm kind of chicken. So many people in the church insist God created the world in six consecutive days, and they will label anyone who dares say different as a liberal or a heretic. I hate to tell you, but there have been times when we preachers had to be quiet about social issues or political stances or Biblical truths."

Gabriel reached over and patted the young preacher on the back. "I understand., Even I had to stay quiet about Lucifer. From the first, I knew he was a bad seed, but He was God's child just as I was. I wanted to give him a chance. Plus, I didn't want to start a squabble in Heaven, any more than you want to start one in the church."

"So, Phase One: Light is explained in detail in Phase Four- Sun, Moon and Stars. Phase Two of Water and Sky set the stage for Fish and Birds in Phase Five. Dry Land and Vegetation take place in Phase Three and lead naturally into Phase Six when animals start to creep across the earth and make ready for the ones made in God's image, Adam and Eve," I explained.

Gabriel was nodding his head, then he abruptly stopped. "I think you will notice Phase Six says He created Man, although the Hebrew word is *Adam*- it means mankind. That is further noted when it says, 'Let us make man in our image, in our likeness, and let *them* rule over the fish, etc.' The best translation is Let us make *mankind* in our image, in our likeness and let *them* rule...'"

Sandra put her head into both hands in deep thought. Sonny was still trying to piece it all together. I sat with a satisfied smile on my face. Finally, Sandra said, "Are you saying God created mankind in His image and for them to rule? Did I miss something or is Adam not a part of mankind?"

"You didn't miss anything- you heard the Scriptures correctly. On the Sixth Day God created the animals. Then what did He do?" Gabriel asked.

"I know that one," Sonny said. "On the seventh day He rested."

"Close but you are missing the point. After everything was created, then God made 'man, male and female He created them.' It seems quite obvious- Man was a special creation. God 'made' the animals in the Sixth Phase, but He 'created man in his own image. Male and female he created them.'"

"So?" Sonny asked.

"So, man is created in a special way, 'in the image of God.'" Gabriel let it set in and then continued, "Animals are not made in His image, only man was created in His image."

"I'm not sure I understand," Sonny said. "We are taught in school that mankind is simply the result of evolution. We have more skills and intellect, but we are still only animals."

"That's as goofy as saying we angels are nothing more than an advanced animal in Heaven," Gabriel answered.

"You have animals in Heaven?" Sandra asked. "Is it true all dogs go to Heaven?"

"Yes and No," Gabriel answered. "We do have animals for you remember the lion will lie down with the lamb. We do not have all dogs, uh, thank goodness. Their yelping would make Heaven too noisy! I'll show you in a few moments how the Garden of Eden was Heaven on Earth. You recall there were animals there along with fruit trees and rivers."

IMPORTANT

Man was

Created

In the Image

Of God

"So Adam and Eve were not the result of evolution?" Sonny asked.

"Of course not, the Bible says 'God created man.'" Gabriel explained. "I will explain it to you..."

Sonny popped in, "In due time, Sandra dear, in due time."

Gabriel's love for us three humans radiated toward us as we were putting the pieces of the puzzle of creation and discovering truths we had never seen. "I think we will table that discussion because I want you to see how life began on planet earth."

+ + +

For since the Creation of the world God's invisible qualities-

- His eternal power and divine nature -

have been clearly seen,

being understood from what has been made,

so that men are without excuse.

(Rom 1:20NIV)

6.5 Billion B.C.

PART **4** CREATION OF LIFE

CHAPTER 25
LIFE BEGINS

The patio remained beneath us. Also accompanying us were the table, chairs and what was left of the sandwiches- not much, and cookies- not any. As we sped forward in time, more sandwiches appeared and the cookie jar was filled along with our Coke cans. No one seemed to notice this minor miracle. Huge lightning storms roamed across the muggy earth and volcanoes exploded hurling tons of debris into darkened skies. The sky which had been a putrid green brightened and turned brilliant blue. Below us a great ocean stretched around the world. There was barren land, pock marked by thousands of volcanoes and scarred with a million meteorite strikes.

"It looks like the moon with water," Sonny said. "Is this what the earth was like back then?"

"This is the earth back then," Gabriel answered. "Sandra, give us a time line."

With no hesitation, Sandra recited, "The Big Bang was 13.7 billion years ago, Earth was formed some 6.5 billions years in the past. Most Scientist believe life began about 2.5 billions years later. So it's about 4 billion years B.C."

"Wait a minute, don't you need to add two thousand years to bring us up to date?" asked Sonny.

"Well, if you must be picky, 4 billion plus 2 thousand comes to 4.0002 billion."

"Good, I think you scientists need to keep the box scores correct," Sonny said.

Sandra stood as she became the lecturer and stated, "There was inanimate matter on earth from its beginning- lava, rocks, dirt, water, etc- but nothing alive. Nobody really knows how life began.

"We do," Sonny answered, "or we will when Gabriel explains it. Maybe it would be better to say, 'We know *Who* did it.'"

Sandra looked at me and asked, "Darwin suggested life probably began in a small warm pond where all the elements necessary for life existed? There are all kinds of theories floating around for the beginning of life: Primordial Soup Theories, Deep Sea Vent Theory, Bubble Theory, Iron-sulfur World Theory, Radioactive Beach Theory, etc, etc.

"Why are you running all of this past us?" Sonny asked. "If you believe God did it, why worry about what others are saying?"

"Because the *Others* are teaching our children and our young people life began from inanimate material without God's help," I answered quickly. "Plus, they are not allowing any concept of Creationism nor Intellectual Design to be taught in the class room."

"Enough of this," Sonny said. "My head is spinning. Gabriel, you said this scene of the barren earth is where life started. Right? So show us what happened."

+ + +

WATCH CLOSELY AS LIFE IS CREATED

The Son God appeared below us. He reached into the waters and began to grind his fingers. He was delicately squeezing the water into something living, just as He has taken energy in Heaven and formed an angel.

Sandra took her teaching role again and said, "Scientists believe that somehow the atoms and molecules came together with all that was necessary for life, but they needed some great force to transform inanimate particles into life."

"What will it take?" Sonny asked. "A bolt of lightning?"

"Some great force of energy," Sandra replied.

"Isn't Energy what the Son is made of? And I don't mean *S U N*, but I mean *S O N*," Sonny joined in her enthusiasm.

It happened.

As we watched, the fingers of the Son carefully lined the amino acids up in a long protein molecule. Then he fused the DNA with it and a surge of white energy shot from His fingers and the two combined. Carefully he performed this over and over compacting them into a tiny object that pulsated for a moment, then moved slowly through the warm waters.

"That, Sonny Miller, was the beginning of life," Sandra said reverently.

"What is it called?" Sonny asked, as the tiny organism wiggled.

"A single cell prokaryote," Sandra whispered. "Science has discovered evidences of them from about four billion years ago, and they are thought to be the first form of life."

Soon others were produced and began to wander like sheep looking for a shepherd. Sonny was amazed and confused by all of this chemistry. He watched the microscopic forms move slowly back and forth. One seemed to grow larger than the others. Suddenly it began to bulge on either end as if an invisible belt were drawn too tight around its middle. Gradually the center grew smaller and smaller until it broke in two. Both tiny cells shivered, then slowly moved apart.

"Reproduction!" Sandra whooped. "This demonstrates the emergence of life."

Sonny jumped when Sandra yelled out so loudly. "Whew, you scared me. I thought a shark was about to destroy them all." He thought for a moment then dropped his voice to mimic a robot and monotoned, "Define life!"

+ + +

THE DEFINITION OF LIFE

Sandra grinned at her boyfriend who often acted dumber than he really was

.

Webster's Dictinary defines life as"
The ability
1- to grow,
2- to reproduce
3- to change, or adapt

She continued, "There are other characteristics, but these are the big three."

"Wait another minute," Sonny said. "You didn't include *evolution!*"

"But I did," she smiled. "*The ability to change or adapt* is what Charles Dawin called *evolution*. The problem with his new term was that it left God out all together. He did not believe in the Creation of the earth or man with any help from a divine source. It was all a matter of evolution, survival of the fittest, etc.

I added my two cents worth, "Darwin's biggest failure was to realize that all life has the ability to adapt. Later Scientists would add Radiation and Mutation to the necessities of evolution. But I believe God created life, then used the law of **ARM.**

"**ARM?**" Sonny asked, if that some type of war God used?

I laughed, "No it is the process God uses higher begins or better breeds!"

"Let me explain:

A creature follows God's laws and becomes a fish. It then
ADAPTS – fins and a long tail.
RADIATION – from a solar blast and changes it to develop teeth.
MUTATION- happens in a fish egg and it is enabled to breath air.

Sonny catches on and says, "So that explains how creatures change shapes, forms, species, etc."
"Basically, yes," Sandra said.
"But you have to include God's design for the fish. He built into the DNA of all creation a blueprint for what they are to become through Adaption, Radiation and Mutation."
"That's exactly the way God started when He created angels," Gabriel said.
"However the first step in building us was to change energy into life and give us our A.N.A., as I told you is much like you D.N.A. But our lives do have a design and a designer, a creator who would fashion it into exactly what He wanted. For starting in such a small way, well, that's the way God chose, to start with the atoms and build up to Adam.

"It was God's design for this first organism to culminate into all forms of life, except man. He wonderfully designed it to branch off into plants, animals, bacteria, fungi and other forms. Darwin taught that this resulted in man." Sandra said. "Darwin called it 'The Tree of Life.'"
"How dumb," Sonny said. "Everybody knows the Tree of Life is in the Garden of Eden."
"*WAS* in the Garden of Eden," I corrected.
"*WAS*? All right, who moved it?" Sonny asked me.
"Not me! The book of Revelation clearly tells us the Tree of Life is in Heaven," I answered.
"But we are not ready to talk about that yet," Gabriel interrupted. "All in due time. Darwin called his theory of Evolution, *The Tree of Life*. He rightly believed life had a common ancestor. His concept has been reshaped to look something like this:"

DARWIN'S EVOLUTIONARY TREE OF LIFE

"As you can see, this concept has man and ape at the top of the animal branch," lectured Professor Gabe. "But this puts man, birds, trees, and apes all about the same level. God did not makes pine trees, monkeys nor mockingbirds in His image. Since you have seen God's form, check and you will see that none of the above look like God."

"Now let me show you how it really was and is," said Gabriel, as he presented a new slide:"

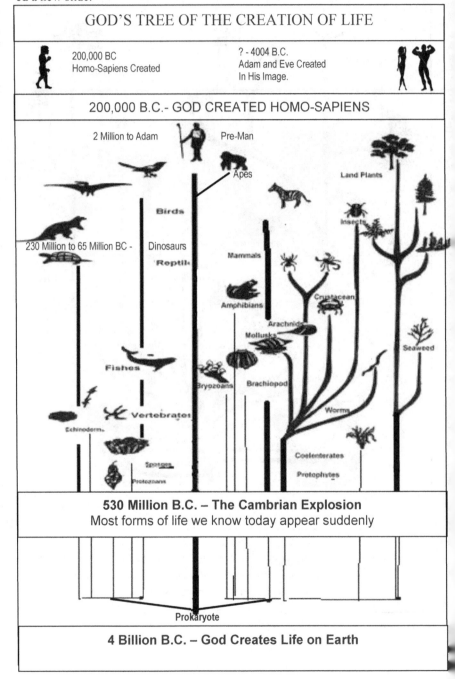

GOD'S TREE OF THE CREATION OF LIFE

200,000 BC
Homo-Sapiens Created

? - 4004 B.C.
Adam and Eve Created
In His Image.

200,000 B.C.- GOD CREATED HOMO-SAPIENS

2 Million to Adam

Pre-Man

Apes

Land Plants

Birds

Insects

230 Million to 65 Million BC -

Dinosaurs

Reptiles

Mammals

Amphibians

Crustacean

Arachnids

Mollusks

Seaweed

Fishes

Bryozoans

Brachiopod

Vertebrates

Worms

Echinoderm.

Sponges

Coelenterates

Protozoans

Protophytes

530 Million B.C. – The Cambrian Explosion
Most forms of life we know today appear suddenly

Prokaryote

4 Billion B.C. – God Creates Life on Earth

As you can plainly see, man did not come from the monkey, but monkey came from the main stem of pre-man," Gabe announced.

"Why do you keep calling it Pre-Man?" Sandra asked. "Shouldn't it be Proto-Man? Proto-man means 'First man,' Pre-man means 'Before man.'"

"I'm talking about Pre-man, the 'Before man" animal that roamed the earth before God created man in His image. The first man created in God's image was Adam, then the first woman, Eve."

"According to your chart, man was not created in God's image until Adam," Sandra said. "What happened to all of those fossils we have found that are older than that?"

I was glad to answer that one. "Scientists will tell you that all of them became extinct. The good old Neanderthal Man held on the longest, he didn't fade from history until about 35,000 B.C. But before that time a pre-man had developed called, *Homo-sapiens*."

"Aha," Sonny said, "we are taught that Homo-sapiens developed into modern man."

"Until Adam, there were pre-men who were made in the image of man. But only Adam lost that Image, when he disobeyed God. And it took the Son to come and show us what it is like to be in God's image. Through his death and resurrection, He made it possible for us to become Children of God, in His Image again."

But as many as received him,
to them gave he power to become the sons of God,
even to them that believe on his name:
Matthew 10:40

Sandra bit her lip, thought a minute, then said, "I doubt if science is going to believe this. You are saying that man appeared much, much later than most animals?"

I answered, "Sandra, this is hard to understand, but if you read the Bible, it is very clear in Genesis, the first chapter, that God *made* the animals. After that He *created* man *in His image*. That is very important for us Christians to realize we are not animals; we were not made like animals; we did not come from animals; we were created by God."

Sandra shrugged and said, "I assume this will be clarified later?"

Gabriel added, "Certainly."

"How did all of this come about?" Sonny asked. "Can you do a show and tell for us?"

"Why not," Gabriel smiled. "We'll do a fast forward through history. Sandra, you're keeping up with the math, so where are we now?

Sandra didn't need to consult any notes. "Life began around 4 billion B.C."

"In that case, we have plenty of time,' Gabriel joked. We watched the blue sea begin to churn as small creatures in various shapes and sizes emerged. Life resembled an aquarium of long, long ago. There were billions of shapes flittering around, most of them no larger than the head of a pin.

"Whoa, that's a long, long time."

"But God is..." Sandra began

And he chimed in. "... in no hurry."

As we flew forward in history fish and birds appeared. Then animals began to crawl across the earth.

"Are we up to the dinosaurs yet?" Sonny asked.

"Nope, we have to wait until 230 millions years B.C," Sandra replied.

"Well, let's just scoot on up there, that's one scene I don't want to miss."

Gabriel beamed at his students then asked, "Sonny, do you know how babies are made?"

The big football played blushed, then looked at Sandra. "Well, yea, I have never experienced it, but we have learned about sex."

"O.K.," Gabriel answered, "now what happens to make a baby."

"One of the lucky sperms outswims all the rest and makes it to the female's egg. There fertilization takes place and the egg takes place and begins to divide into cells, then more cells, and each one has DNA that tells it whether to make a leg or an arm, a heart or a kidney. But none of these cells look like a human being. At first this is just a tiny creature, way too small to see with the human eye. But then it begins to take shape."

"Is that when it, or he or she, begins to look like a human?" Sonny asked.

"No," Sandra said. "By the way do you know what male sperm looks like?"

Sonny blushed and said, "Don't reckon I know the answer to that one, Ma'm."

"People were convinced that human sperm was shaped like little babies. They thought when the sperm was injected into the woman's womb, the teeny, tiny baby just got bigger," Sandra explained. "Later, microscopes allowed us to see that sperm looked like tadpoles- they were flabbergasted."

I added, "Then in time, the developing baby looks like a seahorse!"

"Good news," Gabriel said. "Soon the little seahorse figure changes and develops a head, then tiny arms and legs, and all that is necessary for life."

"Good grief," Sonny said. "There's more to this baby-making than I had ever imagined. Question, is that kind of like evolution?"

I said, "You can call it that, but a better word is growth and adaptation."

+ + +

230 Million B.C.

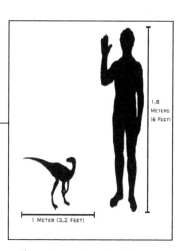

1,8 METERS (6 FEET)

1 METER (3,2 FEET)

CHAPTER 26
WATCH OUT FOR DINOSAURS!

Lush forests covered the earth like the rain forests of today. The sun shone brilliantly against a deep blue sky. The only thing moving were a few clouds creeping in from the southwest. Hovering closer to the land, the group saw rivers flowing peacefully with huge ferns decorating the shores.

"This looks more like the Garden of Eden than the land of the Dinosaur," Sonny said. The words were hardly out of his mouth when we saw a small group emerge from the forest and head toward the water. Furtively they turned their heads back and forth as if afraid a group of terrorists were about to attack. Finally, they hurried to the edge of the stream and began to drink.

"They are Eoraptors," Sandra whispered as it they could hear her and hurry back into hiding. "They were short but vicious."

"I remember them from Jurassic Park," Sonny whispered back. "They're no bigger than a turkey, but I'll bet they could take a bite out of you like a crocodile."

"Funny you should say that," Sandra explained. "Most scientists believe the turkey and the crocodile both evolved from dinosaurs."

"Don't scientists think we descended for dinosaurs?" Sonny asked.

"Not really," Sandra answered. "The more intelligent ones believe the prehuman was a kind of rat, or small mammal living through this period."

"Well, Gabriel, were we- they- once rats?" Sonny asked.

"Some humans act that way," Gabriel said. "But the answer is 'no.' Pre-man was on a straight line till God decided to make the line extinct."

"Extinct?" Sonny said. "You mean the pre-humans became extinct just like the dinosaurs, the dodo bird, and ...? Uh, I can't think of any others."

"There are long lists of animals which have become extinct. This is a major concern among ecologists today," Sandra said.

"Save the whale! Save the mustang!" I chanted. "One of the biggest examples of hypocrites who should be extinct are those do-gooders who want to save some animal and yet they are in favor of abortion. Figure that one."

Sandra nodded assent to her pastor's comments, then continued, "Fossil hunters can't stand it because they have not come up with any pre-human remains during this period. One reason is simple. There weren't that many pre-humans around. Secondly, not everything that was alive back then left fossils."

"So man was alive with the dinosaur!" Sonny exclaimed.

"Again, Pre-man was around," Gabriel answered. "And there were a few other living creatures alive and well."

In the scene before us, the eorapters were dipping their long necks down, gathering mouthfuls of water, then tilting their heads back so the water could flow down. One stood guard at the rear making sure nothing would surprise them.

"WHOSH!" The water erupted like a volcano as a monstrous crocodile snatched two of the creatures in its powerful jaws. Screams filled the air from the victims and from those fleeing back into the safety of the deep woods. Slashing his head from side to side, the crocodile splashed and sloshed its way back to midstream. Two tiny dinosaurs shrilled out for help, but no help came. Like a nuclear submarine the huge reptile ducked its head beneath the surface. A powerful tail snapped through the air, then slapped down on the water. Waves pounded the shore until they receded into ripples. Then all was still.

"Whoa," Sonny stammered. "Nobody told me crocodiles go back to the days of dinosaurs. They must be about as old as sharks."

"Is this where Adam shows up?" Sonny asked as he looked around at the garden-like woods.

"No, not yet- and he didn't just show up. Adam emerges from the Garden in 4004 B.C.," Gabriel replied casually and then changed the subject, "Would you like to see the T Rex?"

"Wouldn't be a trip to The Old World without it," Sonny answered.

"We will have to fast forward again. We are now at about 200 million years ago. The big bully of this age didn't show up until it was almost time for the final curtain. We'll take it up to 65 million years B.C.," Gabriel said. "We'll look at T Rex and then watch as all dinosaurs stumble into oblivion."

+ + +

T-REX

Again there was the blur and the whir as we shot forward. When we were able to see once more, the landscape seemed about the same. Trees were different, some looking more like palms than the strange trees that had preceded them. As we were able to see, smell and feel the scenes before us, we all took a few deep breaths.

"Smells more like the good old days, when we would go camping in the woods," I said. "We'd take a tent, some bed rolls, hot dogs and marshmallows. There was just an aroma to the air which was fresh. You could not smell gas fumes nor the neighbor's garbage. Our youth pastor would take us on overnight trips. We would even do some spelunking, you know, look around in caves. Sometimes he would tell us the Garden of Eden must have been like virgin forest. If so, I wouldn't have minded spending eternity in the Garden, but to be honest to spend forever in a dull old Heaven didn't create much of a desire in me."

"Heaven does seem dull to people who don't know it is the Garden of Eden that has been elevated to Paradise," Gabriel said.

"Say what?" Sonny asked. "The Garden of Eden is Paradise in Heaven? Has it always been there? How did Adam and Eve get down here? Are you pulling my leg?"

Gabriel didn't have time to answer before a growl exploded beneath us. The trees shook and a few broke as a gigantic beast swaggered into view. Green eyes glared around as if looking for us three humans and one angel. Another roar erupted so loudly that Sandra had to hold her hands over her ears.

"Oh, my word, it sounds awful and smells worse," she wailed. "I'm going to be sick, that thing smells like rotten dead meat."

"Good identification," Gabriel said. "I would like to introduce all of you to Mr. T. Rex, or better know to scientists as Tyrannosaurus Rex, king of the dinosaurs. Just in case some of you might care to note, the one below is some 45 feet long, over 13 feet high and weighs a mere seven and one half tons."

The beast howled again and swung his head to and fro looking for something to eat. Sniffing like a hound dog, he pushed brush aside and came upon two-thirds of an animal that had been killed and partially eaten. Throwing his head back the creature roared again as if claiming this treasure for himself. Then he nudged his giant jaws down, ripping the rotten meat from the bones of the corpse.

Nobody spoke as we watched in awe at this killing machine feasting on someone else's kill. "I thought T. Rex was the monster serial killer of prehistoric days," Sonny asked. "What's he doing- salvaging?"

"He is coming back to have leftovers from an animal he killed a few days ago. But he put terror into everything that walked or swam or flew."

Sandra asked Gabe, "I just imagine you have some kind of slide to show us just how big those dinosaurs really were."

Gabe nodded his head, flipped the computer- an image covered the screen.

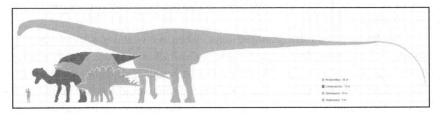

"Good," Sandra said. The little man on the left is about your size, Sonny. Well, maybe not so muscular, maybe more like you, Brother Chris."

I jerked back as if slapped and said, "Well, *thank you*. I've been, uh, sick."

Sandra merrily rambled on. "The dark dinosaur is T. Rex, at about 45 feet. The longest is Amphicoelias. almost 200 feet long."

"Good grief, that's almost as long as a football field," Sonny said.

Gabriel listened to the youngsters, looked back down at the thrashing dinosaur below us and asked, "By the way, Sonny, do you recognize where we are?"

"Iraq? Africa? Europe?" Sonny guessed.

"North America!" Gabriel shared. "Most folks don't that know T Rex walked the trails where cowboys would some day drive cattle and fight Indians and win the West."

"So these are their last days," Sandra asked. "We have quite a few theories on their extinction. One I like best is the cartoon of some dinosaurs smoking cigarettes with the note, *What Really Killed Off The Dinosaurs*."

Gabriel grinned. "I chose this particular moment in the history of Planet Earth for a special reason. We are above what you now call Texas- the time is about 65 millions years ago, and if my eternal watch is correct, here it comes."

We followed Gabriel's gaze and saw a fireball headed straight toward us.

"Duck," Sonny cried as he shielded his head. The red hot rock shot right through us and headed toward the earth. For a moment we forgot we were only spectators in another dimension. As it receded, the bright red trail fanned out about us. We wiped our brows grateful we were still in transfigured bodies.

"Who-eee!" Sonny shouted. "That was bigger than any dinosaur. It was, what, two miles, five miles wide?"

"Nine miles to be exact," Gabriel explained. "Cover your ears!"

First we saw the explosion like a thousand atomic bombs. Smoke begin to rise before the horrific sound followed. Dust kept ascending into the air and began to drift over the entire earth.

"There went much of the Yucatan Peninsula," Sandra said. "But the good news is the Caribbean Sea will get much larger. The bad news is there go the dinosaurs. We honestly don't know if the explosion caused severe cold or extreme heat to kill off most of the plants and many of the living things. But it left a thin layer of sediment around part of the world, and there are no dinosaur fossils found above this strata. The sediment is called iridium."

"Ha! Good name," Sonny said. "Iridium got *ridium* dinosaurs! Good bye and good riddance, I say. It's bad enough to have to play Texas in football out there, but if we had to play a bunch of dinosaurs, I doubt if I'd stay on the team. Wait a minute, what happened to our forefathers during this experience?"

"As you might imagine, Pre-man survived," Gabriel announced. "By this time pre-humans had become quite adaptable. Dinosaurs were not. Pre-humans lived, dinosaurs died."

The sun began to set behind dark red clouds. Lightning was playing hop scotch over the horizon, and the fragrance of death was already beginning. Great flocks of birds flew past us squawking for their very lives. Below hundreds of dinosaurs and other animals were fleeing. Some creatures looked familiar while others looked like they belonged on Mars. The sky grew darker and everything faded away.

+ + +

T-Rex
45 feet long, 13 feet high, 7 tons

CHAPTER 27
MAN TAKES THE STAGE

A ccustomed to time travel our group barely noticed we were moving again. Our minds were boggled with Eternity and billions of years, the rise and fall of animal kingdoms and a whole lot more history. It was like reducing the encyclopedia down to a big pill and trying to swallow it and understand it at the same time.

The sun emerged from the East as it had billions of times just as God had scheduled. Greenery covered the earth below us like a giant carpet. Trees looked more familiar and animals roamed freely on the giant plains. Huge rock cliffs stood sharply on each side of a valley. A peaceful river flowed lazily past. A herd of giant mammoths plodded toward their drinking hole while herds of grazing animals watched without running. Forests were luxuriant, and flowers scattered colors like the palette of Van Gough.

"I like this place," Sonny said breaking the silence. "It would be a good place for us guys to go hunting. And I'll bet there are fish in that river you would not believe."

Five or six figures stepped out of the woods and began to follow the mammoths. They carried sharpened sticks. A few clutched stone axes. Quietly they followed the giant beasts toward the river.

"The time is less than 200,000 years ago," Gabriel announced. "Sonny and Sandra, I want to introduce you to Home Sapiens, your ancestors."

"Where did they come from on the evolution tree?" Sonny asked.

Gabriel mused for a moment, then said, "I think I will answer your question after we visit the Garden of Eden. If I told you now, you would not believe me. You will notice the men have a great deal of body hair. They do not cut it for it provides them with protection from the cold."

"I know a few defensive tackles who are as hairy as that group," Sonny said. "However, football players today are a whole lot bigger than this team." Then he yelled, "Go get'em, Grandpa! Don't' let that wooly elephant escape. He'll feed the team for a whole winter." Then he turned to Sandra and asked, "Do you have any idea what mammoth meat tastes like?"

"Better than T. Rex's," she responded. "Look, the guys are driving the mammoths away from the water toward the cliffs. Now they're separating a young one and yelling at him and punching him toward a gap in the cliff."

"They need a better defensive coordinator," Sonny said. "They let the whole herd escape except for one little fellow."

Gabriel remarked, "They know what they're doing." We watched them as they jumped and jabbed until they forced the young mammoth into an opening in the cliff. The hunting group poked and probed to keep him there.

"Well, looka' there!" Sonny said. "The whole family is involved in this hunt."

Above the terrified beast, several men, women and children began to push huge boulders down. The animal fell quickly as the rocks rained upon him. Then the hunting group swarmed over the creature, stabbing at certain spots, until he ceased to wiggle. A shout went up much like one from a modern football stadium when a touchdown is scored.

Sonny shook his head in disbelief. "Their defense may be weak, but their offense is terrific. How did they get so smart to trap an animal and then kill one that is twice their height and probably weighs a couple of tons?"

"Humans have always had good minds," Gabriel remarked. "The problem is not their lack of brains, but their misuse of their mentality and their morality."

"What do you mean by that?" I asked.

"Watch," Gabriel instructed. The hunters danced around the fallen mammoth, then an old woman climbed down the rocks and stood before them. She was as naked as a jay bird. Claws, bones and feathers hung around her neck. Grabbing the necklace she held it up and we saw it was a decorated cow's tail. Holding the neck piece before her, she jumped up on the dead animal, lifted her arms and began thanking the god of her necklace for the kill. The men began shrieking, dancing and bowing before her and her "idol."

"I assume they are *not* worshipping God the creator," Sandra said.

"According to my professors, man has not yet invented God," Sonny stated, "They probably have never heard about him."

"Oh, they know about Him, really well," Gabriel said. "They just refuse to worship Him. Your professors are correct about men inventing gods, or should I say, false gods. All false gods are man-made. I warned God about giving human beings free will. God is so full of love and peace, He wanted to give them the same opportunity He gave Lucifer."

"Lucifer!" Sonny exclaimed. "How does he fit into the picture?"

"It didn't take the devil very long to discover Planet Earth," Gabriel answered. "He still didn't know God's final plan, but he had an instant dislike for humans. He felt superior, for he was made in heaven and they were made on

138

earth. Here's the problem you see before you. Mankind, or Homo Sapiens, as you are called at this first point of your history, used their brains and God-given abilities to track and kill game. Do they glorify God? No. They dance and worship a cow's tail. It makes no sense to me."

"Didn't God make man to enjoy His love, joy and peace?" Sandra asked.

"Yes," Gabriel answered, "but love quickly turned into lust. Joy deteriorated into killing animals or getting drunk or having wild sex. Peace was only when your stomach was full, and the enemy was not knocking on the door of your cave."

"Boy, am I confused," Sonny said. "Here I have been thinking Adam was the first man, and Satan didn't show up until chapter three of Genesis. Gabriel, I think I've had enough human history to set the background. How about let's get to the Garden of Eden and see if you can straighten me out."

"Sure," Gabriel said. "Let's get going. You will have to excuse me, but I don't get to guide this tour often, so I'll point out some interesting points along the way."

Below us a river snaked down a valley, winding round and round and round. "This is the River Jordan, to the North is the Sea of Galilee, to the South you may view the Dead Sea. The time is 10,000 years before Jesus will walk this land. There in the valley you will notice a new town is being built. That is Jericho, one of the oldest cities known to man."

10,000 BC
Jericho is Built by Advanced Pre-man
Houses built of sundried brick, Pottery

The group gawked at the scene below as Gabriel continued, "Already mankind is building houses of sundried brick and is even producing some pottery at 10,000 B.C."

We hurried along like we were on a moving sidewalk at O'Hare Airport in Chicago. "We're now passing over the Sixth Millennium B.C., that's 6000-5000 B.C. for those of you who may have trouble converting time."

6000-5000 BC
Villages, Buildings, Furniture with Paintings
Bread, Canoes, the Plough
Temples to False Gods

Buildings and villages were scattered over the landscape. In places, canoes were being paddled up rivers. Sandra exclaimed, "Look in the house- they have furniture and paintings on the walls. I can smell home-baked bread in the oven. In the garden, there is a plough. Never did I figure mankind was this advanced six thousand years ago."

"Too far advanced," Gabriel said. "See those temples over there in Mesopotamia. That's where we are headed; it's near the Garden of Eden. Those temples are not Houses of God. They are shrines built to strange and savage gods. Man created the false gods and now he is worshipping them."

"One more pause and we're headed in for our destination. We are now in the Fifth Millennium B.C., again that's 5000 to 4000 B.C. or as you humans love to say, *B.C.E., Before the Common Era*, whatever that means. The wheel is invented, at least in part of the world. For some reason American Indians never got the hang of using the wheel for transportation Weapons are made from copper, and worst of all the priesthood appears. They're the ones who instruct humans to worship false gods.   It's time for us to look at God's Garden.

"Oh, I need tell you. Of all the pre-human begins on the earth at this time, not a single once worshipped the One Creator God," Gabriel added as we zoomed forward.

+ + +

Now faith is being sure of what we hope for

and certain of what we do not see.

This is what the ancients were commended for.

By faith we understand that the universe

was formed at God's command,

so that what is seen was not made out of what was visible.

(Heb 11:1-3NIV)

?- 4004 B.C.

PART **5** THE GARDEN

CHAPTER 28
THE GARDEN OF EDEN

A s we rushed through time and space we heard chants and screams. Clothing now donned the human beings along with headpieces of skulls or cloth or metal. Some wore jewelry of gems or gold. Laughter would boil up from time to time only to be drowned in clashes of spears and axes and screams of the dying. Although we never caught sight of him, the hoof prints of Lucifer were evident over all of this part of history.

The scene grew dark and quiet as we stopped. Gabriel cleared his throat as if he were about to make the most important speech ever heard, then said, "You are going to see the Garden of Eden in 4004 B.C. I am forewarning you it will be the most beautiful sight you have ever seen on earth. You will see the finished product, then we will back up in time so you can see how it was made- also the why and when. So without further ado, whatever that means, I present to you, The Garden of Eden."

At first all we could see were blue mists rising slowly and softly from some land below us. Before we could see, we were able to smell. As usual Sonny was the first to remark, "Wonderful aroma. It's hard to describe, kind of a combination of Dreamland's barbecue and Thanksgiving dinner at Grandma's."

Sandra put her hand over her mouth to keep from laughing. "It's probably all in the nose of the be-smeller. To me it's a trip to Hawaii, with flowers overflowing with perfumes. It's heavenly."

"Whatever it is," I added, "it's like nothing I've ever encountered. It smells like the good old outdoors. It's spring time and there's the scent of new life, a new start for the year. It's, uh, it's ..."

"The Garden of Eden," Gabriel completed. The blue mists parted and below us a kaleidoscope of colors shimmered and glistened in the sunlight. Soon we could not only see flowers of every size and shape but also trees covered in blooms. It was like an art exhibit at the Louvre. Cherry blossoms drifted in the air and fell like pink snowflakes. Flowering pear and peach and apple vied for first place in the beauty contest. Some trees were more mature as they offered brilliant red apples, deep golden pears, peaches of more shades than the visitors had ever seen. Clusters of purple grapes mingled with yellows and greens. The whole area was ablaze with color- but not just the natural color of botanical gardens. Colors glowed as in a Disney movie.

"The river," Sonny shouted. "It's the same shades of color as the seas off Hawaii- green and lavender and every shade of blue. Up there, look, Sandra, waterfalls on the mountains! Aren't they the most gorgeous sights you've ever seen? Now I could stay a long time in this place and never get bored. Now if I had been Adam and, Sandra, if you had been Eve…"

He stopped as deer moved toward the river as gracefully as dancers in Swan Lake. Beside them came a lion and a tiger. "Watch out!" Sonny yelled. They could not hear him nor did they need to. A lamb waltzed out beside the lion and they played together like two frisky puppies on the front lawn.

"Hear the music," Sandra said dreamily. "It reminds me of the sounds of Heaven. Listen, the water is playing the piccolo and flutes; the waterfall is adding the percussion, and the wind in the trees are like the brass section. Listen to birds soaring over, adding their songs to the symphony."

"And you can actually feel it," I added, "I'm experiencing a sense of joy that even exceeds my wedding day."

"I feel like I just won the Super Bowl," Sonny said.

Sandra swayed her head back and forth, "And I won the Mrs. America contest, and gave birth to twins, a boy and a girl. I love them so very dearly."

"Why would anyone ever want to give up this place?" Sonny asked.

Before Gabriel could answer a strange creature flew overhead as if it were searching for some special somebody. It was not a bird- there were no feathers. Several shades of orange and gold covered the sleek body. About twenty feet long, it sailed gracefully on butterfly wings over Eden.

"What's that?" Sonny asked.

"Whatever it is, it's beautiful in a fascinating way," Sandra exclaimed.

"That," Gabriel said, "is part of your answer and part of the problem. Would you like to see the two main characters in this drama?"

"Whoa," Sonny said, "you mean Adam and Eve? They're, uh, not going to have any clothes on, are they?"

Sandra replied, "Well, Sonny, you don't have to look!"

"It won't hurt to look," Gabriel responded. "Remember you are now in a transfigured state. When you see them, you will not be worried with hormones and sexual drives. You will see them as two small children just emerging from a bath, or maybe still enjoying the tub."

We moved down a pine straw path, flanked by ferns and flowers. Butterflies glowed like neon signs. Hummingbirds were singing lullabies. As we went around the curve, a pool appeared before us, and we heard laughing and splashing like two people diving into a pool. Again the atmosphere of love fell over all of us.

Then there they were- the first man and woman.

+ + +

CHAPTER 29
ADAM AND EVE

Adam and Eve

A dam and Eve were both evidences of God's good taste in creation. Eve had blonde hair that sparkled golden in the water.

"I wouldn't want to be in a beauty pageant with her,' Sandra sighed. "She is out of this world gorgeous."

"But not as pretty as you are," Sonny said, as he admired Eve's brilliant white teeth, her slender body and her light golden tan. Since she was in the water, he wasn't even temped to look at the parts of a woman he was not supposed to look at.

He turned his attention to Adam and gave a low whistle. "Wow, I never saw that coming," he said to Sandra.

As she saw Adam emerge from the water waist up, she whistled also. "My word, who would ever have imagined? I always had Adam as some normal guy or even a young Moses. But would you look at that?"

Adam flipped water back toward Eve as he flashed a million dollar smile. It was his physique that stunned us. "He looks like Superman without a cape, or anything else on." Sonny said. "I never expected Adam was into body building."

"God is into body building," Gabriel explained. "What did you expect his images to look like- a video game nerd?"

Adam tossed his black hair away from his face and we saw his eyes. They were unlike any we had ever encountered. His eyes were dark, yet they had flecks of green and gold with specks of blue sparkling through them. They were happy eyes hidden behind the longest black lashes Sandra had ever seen.

"His eyes are a mosaic of all mankind who will follow him," Sandra whispered. "Don't guess I ever imagined him with a trim mustache and beard."

"He looks like Jesus," Sonny exclaimed. "He looks just like the pictures we have of Jesus."

Adam sniffed inhaling the perfumed air around him.
He asked in a clear baritone voice,
"Don't you think it's about time for supper?"
Teasingly, Eve replied in her voice of silver bells,
"What would you like tonight?"
"Chef's choice!" he answered.

Sonny said , "Big deal! What's to eat besides apples and pears?"
Gabriel responded, "Sonny, were you not listening.? God didn't create Adam
and Eve as dumb bunnies. They have all the intelligence of mankind. They
have fire and they can bake bread. Part of the Eden you haven't seen is the vegetable garden. Also there are pastures of livestock that need tending, milking,
feeding, shearing. That's where Adam has been busy all day. He's just come
home, having his bath, and ready to sit down to a good meal."
"No meat," Sandra said. "Man didn't eat meat until later."
"True, but a good cook can make a wicked vegetable plate." I answered.
"My grandma cooked turnips, black eyes peas, fresh corn, home-ripened tomatoes, smashed potatoes and cornbread. It was a meal fit for a king."
Eve jumped from the pond and raced down the pathway, her backside toward her viewers. Adam laughed, leaped out and chased after her. A hut stood
on the edge of the pond. We had been so interested in Adam and Eve that we
had not noticed their home. Looking like a habitat for Tarzan and Jane, we saw
it was made of bamboo. Flowers bloomed beside the open door. Inside we saw
furniture Adam had made from the trees in the Garden. The table had only two
chairs but that was enough, for they were the only two humans in their world.
Plates were made of pottery. A pot hung over the fire and from the smell, it
seemed to be some type of veggie stew. Huge hunks of bread lay in the Indian
type oven beside the fire.

Adam had a seat as Eve brought the pot of food over.
She picked up a wooden spoon, but before she took a bite,
Adam reminded her, "We need to pray."
Eve sighed and rolled her eyes upward, but Adam bowed his head and
prayed, "Father, we thank you for our blessings, for this garden, for this
food. Bless us with children so we can share our love with them, Amen."

"Children?" Sonny asked. "You don't mean they had discovered, uh, sex?"
"What a silly question!" Gabriel said. "You have a nude man and woman
running around in a beautiful garden. They are both young and hot blooded,
what do you think they were going to do? Become a monk and a nun?"

Sonny blushed and said, "Well, I just, uh, thought, maybe like Mary and Joseph they waited until, uh, after Jesus was born."

"If Adam and Eve had waited until after Jesus was born," I added with a chuckle, "then Jesus would never have been born."

Sandra said, "Oh, I'll bet they didn't even call it sex- and none of the ugly words you guys use to describe it. I imagine they called it love."

"Correct," Gabriel said. "God gave them emotional love and expanded it so they could experience physical love. In your day, Hollywood calls it 'making love,' but what they call *love* is nothing but lust, adultery and fornication."

Sonny eyed Sandra, "You really are as pretty or prettier than Eve. Some of these days I'll be able to make, uh, express my love to you."

Sandra nodded, 'Right. *Right* after we are married. Remember God performed a wedding ceremony when he made Eve the wife of Adam. Besides, you've never officially proposed."

"Just wait till after graduation!" Sonny said and gave her a hug. Then he looked at Gabriel and said, "Now explain all of this to me. We have the earth created 6.5 billions years ago, then life pops up a couple of billions years later. We see some kind of man running around covered with hair at 200,000 years B.C. Men have built Jericho by 10,000 B.C. Here we are at 4004 B.C. and Adam shows up. Isn't that like getting the cart before the horse."

"It is, if you are dealing with carts and horses," Gabriel answered.

In the background we could hear Adam and Eve talking.
Adam told her, "Tomorrow I've got to tend the animals
and it's your day in the vegetable garden."
Eve smiled a bit too much as she replied,
"Oh, I'll take care of those plants;
I want you to go with me tomorrow to the fruit orchard.
I saw a delicious fruit today, and I want to show it to you tomorrow."
"Is it a new fruit?" Adam laughed.
"I'll bet it's an old one you've forgotten. Where is it?"
"Oh," Eve dropped her eyes and said, "It's a secret. You know how
we've come up with new varieties of beans. This just may be a new fruit."

All three humans were silent when she said this. Sonny finally yelled, "Don't Adam! Don't go with her! Don't eat that fruit!"

"They can't hear you," Gabriel said. "Even if they could, I doubt if they would pay much attention, for that is exactly what God had told them." He shook his head sadly as if preparing to make an appearance at a funeral for a loved one. I think I'd better explain this to you."

CHAPTER 30
A SPECIAL CREATION- EDEN AND ADAM

W e're going to have to do a rewind," Gabriel said. "We are going back to the time before 4004 B.C." The Garden disappeared into a blue haze that slowly turned dark brown.

Gabriel had us sit down on our traveling patio at the table with chairs while he spoke. "You saw how God created the Universe. He then slowly began the creation of earth- then life. As I have told you a number of times, God is in no hurry, and what seems like a billion years earth time is a short period in Heaven. God set out to create life on a natural basis. He first made atoms, then molecules. Then he joined amino acids and nuclei acids to form life. Don't ever forget- He had a purpose. Eventually He would create man."

"Also, keep in mind Lucifer had defiled and contaminated Heaven. Although he and a third of the angel population were cast out, the stains remained. You heard Lucifer hint that Heaven could be cleaned only by a sacrifice and angels can't die," Gabriel said.

"Got it," Sonny said, "but I don't know yet what it means."

"You will," Gabriel continued. "The Triune God had created angels first. He loved the love, joy and peace they shared, but they had only the knowledge of good. So, He created another type of angel, called Cherubim. Lucifer belonged to this group and they had the knowledge..."

"Of good and evil," Sonny added. "That led to the war in Heaven and Lucifer and his cohorts were cast out. Along with God's word, 'Let There Be Light!'- they caused the Big Bang. Ultimately this led to the creation of the sun and the earth."

"Very good," Gabriel said. "It is God's nature to create, so He created life. He wanted a duplicate of Heaven, with all the pleasures and joys. Of course there were plants and mountains and rivers. He decided to add animals, some to be pets and some to work."

Gabriel paused to gather our attention. "God also created Pre-man. But things went wrong, bad wrong. They fought, they killed, they stole. Pre-man never developed beyond the animal stage. From the fossils of these creatures, you can tell they are nothing more than slightly advanced apes. So, God decided to try again. This time He would take a different course," Gabriel stated.

"But that's not what the Bible says," Sonny said almost angrily. 'I told you, the preacher at that little church I attend in Tuscaloosa. He condemned any idea of Evolution and anybody who dared suggest that Adam was not the first man created."

"Then perhaps your little preacher needs to examine the Bible more closely," Gabriel said. "Let's see what it says." He punched his computer and the verses appeared.

Genesis 2:4-7

4- This is the account of the heavens and the earth when they were created.
When the LORD God made the earth and the heavens--
5- and no shrub of the field had yet appeared on the earth
and no plant of the field had yet sprung up,
for the LORD God had not sent rain on the earth
and there was no man to work the ground,
6- but streams came up from the earth and watered the whole surface
of the ground—
7- the LORD God formed the man from the dust of the ground
and breathed into his nostrils the breath of life,
and the man became a living being.

(NIV)

"Let me fill in some background. Genesis One gives us the Six Phases of God's Creation. In the first part of Creation, we saw how the Phases fell into the exact order of creation as scientists have discovered."

On the Sixth Day God made the animals. Lastly he made man. To phrase it carefully, He *created* man as a Special Creation."

Adam was a Special Creation

"A Special Creation?" Sonny shouted. "That sounds interesting!"

Gabriel continued, "In the second chapter of Genesis we have a detailed account of the Creation of Man. Chapter one of Genesis tells us that before man was created, there were all kinds of plants, birds, fish and animals running around."

"But then in Genesis Two comes this amazing story of dry land, no vegetation and no man. There are not even any animals.

"Some say 'Genesis Two' is only a summary of the sixth day. Well that doesn't fit, because God made vegetation on the third day. I'm surprised that your scholars have not understood this is a Special Creation for a special place,

Eden, and two special people, Adam and Eve."

"My professors will never buy that," Sonny shook his head.

"It's not for sale," Sandra said. "Calm down, Sonny, and listen to the one who was there."

"I'm not trying to destroy your faith, Sonny. I'm trying to help you understand it," Gabriel said. "Much of what we call correct doctrine has been dreamed up by some dissatisfied person who is angry at the Catholics or the Protestants or the church or mankind. So he decides on something and makes everybody else bow down to it. Today Science is attempting to do this. Their creed is 'We believe in Evolution and Creation without a God, and if you defy us, you are an ignoramus and a fanatic.'"

Gabriel continued, "However, before we wear our arms out throwing stones at scientists, let us be aware the church does the same kind of closed thinking. You hear preachers declaring 'All evolution is of the devil, and anyone who believes it is doomed to Hell.' So we have a war between two sides and neither one is completely right, and both are partially wrong. Let me take the Scripture and try to help you understand. This Special Creation is for a special purpose.   "

Gabriel paused to make sure the young students were following, "Two thousand years ago Jesus was the result of a Special Creation, a Virgin Birth. He became the last Adam, am I correct?"

"Sure, no problem," we three echoed.

"I want you to understand God performed a miracle with the first Adam. God wanted a role model man and woman to show all of mankind how they were to act and behave. Also he needed a preview of the coming Adam who would be the Great Sacrifice."

"Oh, I'm beginning to see the light," Sonny said. "The first Adam was made good- but he fell into sin. The last Adam was the Son, and he was the perfect sacrifice for the sin of the world."

"And the sins of Heaven," Gabriel answered. "So God took a piece of earth where there were no shrubs nor plants nor man. Now where do you think this place is?"

"Probably somewhere in Iraq," Sandra answered. "But men have searched for the Garden of Eden through the years. Christopher Columbus thought he found it in South America. In his journals he writes of the beauty of one of the coastlines there and is convinced he had found the Garden of Eden- complete with flowers, rivers and a waterfall. Of course, he also thought he had found the West Indies."

"Didn't we study about Ponce de Leon looking for the Garden and thought he had found it in Florida?" Sonny said. "He believed the Fountain of Youth was in the Garden and finding it would make him and anybody else young again."

I added, "The Mormons swear the Garden of Eden was located in our back yard - in America."

Sandra, sounding much like a school teacher who knows her subject, remarked, "We are pretty certain today the Garden was in Southern Iraq, somewhere south of Baghdad."

"Good guess," Gabriel said. "But none of those fit the Biblical description. Again, let's look at the Bible:

+ + +

CHAPTER 31
WHERE WAS EDEN?

G abriel showed us another slide and give us time to read it.

> **Location of the Land of Eden Genesis 2:10-14**
> 10- A river watering the garden flowed from Eden;
>   from there it was separated into four headwaters.
> 11- The name of the first is the Pishon…;
> 13-The name of the second river is the Gihon…;
> 14- The name of the third river is the Tigris…;
>   And the fourth river is the Euphrates.
> (NIV)

Gabriel read the verses to us, skipping over remarks about gold, etc. "It is quite obvious Eden was at the source of four great rivers. Sandra, the location in Southern Iraq doesn't fit that picture- that's only where the Tigris and Euphrates pour into the Persian Gulf. Let's take a look at a map."

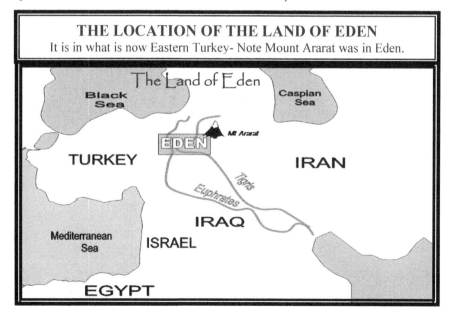

THE LOCATION OF THE LAND OF EDEN
It is in what is now Eastern Turkey- Note Mount Ararat was in Eden.

"You will notice that it is quite obvious Eden is not in Iraq at all, but instead was located here in Eastern Turkey, where now two rivers begin: the Tigris and the Euphrates. Thousands of years ago, the two other rivers also flowed from this area. So Eden is the dark spot at the top of the map. To make it simple, I have it marked 'Eden.' However, it's correct name was 'The Land of Eden.'" Gabriel pointed to the spot with his laser marker.

"Today this area is pretty well barren like much of the land you see on television of Iran, Iraq, Turkey, Afghanistan. It was barren desert in those days before God decided to create Eden on earth. When you zoom in closer, you will find Lake Van in this area."

"Let's go back in time now and see just how God created the Garden and Adam," Gabriel said. Seeing the stare from Sandra, he quickly added, "And, of course, the ultimate in God's creation, Eve."

She smiled approval of including Eve.

The dingy brown of the scene was a sandstorm. Below us ugly, cracked land appeared with no sign of a plant nor an animal. A geyser erupted in front of us; and water shot into the air, watering the land around us like a gigantic sprinkler.

+ + +

Adam

CHAPTER 32
ADAM IS CREATED

The Son materialized before us. As he turned toward our group we could see his features more clearly. His eyes were dark with flecks of gold, green and blue. His smile was contagious. His build was the same as the first Adam. Sandra thought the two must be twins. Looking at her boyfriend, she squeezed his biceps and realized with a beard and mustache he would resemble their triplet.

ADAM IS CREATED, Genesis 2:7
7-the LORD God formed the man from the dust of the ground
and breathed into his nostrils the breath of life,
and the man became a living being.
(NIV)

The Son reached down and grabbed a handful of dirt- then he began to grind it between his fingers.

"What's He doing?" Sonny asked.

"He's making atoms before He makes Adam," Sandra answered. Soon a boy child emerged much like a newborn baby who quickly changed through childhood, teenage, and finally into manhood. Glossy hair grew on his head, his lips and his chin.

The Son examined him as an artist inspects his masterpiece. Then He lifted the new man gently toward him as if he were going to give the kiss of life- instead he held Adam's nostrils close to him. Suddenly the Son, dressed in red, changed into the Godhead, all in white. Blue electricity and white energy shot from God to the Man. "He breathed into his nostrils the breath of life, and the man became a living being."

Adam's eyes blinked open and he looked into the eyes of his Creator. As the two stood there, they were as alike as mirror twins. Adam smiled and said, "Thank you."

The Son smiled back at him and said, "I love you."

Like the end of a romantic movie, the scene slowly faded away.

Sandra sighed, "Love stories always make me cry. This is just so beautiful."

Gabriel raised his eyebrows then said, "Let's learn an important lesson from what we just saw. Sonny, how did God create pre-man at the beginning?"

"Well, we don't really know how," Sonny said. "But to us it seemed as if over time they just appeared."

Gabriel waited a moment then asked, "In the creation of Adam, what difference did you notice?"

Sonny thought, "Adam was like a fast-food specialty!"

Gabriel laughed. "The creation of Adam was pretty fast compared to the beginning of life. But what else was different?"

"I know," Sandra said. "God breathed into him the breath of life."

"Bravo," Gabriel clapped. "That is the difference. Animals came from a long line of one-celled organisms. So did plants and everything that has life- except for man. God breathed into man the breath of life, and he became a living soul."

"So, does this make us better than puppy dogs and long tailed monkeys?" Sonny asked.

"Well, all of God's creation is special. But can you think of one other aspect that was different about Adam's creation?"

I finally answered, "Adam was made in the image of God."

Sandra and Sonny nodded as Gabriel said, "Humans are a special creation made in the image of God. Dogs and monkeys were not made in the same manner. They are different. Of course, with this difference goes a great, great deal of responsibility for mankind."

+ + +

CHAPTER 33
ADAM GOES TO WORK

The Son

G abriel said. "One main responsibility of mankind is to work! God didn't put man here to sit around idly in a lazy boy chair. Now watch as the Son gives Adam a job and then helps him with it. In no time at all, they are planting the tree orchard."

The Garden and Its Trees Genesis 2:8-9
8- Now the LORD God had planted a garden in the east, in Eden;
and there He put the man He had formed.
9- And the LORD God made all kinds of trees grow out of the ground--
trees that were pleasing to the eye and good for food.
In the middle of the garden were the Tree of Life
and the Tree of the Knowledge of Good and Evil.
(NIV)

Watching the Son planting the Garden was like watching an old silent movie where they speeded up the action. The Son and Adam worked together as a farmer and his son- except in fast motion. The Son created seed from the dust. He shared them with Adam. As soon as they dropped the seed onto the ground, green sprouts emerged, wiggled, then grew quickly into trees, plants and vegetables. One area was set aside for fruit trees ablaze with multicolored blossoms: the cherry, the flowering peach and apple. Once again the earth began to smell like high Heaven.

'Why does He work so fast?" Sonny asked. "You told us God is in no hurry."

"I didn't tell you He couldn't get in a hurry, if He wanted to," Gabriel replied. "Sometimes God will shortcut history. For example, Jesus fed five thousand one day. Do you remember what he started with?"

"Some fish and bread," Sonny answered.

"Two fish and five loaves of bread," Gabriel answered. "He took those two fish and short-circuited history. Just as two fish in the sea can produce enough offspring to feed thousands, Jesus just hurried up the operation."

"Is that what He did with the water into wine?" Sandra asked.

"Clever. Yes, water comes down from Heaven, soaks into the ground, then into the roots, up into the vines, out into the grapes, then into wine."

"How about healing the sick, the blind, the lepers?" Sonny asked.

"Shortcuts to Heaven," Gabriel said. "In Heaven there will be no sickness."

"And Lazarus?" Sonny asked. "He was a sure-enough short cut to Heaven."

"The miracles don't sound so unbelievable when you understand God can get in a hurry when He desires," I laughed.

"The creation of Adam was a telescoping together of history," Gabriel told us. "You saw the Son squeeze from the dust atoms and molecules necessary for life. Within minutes four billion years of evolution whizzed by and Adam emerged. He had all of the 'living' molecules: bones, organs, blood vessels, nerves, brain, heart, everything to live. But you noticed he only came to life when he received the breath of life from God.

+ + +

CHAPTER 34
THE TREE OF LIFE

The scene glittered like a diamond sparkling and casting a spectrum of color across the ground. Bending over, the Son carefully dug a hole for a jewel.

The Tree of Life-
(Notice the Cross)

He planted it and pushed dirt over it. He grabbed a handful of water spurting into the air and sprinkled it carefully over the jeweled seed. For a moment the ground was still. Then a minor earthquake shook the Garden as a translucent shaft arose. Twisting, it grew. Crystal leaves sprouted from its silver trunk. Soon the tree was covered with silver foliage and gleaming golden fruit. As we watched, the tree grew taller as if it were striving to reach Heaven. A large limb emerged on either side. Finally it stopped. Sandra and Sonny gasped as they realized it was in the shape of a great cross.

"This is the Tree of Life," the Son spoke softly to Adam. "Always remember its mother was located in Heaven. Angels eat of this tree for their eternal life and energy. This is the source of eternal life."

Sonny waited patiently for a "No Trespassing" sign to be posted, or for the Son to warn Adam that under no circumstances could he have a bite of that fruit. But nothing was said. Adam looked at the tree longingly but did not touch it.

The Son then pulled a seed from his pocket and held it up for Adam to see. It was half black and half white. Using His finger, He dug a hole, planted the seed, then we watched it shoot up like Jack's beanstalk. It didn't make it into the clouds, but it was taller and more beautiful than other trees around. Fresh fruit popped forth on its mighty branches. The fruit glistened every color in the sunlight and seemed to have an unearthly attraction about it. "Come and eat me," we could almost hear it murmuring. It smelled delicious.

"This is the Tree of Knowledge of Good and Evil," the Son told Adam. "You are free to eat from any tree in the Garden, but you must not eat from the Tree of Knowledge of Good and Evil, for when you eat of it, you will surely die."

"Professor Gabriel, you'd better explain this to me," said Sonny. "I'm not getting all that is happening."

"Really, it's quite simple," Gabriel responded. "God has just created Adam, and He also provided him with plenty of food; every fruit in the Garden was his. But God has also made Adam as a role model. Unlike the Cherubim and Lucifer, man was not equipped with built-in radar for good and evil. God realized Lucifer had used the knowledge of evil to make war in Heaven. Man is created in the image of God, but without knowledge of good or evil."   "You mean, man has no conscience at all?" asked Sonny.

"More than being motivated by conscience, Adam was to be steered in the right direction by freedom, love and rules. He was given freedom over all the Garden, and you have seen how beautiful it was," Gabriel stated. "But he was to OBEY God not to DISOBEY Him. The tree was the test for good and evil. Adam failed the test when he broke God's rule and ate of the tree. Four thousand years later the last Adam would face the tree, perhaps of good and evil, in the shape of a cross. He obeyed the Father and was able to undo the damage of the first Adam."

"Whew, that's heavy," Sonny exhaled deeply. "But it makes sense. What happened next?"

"You ought to know that one," Sandra said. "Adam got lonely. He needed a friend, some companionship."

"Is that when God created dogs?" Sonny laughed.

"Dogs and the rest of the critters," I answered.

+ + +

CHAPTER 35
ANIMALS ARE MADE FOR THE GARDEN

While Adam slept that night, the Son was busy. We humans could not see much in the darkness, but we could dimly discern the Son was excavating dirt, squeezing it into shapes, and patting it on the back. All types of squeals and grunts were heard through the evening. Slowly the scene faded into view.

> The LORD God said, "It is not good for the man to be alone.
> I will make a helper suitable for him."
> Now the LORD God had formed out of the ground
> all the beasts of the field and all the birds of the air.
> He brought them to the man to see what he would name them;
> and whatever the man called each living creature, that was its name.
> So the man gave names to all the livestock,
> the birds of the air and all the beasts of the field.
> But for Adam no suitable helper was found.
> *(Genesis 2:18-20NIV)*

By the morning light we saw enough animals lined up to fill the San Diego zoo several times. Strangely enough, they stood two by two. We watched as Adam received his instructions from the Son and began to name them as they streamed by.

Sonny said, "That ought to keep him busy for a long, long time. How many animals and birds are there? Why were there no fish? How did he think up all those names?"

"You must remember this was the Special Creation," Gabriel reminded him. "All the mutants and varieties of animals were already running around loose outside the Land of Eden. Here were the complete animals: cows, horses, goats, sheep. These are how God intended them to be from the beginning. There weren't many birds in the Garden: some peacocks for show, doves to coo in the evening, the raven, the robin, the eagle, etc. All the animals were there which would be classified as the main species of birds and animals. Later you will understand this better."

Sonny reached down as if counting the animals. In a deep voice he imitated Adam. "Okay. you are a fox, you are a cow, you are a pig, etc, etc. Right?," "Right,' Gabriel answered.

"So when Eve asked him why he named the big fat one a hippopotamus, he answered, 'because he looks like a hippopotamus.'" Sonny laughed because he thought he had pulled a good one on Gabriel.

Looking like a British waiter, Gabriel quietly said, "That's exactly what happened." When Sonny gave him the I-don't-believe-you-look, Gabriel laughed and said, "Just kidding. It did take him some time to name all the animals of the Garden. You will notice there were few fish there. Some insects made it, like the butterfly and the moth. However, roaches, ants and fleas were not included in the Garden."

Sonny raised his hand. "Question, where did all of the bugs come from then? Did God make them later?"

"All of these existed outside Eden. They are the products of a changing, evolving world. Man was created in a special way in a special place with special animals and birds around him for companionship. Who would want to be friends with a scorpion or a spider?" Gabriel answered.

Sandra says, "But for Adam no suitable helper was found. That sounds so lonely- it's like being castaway on a beautiful island. Or like being a Robinson Crusoe without a Friday. All alone! That's so sad."

"You pretty well know the story from there, although you have difficulty believing it," Gabriel said. "Since mankind is now into cloning and such, it might be more reasonable and possible for modern mankind to understand. Let's take a look at the arrival of woman."

+ + +

CHAPTER 36
EVE

Eve

G abriel quoted the Scripture as accurately as a retired Baptist preacher.

But for Adam no suitable helper was found.
So the LORD God caused the man to fall into a deep sleep;
and while he was sleeping,
He took one of the man's ribs and closed up the place with flesh.
Then the LORD God made a woman from the rib he had taken
out of the man,
and he brought her to the man.
The man said, "This is now bone of my bones and flesh of my flesh;
she shall be called 'woman,' for she was taken out of man."
(Genesis 2:20b-21 NIV)

"Would you like to watch this operation?" Gabriel asked.

"Wouldn't miss it for the world," Sandra said. "This is one part of the Bible story with which I have trouble."

Below us was a sad-faced Adam, utterly exhausted. In the background were two of every major animal you could imagine.

Adam was remarking, "First, I had to take care of all the fruit trees, now I've got to herd cattle, feed pigs, shear sheep, gather eggs."

A spotted dog wandered over to Adam, licked his hand then rubbed up against his leg. Adam stooped down, petted the animal, which prompted a female dog to rush over for attention. Soon, most of the animal population was crowding in wanting a pat, a hug, a word of encouragement. When the skunks came too close, Adam shooed them all away and said, "Forget it. I don't think any one of you will do- and all of you together is too large a crowd..

With that, Adam took a bite out of a pear, chewed it as his head swayed and his eyes floated back and forth. In a moment he was fast asleep. All of the animals seemed to lose interest in him, so they wandered off to find some place for the evening and perhaps to locate some food for supper.

As he slept, the Son appeared beside Adam. You could see the look of deep compassion the Creator had for His Creation. With a gentle hand, the Son wiped the dust from Adam's face, then cleaned off his side. Without anesthesia or a knife, the Son reached into his side and pulled out a rib."

Sonny could not be quiet, "Daddy always told me Eve was not made from the foot of man so he could step on her, nor the head so she could boss him, but from the prime rib so she could be by his side."

All the rest of us smiled then motioned for him to be silent. The Son carefully closed the wound in Adam's side. He held the rib up into the sunlight. Examining it carefully, he held it in his hand and squeezed. A flash of lightning shot from his hand along with a deep rumble of thunder. White sparks continued as he clinched his fist tighter and tighter.

"That's a switch," Sonny quipped. "He's making atoms and from them He's going to make Eve."

This was a different process than Adam's creation. Or maybe it was just faster. Soon a striking young lady lay on the ground. She was covered with perfect skin, shoulder length hair and a just-what-the-doctor-ordered figure. She was complete, except she looked like a mannequin in a store window without any clothes. Gently the Son raised her toward him and breathed into her the breath of life.

Sonny could not keep quiet, "Looks like He has a new, improved model."

Eve opened her eyes and glanced around. Closer now we could see the sky reflecting in the deep blue of her eyes. Something else danced there. Happiness? Joy? Mischief? Looking back into the face of the Son, she asked, "Where am I? Who am I? What am I doing here?"

"Typical woman reaction," mumbled Sonny.

Like a father escorting his daughter down a wedding aisle, the Son led Eve to the sleeping Adam. He nudged him with His foot- Adam's eyes shot open.

"I wonder what kind of animal he thinks she is," said Sonny.
"Be quiet," Sandra smiled.

The Son did not have to introduce them- they gazed at each other for a few moments. A trace of a smile twitched on Adam's lips indicating something far better than a puppy dog had arrived. Eve was obviously impressed with the good looks of her companion, as she shyly dropped her head, then raised her eyes back toward him.

Cautiously, Adam reached out his hand to her shoulder. You could feel the love radiating from him like heat from an old fashioned stove. He touched her hair, she blinked her eyes. Then he took both arms and drew her closer to him.

"CUT!" I yelled. "Stop the Action! Don't look, Sandra and Sonny!" As the scene faded, I breathed deeply and shouted "I pronounce you husband and wife in the name of the Father, the Son and the Holy Spirit. You may kiss the bride. Whew!"

Gabriel grinned at me, "Not to worry, pastor, God took care of the vows, don't you remember?"

The man said, "This is now bone of my bones and flesh of my flesh; she shall be called 'Woman,' for she was taken out of man."
For this reason a man will leave his father and mother and be united to his wife, and they will become one flesh.
The man and his wife were both naked, and they felt no shame.
(Genesis 2:23-25 NIV)

"So, they got married and lived happily ever after," Sandra said. "What a beautiful love story. They were never real people to me until now- they were like paper dolls cut from a religious book. It never dawned on me the intensity of their love for each other. Nor did I imagine they had to have a place to eat and sleep and cook. They were just two characters running around with fig leaves for a few days until the serpent showed up."

I wiped the sweat off my brow indicating the scene with Adam and Eve had gotten rather "steamy." I added, "I'll bet you never realized they had, uh, physical attraction for each other."

Sonny popped in, "That had never crossed my mind. But I can assure you from now on whenever I see their pictures, I'll have a better knowledge of what was going on in their minds."

+ + +

CHAPTER 37
HOW LONG WERE
THEY IN THE GARDEN?

Gabriel walked over to Sandra and whispered rather loudly, "Adam and Eve were in the Garden for a while. Would you like to guess how long?"

Sandra said, "Uh, seven days? Maybe they made it a week before they fell."

"No way Eve made it that long," Sonny said. "Let's see this probably took place on a Friday to give them a long weekend for a honeymoon. I'd say that red hot babe made it all the way until Monday. Any way, it wasn't long."

"Not even close," Gabriel answered. "They were in the Garden two hundred thousand years, earth time."

"Two hundred thousand years? No way," Sonny answered. "She would have been an old hag, and he would have had to have a wheel chair to be driven out of the Garden."

Gabriel asked, "Doesn't the Bible say a day is as a thousand years?

'For a thousand years in thy sight are but as yesterday when it is past, and as a watch in the night. Psalm 90:4 (KJV),'"

"Oh yea," Sonny smiled. "So the Garden was under heavenly daylight saving time. Let's see now, if one day equals one thousand years on earth, then they were in the Garden, hmm, only 200 days!"

Gabriel smiled at the sharpness of the young athlete. "There are a few things I did not tell you about the Garden Eden was a colony of Heaven on earth. You experienced this with your senses- the smells, the sounds, the beauty. To make it simple for you, the whole Land of Eden, including the Garden and the mountains around it- all were in a heavenly bubble. No one could enter and no one could leave. Here God had a perfect Kingdom on earth for two hundred thousand years."

"Earth years!" Sonny added.

Gabriel nodded then searched for the right words. "By the year 200,000 B.C. it was quite obvious something had gone badly wrong with Pre-man. Scientists today are still looking for fossils to prove you are cousins to the ape.-

maybe even the grandson. Some people even faked evidence to prove evolution. For example, the Piltdown Man was proved to be a forgery. In 1912, the scientific world went bananas over a fossilized human being found in England. Later they found he was nothing more than an orangutan's jawbone and the skull of a modern man."

"The Neanderthal man is still news, claiming he went back some 600,000 to 300,000 years B.C. Unfortunately for science, he became extinct some 30,000 years ago. So did a bunch of others, such as the Cro-Magnon man.

"Homo Sapiens arrived on the scene in 200,000 B.C." I said.

"That's the same time as Adam!" Sandra said excitedly.

"I've still got a few missing links," Sonny said. "If Homo Sapiens arrived the same year as Adam, why didn't they know each other? Why didn't Adam appear until 4004 B.C.? We've got more questions than answers."

"You remember the scene of the men hunting the mammoths. I told you the time was a little less than 200,000 years ago. Those people were intelligent and physical. They had been created by God in a similar way as Adam and Eve. But God did not make them in His Image. In fact, he made them incomplete, just like a fetus or an embryo before birth."

Both college students stared at Gabriel as if he had just been preaching heresy. "What?" they both asked.

"Calm down," I told them. "It shook me when I first heard it. But Gabriel will explain it all later- and believe it or not, it will make sense. Just trust him."

Gabriel continued, "However, as I told you then, it didn't take long for those early homo sapiens to be warped almost beyond repair. They were given all the resources to love each other and to love God. What I didn't show you were the wars they waged as well as the hundreds of idols they worshipped. You were spared from watching them sacrifice their babies and young virgins and even strong warriors."

"Satan had already gotten to them," I explained. "He had implanted in them selfishness and pride and envy. Oh yea, he also gave them the necessity of a blood sacrifice. It became twisted and perverted into a blood sacrifice of one of their own."

"So God realized one group He had made in His image needed better protection," Gabriel said. "As I showed you, God took barren land and made it into Eden. He protected it on all sides with mountains plus an invisible wall so nothing could slip in and ruin it. He created the Garden for beauty and to make a home place for His creatures- the Land of Eden. Then He built a Garden in the East of Eden. There He built His Kingdom on earth, and it lasted 200,000 wonderful years."

"Was Jesus hinting at this when He taught us to pray in the Lord's Prayer, 'Thy Kingdome Come, Thy Will Be Done, On Earth As It Is In Heaven?'" Sonny asked.

Exactly, my young genius," Gabriel answered. "God has placed within each of us a kind of gene that longs for a return to Eden. In Christians He places the hope for Paradise for the future."

"Well, that's neat," Sonny said. "But I'm still not getting it."

"Do you remember the location of Eden?" Gabriel asked.

"Sure, it was north of Iraq, on the eastern side of Turkey. It's not much of a garden spot today," Sonny answered. "I don't think I mentioned that it was only fifty miles from a very famous mountain," Gabriel smiled his secret smile at us.

"Mount Sinai?" Sonny asked.

"No, but one just about as famous- Mount Ararat." "Mount Ararat? That's where Noah landed the ark," Sandra said.

"Close, but to be exact, Noah landed the ark in the Ararat mountains, or in Hebrew 'RRT' mountains," Gabriel said. "The apples never fell far from the tree. God set aside an area just as your government will designate some lands as national parks and others as military testing grounds. Eden was a bit of both. His land was a rectangle about one hundred miles long, large enough to take care of all the civilization that would live there before the flood."

"So, Eden was about the size of modern day Israel." Sandra said.

"Was all of it the Garden?" Sonny asked. "No, the Bible states that the Garden was 'in the east of Eden.' You'll see, the Garden was not very large," Gabriel answered.

"Why didn't the Garden fill all of Eden?" Sonny asked.

"Do you remember God had to make a place for Lucifer and his followers when they were cast out of Heaven?" I asked.

So, God made the World of Eden which was outside the Garden- it was the place Adam and Eve would be cast when they sinned and had to leave the Eden," Sonny answered.

Gabriel nodded his head in approval, then went on to explain. "All the Land of Eden was protected from the rest of the world. You would say it was where God had his specially chosen people. No one could enter or exit the land of Eden. And a small part of the land was the Garden. Inside it was Heaven on earth- no problems, no hurts, no cold, no diseases...."

"No dress codes," Sonny grinned. "You know, I'm glad we are going to have white robes in Heaven, I'm not sure it would be wise to have everybody in Heaven running around in their birthday suit."

Everyone laughed. Then no one said anything for a while- we could not think of anything to say. This was all so mind-boggling to us. We had thought the Land of Eden and the Garden of Eden were the same. Never had we been told the Garden of Eden and Mount Ararat were within spitting distance of each other.

"What did Adam and Even do for those thousands of years?" Sonny finally asked.

"To them it was only like 200 days. As to their activities, they did the same thing you will do in Heaven for millions and billions of years," Gabriel answered. "They loved. They laughed. They worked. Adam took care of the animals and did the farming. Eve handled the flower gardens and the fruit trees."

"Uh oh," Sonny said. "So Eve was in charge of the fruit orchard. I see where this is leading. Wait! Another big problem, Gabriel. If this were a protected area, how did Lucifer get in to tempt them?"

"About the same way he comes in today," Gabriel answered.

+ + +

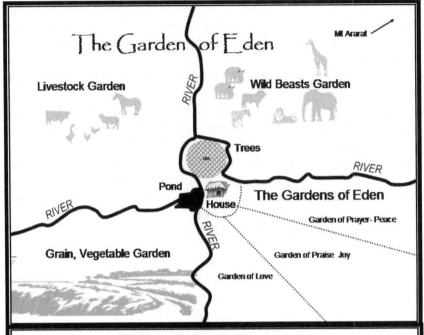

The Garden of Eden

Mt Ararat

Livestock Garden

RIVER

Wild Beasts Garden

Trees

RIVER

Pond

The Gardens of Eden

House

Garden of Prayer- Peace

RIVER

RIVER

Grain, Vegetable Garden

Garden of Praise Joy

Garden of Love

THE GARDEN OF EDEN

The Land of Eden was located in what is now Eastern Turkey
at the foot of Mount Ararat.
The Garden of Eden was at the North East side of Eden.
A river ran through it, but it split three way in the center
and divided the Garden into four distinct areas

1- Livestock Garden
2- Wild Beasts Garden
3- Grains and Vegetables Garden
4- The Gardens of Eden
  a- The Garden of Prayer and Peace
  b- The Garden of Praise and Joy
  c- The Garden of Love

Many trees were in the middle surrounding the Tree of Life
and the Tree of Knowledge of Good and Evil.

CHAPTER 38
A TOUR
OF THE GARDENS

Sandra sniffed, shrugged her shoulders- then looked coyly at Gabriel. Clearing her throat she said, "Uh, Gabriel, before we encounter Lucifer again, would it be possible for you to give us a tour of the Garden? So far all we've seen is a pool, a little hut, and, well, that's it. I thought it was the most beautiful spot on earth and would really like to take a look around while we are here."

"Sure," Gabriel said as they ascended back up into the sky. "Eden was a special place- like the Temple of God would be. But the Garden was comparable to the Holy of Holies. It was like, well, like the Lord's Prayer- 'Thy Kingdom come, Thy will be done, on earth as it is in Heaven.' The Garden of Eden was a colony of Heaven on earth. Though John Milton wrote about it in *Paradise Lost*, he never captured it's beauty. There are thousands and thousands of paintings of the Garden- ranging from Walt Disney scenes to pictures of clouds over rain forests. None of them come close to the real thing. So now you can take a peek."

"Wish I'd brought my camera," Sonny whistled as we gazed down at the scene below us.

"As I told you, it would have burned up in this dimension in which we are traveling," Gabriel said. "Plus, God would not want you to take photographs to try to show what Heaven and the Garden were like. There is no way you could capture the scenery, the feeling, the smells, the tastes, the peace and love and joy. You can only know that through Christ. Mankind has not invented any machine nor a gadget capable of confining Paradise to a piece of paper or film."

"Oh," I sighed as I gazed at the scene below. "I had forgotten how out-of-this-world beautiful this place is- uh- was- hmm, shall be."

Sandra said, "Looks like it's all fenced in. "There are mountains around all of Eden. It reminds me of the great meteor crater in Arizona. We saw pictures of it- it's a mile wide. How large did you say Eden was?"

Gabriel answered, "One hundred miles long and one hundred miles wide. That's about the distance from Birmingham to Montgomery and all the land over to the Georgia state line."

Sonny was awed by the beauty, but then noted, "There's not a single village in the whole place. I can't spot an animal nor a cave man. Nobody. There are trees and bushes and a river running through it. But that's all."

"Up there," Sandra said. "Look up there to the north east- right at the foot of Mount Ararat. Can you see the Garden now?"

On cue, Gabriel had our foursome glide over the designated area. Again mountains flanked the north and east sides. From above it was difficult to tell if the south and west sides were small hills or thick rows of trees. Whichever- the land inside was quite different from that outside.

"It doesn't look so big from up here," Sonny said. "It's like looking down from an airplane, unless you can see a car or house, it's hard to determine sizes."

"The Garden is nine miles square,' I said. "I can remember from my first visit that is it three miles by three miles."

"Any symbolism there?' Sandra asked.

"Probably," the preacher replied. "The concept of the trinity is deeply embedded in all of the universe. For example, mankind is made of body, mind and spirit. Freud told us we are id, ego and super ego. Later we learned we are child, adult and parent wrapped up in one body."

"Don't forget how we are all three dimensional," Sandra said. "If it weren't for that, we would be stick figures stuck in the ground."

"Enough philosophy," Sonny said as he gazed down at the scene below him. "You were right, Brother Gabriel, it is out-of-this-world beautiful. Even though we are up about the height of a jet liner, I can tell there are animals running around on the northern part of the Garden."

Gabriel followed Sonny's pointed finger and said, "Yes, that's where the wild beasts roam. You remember God made livestock and wild beasts. Even though they get along well together here, they still have the areas that suit them best. There in the northern area are plains and jungles and a river."

"And waterfalls. The water flows from Mount Ararat, then bounces and bubbles its way through rainbow falls into the Garden," Sandra said.

Sonny stared, then said, "I see elephants, hippos, lions and zebras. There in the trees are monkeys and all sorts of critters. It looks like one of those drive-through safaris. You have some animals but not all of them."

"That's right," Gabriel said. "Below are the special animals God made for the Garden. If I were to take you higher and we could roam over Africa or Australia or Alaska, you would see many varieties of animals that changed by A.R.M."

"A.R.M.," Sonny said, "Adaptation, Radiation and Mutation."

"Right," Sandra continued. "That's the reason Darwin found turtles and birds that were different on the Galápagos Islands."

I added, "It ended up a five year trip around the world."

"And I assume we will understand later why all the mutations and different species are not in the Garden," Sonny grinned.

"Exactly," Gabriel said. "Now if you will look to the west, you will see the livestock of Eden. That's where Adam spent most of his time."

Sure enough, below us we could see herds of cattle standing on the grassy land, chewing their cud. Horses raced back and forth as if seeking some way out of their domain. Sheep and goats grazed peacefully beside lakes and ponds. There was a shriek and a grunt and a bunch of pigs came running over the hill as if the devil were after them. Again the same river wandered back and forth across the land supplying the needs of the flocks.

I took over the role of tour guide and said, "If you'll look to the south, you'll see the farm area. Adam was also a pretty good farmer- but you remember he learned from the Son back at the beginning when they planted trees together."

"That looks like wheat fields below," Sandra said as we veered southward. "And over there- that's corn. I didn't think they had corn until they brought it back from America."

"Well, you need to remember God planted vegetation all over the world," I answered. "In some places the crops thrived, in others they disappeared like dinosaurs. Now if you want to remember the old south, look at that field."

Sandra and Sonny both gazed down at a spot that looked as if giant snow flakes had fallen on the bushes. Sonny cried out, "Cotton fields! My grandpa grew cotton on the farm where I lived."

"All of this is prettier than National Geographic could imagine," Sandra said. "Hmm- the first couple must have been pretty busy- for look at all the vegetables! Beans, peas, corn, okra, lettuce, carrots. It must have taken forever for just the two of them to take care of the animals and the fields."

"Well, God didn't design mankind to sit in front of a TV all day," Gabriel said. "Man was made to work."

I stared at the huge garden below him. "One good thing," he said, "no weeds grow in Paradise!"

Sandra laughed, as she glanced over the perfect rows of grains and vegetables. She also remembered how they had been taught that the world has enough space to supply all the food needed for the hungry. It's just that the workers are so few. Suddenly she said, "Gabriel, this is awesome, but I think you are holding the really gorgeous spots back for last."

"Just like God's holding the best for last," I sermonized. "You know, like when the whole battle is over, the winners win Paradise."

"You are correct, Miss Sandra," Gabriel said as we hovered over the center of the area. "And you also make an 'A,' Brother Chris. The Bible promises you that the eyes haven't seen, the ears haven't heard, and the mind cannot even imagine the beauty of Heaven."

"Why this big circle of trees at the very center?" Sonny asked. "They seem to get thicker and thicker as they reach the middle. Wait- now I can see. It looks like a giant bulls-eye right in the hub. It's a tree- I've seen it before. Think, think, think."

When we dropped down low enough that we were in the air beside the central tree, Sonny said, "The Tree of Life. Ha, I couldn't tell from the top, but now I can see the strange cross shape it has. And the tree beside it- that's got to be the Tree of Knowledge of Good and Evil. I remember when it was planted, and who can forget the multi-colored fruit?"

The two trees faded quickly from sight as we moved southward. Sonny said, "Wait a minute, Gabriel, I wanted to examine that last tree more closely."

"Too many have examined that tree too closely and been caught in its trap like a bug in a spider's web," Gabriel said. "I don't want to focus on just those two trees- for the Garden was much, much more. Look at all the trees that grow out from the center. Recognize any of them?"

"Sure," Sandra said, sounding like the science teacher she would soon become. "Up there are the fir trees- pines, cedars and spruces. Next to them are the broadleaf or deciduous trees- oaks, maples, elms and many, many more."

Sonny said, "Hey, I can play this game. Below are the tropical trees- palms, ferns, etc. Over there are fruit trees and nut trees and flowering trees. But what is that bunch? I've never seen anything like them."

Sandra looked, shrugged her shoulders and said, "I don't recognize them."

"Look closer," I urged.

"Oh, those are trees and bushes that have become extinct over the 200,000 years since God made the Garden," Sandra said.

"Yep, and there are some new plants that have evolved along the way since then."

"Look, there's where Adam and Eve live," Sonny said. "Their hut is beside the trees- snuggled up alongside the river."

"Well, what do you think, Sandra?" Gabriel asked. "Is it stunning enough for you?"

Sandra bit her lip, scratched her chin, wiggled her nose, then said, "Of course, it's beautiful. But you must remember we just left the glories of Heaven, so maybe I was expecting too much."

Gabriel winked at her and said, "Oh, maybe I forgot to show you the gardens."

"The gardens? As in plural, more than one garden?" she asked.

"Yes, I thought you understood that the Garden, singular, referred to this whole nine square miles of prime real estate. It includes plains for the wild beasts, meadows for the livestock, farmland for the vegetables and cereals needed for the first family. Of course, in the middle we have trees, all clustered around and guarding the Tree of Life and the Tree of Knowledge of Good and Evil."

"But there are more gardens!" Sandra almost shouted. "Next to their house, I see three trails leading back into the forest. Do they lead to other gardens?"

"Hmm," Gabriel hummed. "Why don't we walk down this one and see where it leads?"

The angel took Sandra by one hand and grabbed Sonny with the other. He motioned for me to follow, and we walked down the well worn path, entered the cool green of the trees as excitedly as Dorothy, the Scarecrow, the Tin Man and the cowardly Lion setting out for the Wizard of Oz.

+++

THE PRAYER GARDEN
OF PEACE

We wound around the narrow trail as green-
ery surrounded us, and we felt as if we were wandering through a tunnel into the
deepest jungle. Ahead we could hear wind chimes- soft notes composing a melody. Suddenly we emerged into a quiet meadow. Sunlight painted the clouds
with every pastel shade, yet left the sky behind a soft mellow blue.

Flowers bloomed all along the edges of the meadow- as well as rimming the
trees. Every shade of light yellow mingled perfectly with pale blues and violets
and soothing greens. In the center of the garden a calm lake stretched out lazily
across the landscape. Several willows dipped their lacy branches toward the
cool, clear water. Two swans slowly made their way across the placid scene like
two ballerinas tip-toeing across a stage.

All was still. All was quiet- except for the gentle sound of the wind chimes.

"Whew!" Sonny said, breaking the silence. "I've never experienced any
place like this. It's so, uh, beautiful. So peaceful. I feel I could stretch out here
and sleep for a year."

Sandra inhaled deeply, closed her eyes, smiled and said,

"I wish that there were some wonderful place
In the Land of Beginning Again.
Where all our mistakes and all our heartaches
And all of our poor selfish grief
Could be dropped like a shabby old coat at the door
and never put on again."

"The Land of Beginning Again, by Louise Fletcher Tarkington," I said softly.
"I've used that verse in many a sermon for New Years. It also is good material
for a funeral."

"Would it be good for a wedding?" Sonny said. "I know a lot of folks who
may drop their mistakes and heartaches, only to have their spouse tell them to
pick'em up and hang'em up!"

We all laughed then stood silently breathing in the beauty of the garden and
actually feeling our burdens melting away like a snowman on the first warm
sunny day of Spring. Sonny stretched his neck and back feeling gentle pops as
bones and muscles eased. Sandra knelt and lifted her hands slightly as if she
wanted to pray. Turning to Gabriel, she asked, "What is this place? Does it
have a name?"

"The Prayer Garden of Peace," Gabriel whispered.

"Well, it sure beats going into a closet to pray," Sonny said. "I feel a great urgency to talk to God. Do all of you feel the same thing?" We other two human heads bobbed in agreement. Gabriel smiled like a teacher when his students finally discover some great truth. "When we come into the presence of God there is a natural desire to pray."

Sonny said, "Hey, there's something by the willow tree. I'll go look and see what it is."

He took off running just as he had when he set the high school record for the mile- just as he shot through the defensive lines of both high school and college teams. We others followed- at a slower gait. A low bench sat silently beside the willow. Sonny picked it up, examined it, shook it, then set it down again. "If it's a sitting bench, it must be for midgets. It's not high enough."

Sandra took a quick look at the manmade object in Sonny's hands, then said, "Sonny, don't you remember when you and I visited the Catholic church?"

"Yea."

"And you couldn't figure out why they would stand up, sit down, then kneel down on those funny little benches."

"Oh, this is the Prayer Garden- so this is a prayer bench. I suppose Adam must have made it. Eve doesn't look like she could nail two boards together."

I said, "If you'll look, there are no nails, only pegs."

"I doubt if she could peg two boards together, either," he said. "Wonder what this would fetch on E-bay? 'Praying Bench for sale. Made by Adam.' Bidding starts at one billion dollars."

He examined the work surface again, nodded his approval as if he were a judge of fine furniture. He then placed the bench on the ground, looked around at the others, and knelt down upon it. Sonny began to raise his hands but shook his head, and said. "When I try to pray, my head is like a popcorn machine. I start off pretty well with a 'Dear God,' or an 'Our Father.' I will get out a thank-you for this or that- then something else pops in my brain like what am I am going to eat for supper, or which football play we should have run last week. I'll jerk back and continue my prayer for a few more words or thoughts and then my brain is off to the races again. My mind will be wondering what Sandra is doing right now or which shirt I need to wear on our next date or did I remember to finish all of my homework. Then back to praying for another brief spell until other ideas come barging in. Does everybody pray like that, Brother Chris?"

As a young preacher I honestly faced my young church member and star football player and confessed, "Yep. As long as we are in the flesh, our bodies are going to fight with our spirit just like Alabama and Auburn footballs teams fight from kickoff to the final whistle."

"But I don't want to pray that way," Sonny said. "It's just so many things and ideas keep crowding in."

Gabriel walked over to the athlete and said simply, "Try praying here."

"Right here? In the Garden of Eden?" Sonny asked.

"Right here, in the Prayer Garden of Peace in the Garden of Eden on the kneeling bench made by Adam."

"O.K.," Sonny said as he knelt on the path. "Dear God, I come to you…"

His eyes popped open along with his mouth. "Wow, what was that? I just started praying and a tunnel opened up right into the presence of God. He was there looking at me, listening to me, and I felt a peace that passes all understanding."

"That's what real prayer is," Gabriel coached him. "We close our eyes to block out all the distractions of this world. Then we address God just as you would address the President of the United States."

"I understand," Sonny said. "This was more like a chat room, where you carry on a real conversation."

Sandra knelt down beside her boyfriend and said, "It's really more like you coming to my house, knocking on the door, entering and then sitting down and talking."

"Yea, yea. That's it." Sonny smiled. "It was not an Email nor even a phone call. It was up close and personal. It was, uh, unbelievable." He gazed at the others with the sweet sense of victory. "I think I'm going to try it again."

He knelt, closed his eyes, then began praying, "Father, I am coming into your very presence. On this trip I've seen images of you in Heaven. Your love was so strong when you created Gabriel and the angels: it made me shiver. I felt that same love when you made Adam. Now I know you poured that exact amount of Tender Loving Care when you made me. Wow! I feel your love so powerfully. And underneath that love are your hands, taking care of me and Sandra, and all of us who will allow you to be our God."

He opened his eyes, looked around to make sure he was not dreaming, then continued his prayer. "Lord, there is such a peace in my life and it comes from talking to you and with you. What's that, Lord? You say your peace will go with me and your power will protect me? Hey, Lord, that's like knowing the final score of victory before you even take the field. It's great. Uh, Lord, I love you and I love this new type of praying where I talk to you and not just throw words up again the ceiling or try to impress everybody with my fancy phrasing. I'll be back in touch, Lord. You can bet on that. Amen."

Sonny hopped up, threw his arm up in the air and shouted, "Come on, Goliath! You are no match for me and God. Heck, send on the whole Philistine army."

I laughed, "Sonny, that's one time I can tell you got all pumped up- not from a pep rally but from a prayer rally.   Say, I just thought of something.   This is the Garden or Prayer and Peace.   How about this for a pithy saying, 'Prayer is the Pathway to Peace.'"

Prayer is the Pathway to Peace

Sandra and Sonny applauded while Gabriel nodded approval. Blushing a bit, I explained to my two young church members, "When Gabriel brought me here years ago, I felt the same thrill as you, when I was able to pray straight through to God. I never really thought praying to Saints or statues were the right way to pray, but I set up other idols that interfered. My worst problem was trying to impress people with my wording. Somehow, I figured a prayer that sounded like the Gettysburg Address would catch the attention of God and man than would a simple 'God, I love you.'   It was so easy to pray the right way here in Eden, but as soon as I arrived back at CROSS+ROADS, my praying suffered and struggled and seemed more like a video game on a computer than a talk with God, the Creator of Heaven and Earth."

Sandra put her arm around Sonny's shoulders and guided him back down to the prayer bench.   She placed her smooth hand over his brown tough fingers, bowed her head and said, "Dear Father..."

It was easy to tell she had entered into another world, another dimension, a place where things don't rot and thieves don't steal. A faint golden glow surrounded her as she continued, "I've prayed to you so often, but like Sonny, I now feel as if I'm kneeling at your feet. It's not in fear, but in love. Lord, I love you with all my heart..."

She started weeping- not tears of pain and grief but huge drops of joy. Sonny tried to reach into his back pocket to pull out his handkerchief- then he realized his clothes were thousands of miles and years away. So he took his sleeve and offered it to her. When her teardrops fell upon the white robe he was wearing they turned into diamonds and fell sparkling to the ground.

Sonny broke the spell when he said, "Hey, Gabriel, can I take one of these gems home with me? I'm thinking about giving Sandra an engagement ring one day and ...."

"No!"

"It was just a thought" Sonny stood and stretched.   He saw something under another willow tree. "What's that?" he asked. "Another prayer bench?"

I smiled, "It looks more like an-answer-to-prayer bench for the sheep and goats. It's a feeding trough."

Sonny walked over, pushed the drooping limbs back and knelt down beside the newly found object. "A feeding trough? It looks like a manger from one of our Christmas plays to me."

Sandra finished her prayer and walked over beside him, put her thin hand over his and whispered, "A feeding trough is a manger."

"Oh," Sonny said, a bit embarrassed. Nobody laughed at him, but we did smile a bit. "What's a manger doing in the Prayer Garden of Peace?"

Sandra volunteered, "Adam probably brings his flock here to feed them and so they can rest in green pastures beside still waters."

I knelt beside them and said, "This is a Faith Quiz. Question, 'What other reason could there be for a manger to be in a place of prayer and peace?'"

Sonny cut his eyes toward Sandra for an answer, then exclaimed, "I bet I know- Jesus was going to come some day to feed his flocks. This is a preview or a prophecy."

"Very good," I applauded him. "Anything else?"

Sandra put her face against the rough lumber, closed her eyes as if in prayer, then said, "Peace."

"Peace?" Sonny asked. "How can a manger symbolize...? Oh, I get it- the Prince of Peace would be born in a manger."

Sandra nodded agreement. "But do you remember what the Angels sang that night?"

"I do," answered Gabriel. "I was there. Thousand and millions of us angels filled the skies over Bethlehem. What a glorious moment. We all sang together those wonderful words..."

"Peace of earth," Sonny said, then sang out richly, "Peace on earth, good will to men!"

Sandra said, "I get it now. This manger is a sign that mankind would fall and lose this tranquility - but in the future the young Prince of Glory will come to bring peace back to planet earth. That is just beautiful. Oh, I love this place. I can see why people who have after-life experiences and visit Paradise don't want to come back home."

The chimes begin to play again and Sandra jumped to her feet and began to dance. She swirled through the branches that almost touched the ground, then she swayed beside the tranquil pond. Feeling the music, the two swans glided gracefully toward her swinging their heads to the beat of the music. When she finally finished her impromptu ballet, we all applauded.

Sonny hugged her, then said, "Oh, I see a path through the trees over there. Does that lead to another garden?"

THE PRAISE GARDEN OF JOY

Without waiting for an answer, Sonny raced across the grass and down the path leading through the woods. In a moment he yelled back, "Sandra, hurry, you're got to see this. It's unbelievable."

Dashing across the field, Sandra showed us that she was in great shape. It only took a few minutes to reach the opening and slip through. Gabriel and I followed at a more reasonable pace. I had already had the Garden tour several years ago and knew that Gabriel had helped design the gardens.

Sandra grabbed Sonny's arm and gazed in wonder at the scene before her. She had been to Yosemite and gawked at the waterfalls and mountains. But they were nothing compared to what stood before us. Mountains of lavender and purple stood like Royal Guards in the background. Waterfalls spilled from them in every shade of green and blue. Mists rose from them and floated out across the Garden, watering every plant.

Sandra shook her head in disbelief at the beauty. Then she told Sonny, "There are no rainbows in the mists. But if you look closely, you can see shades of blue and yellow and red- God's DNA in His Creation."

Pools glittered beneath each cascade, and the water gushed out and over rocks, splashing a merry tune as it flowed along. The previous garden was one of pastel colors- this was one of bright shades. Fire red rhododendrons banked the edges of the creeks, brilliant orange azaleas grew wildly, lemon day lilies surrounded tropical flowers. The scene was so happy, Sonny beat his chest and let out a Tarzan call. Then Sandra laughed and thumped her chest in an effort to mimic Jane.

Gabriel and I arrived and stood grinning at the young couple experiencing such merry moments.

"What is this place called?" Sonny asked. "I want to make a reservation here when I get to Heaven?"

"Your reservation has already been made by the Prince of Peace," Gabriel said. "This is The Praise Garden of Joy. Adam and I would come here to laugh and run and romp like children."

"Did Eve even come here?" Sandra asked.

"Sure, but she never learned to enjoy it like Adam," Gabriel said sadly. 'Eve was always wondering what was on the other side of the mountain. Sometimes she would tell Adam she wished there were more geraniums in this garden- or often she would bring exotic plants and place them beside the gurgling waters.

The next week she would dig them up and plant them somewhere else. In the last days she wanted to climb the mountains and ride down the waterfalls to experience a greater thrill. When Adam told her it would be dangerous, she would reply that they were in God's image and nothing could hurt them."

"Well, that was Eve's problem," Sandra said. "I am going to enjoy this moment." She and Sonny joined hands and leaped into the rushing waters. The creek seemed to be aware of their presence and burst forth with a happy tune. The young couple looked across the gorgeous garden and began to sing an old song with a rather peppy tune:

> *Praise God from whom all blessings flow*
> *Praise Him all creatures here below*
> *Praise Him above ye heavenly host,*
> *Praise Father, Son, and Holy Ghost. "*

Slowly, I swayed with the music and added a threefold "Amen" at the end. Then I hopped in the water beside them. It only came up to our ankles, but we all managed to dance a little jig to the tune of the musical waters.

Gabriel watched from the bank. It did him good to see God's children so happy. His eyes misted over as he remembered the good times Adam and Eve had sung the same song, danced the same dance and felt the same elation.

"This is what God wanted and still wants for his creatures," Gabriel told us. "As I told you, God existed in the Trinity for ever with Love, Joy and Peace. He created the angels to share those feelings. Much later, he built a Garden in the East of Eden. He filled it with trees, animals, flowers and a man and a woman. But he meant to fill them with enough Love, Joy and Peace that they could be happy forever. Tomorrow that dream will be shattered into a billion pieces. As the Roman writer, Horace, wrote '*Carpe diem.*' You usually translate it as '*seize the day.*' Horace and I both use the word in the sense of '*enjoy!*'"

For ten or fifteen minutes- earth time- we three humans laughed and rollicked in the garden. To us it seemed an eternity of bliss. Finally it was Sonny who wandered up the creek toward the falls and found a surprise behind a cave. He called out for Sandra to come and see what he had discovered. She waltzed through the falling water as if it were the first snow fall of the season. Gabriel and I followed behind.

Sonny pointed to the wall of the cave and said, "I didn't expect this."

"Neither did I," Sandra added as we moved closer to the ledge cut into the side of the cave. "It's wider than I would have thought. And what is it doing in Eden, especially in the Garden of Praise and Joy? Can you explain this tomb, Brother Chris?"

I walked over and sat on the ledge cut so smoothly into the cool wall. I motioned for them to sit beside me. Putting my arms around both of them, I said, "Gabriel explained this to me on my first trip here. I was stunned for I never thought the idea of death would cross their minds- well, not until the day they ate and fell."

Pointing at the ledge on which we sat, I said, "Adam heard God very clearly when He told them the day they ate of the fruit of the Tree of Knowledge of Good and Evil, they would die. Adam was smart. With Eve he knew it was not 'if' but 'when.' So he slipped up here and made a tomb for two. When Eve ate the fruit- she would die. It would bring pain and sorrow into the Garden just as Lucifer did in Heaven. Adam would bring her here and lay her down in this grave. Then he would eat the fruit and lie down beside her. Eden, without Eve, would not be Paradise."

"So that's the reason he ate the fruit with Eve," Sonny said.

I answered, "That was part of the reason, but Satan tricked both of them. They both ate- they both sinned- they both died."

Sonny thought a moment and said, "Wait a minute, they both didn't die..."

Gabriel broke in, "Wait until tomorrow. You will understand."

"But why is this tomb in the Praise Garden of Joy?" Sonny asked.

Sandra thought a moment then said, "Sonny, ask that question again- but include the word, 'empty.'"

Sonny blinked at her, puzzled, then asked, "Why is this *empty* tomb in the Garden of Praise and Joy... Oh, I get it. I see. Our joy today comes from the fact of the empty tomb. Easter. Resurrection. He is not here, He is risen. I love it."

Jumping on the ledge he made an imaginary microphone with his fist and said, "Ladies and gentlemen, I bring you good tiding of great joy. For the savior who was born in a manger and who died on the cross is no longer dead. The death tomb is empty- He is alive forever more!"

With that Sonny let out a war hoop that echoed back and forth in the cave. "So folks, we can have real joy because Jesus rose from the grave."

+ + +

THE GARDEN OF LOVE

"First, we encountered the Prayer Garden of Peace. If you noticed carefully, it was like daybreak," Gabriel told us as we walked another path that led through the trees toward a third garden. "Then you experienced the Praise Garden of Joy- and it was much like noon."

As he spoke the light began to dim gradually and blue-violet haze settled over the group. He continued, "Now we enter an area of Twilight..."

"The Twilight Zone," Sonny called out- then hummed, "Dum de dum dum."

Sandra gave him a this-is-no-time-to-be-funny look, then said, "This has to be the Garden of Love." She inhaled deeply, tossed her hair gently from side to side and soaked in the deep sensations pulsating toward us like rays from the sun on a summer afternoon at Panama City Beach.

Before us stretched a garden of roses. There was ample light to see the brilliant reds, the calm pinks, the assortment of yellows and the dazzling whites. A path stretched before us and continued up and over small hills.

"I felt a lot of love when we visited Heaven," Sonny said, "but this- this is different. There I experienced a deep love for God and the angels. But now love has flattened out and spread out so I can love people. Brother Chris, I have always admired you and respected you, but now- I can't think of any other words to say, except, 'I love you, man.'"

Sonny wiped a few tears from his eyes and reached out to give his pastor another bear hug. I grunted and said, "Sonny, I'm glad you love me, but if you loved me any more you would have broken several ribs."

Sonny laughed then turned to Sandra. "Sandra, I thought I loved you before we began this trip, but now, I love you a hundred times more."

Sandra threw him a kiss, then asked Gabriel, "So God built a garden of love to magnify the love He had built into us."

"Was it all destroyed when the Garden was demolished and torn down?" Sonny asked.

"Who told you the Garden was destroyed?" Gabriel asked.

"Well, I thought when Adam and Eve were driven out..."

I helped the young athlete out. "Don't you remember how God sent the Cherubim to guard the gates of the Garden after Adam and Eve left?"

"I remember now," Sonny said. "But is the Garden still out there somewhere like the ark on Mount Ararat?"

Gabriel broke in, "You will find out what happened to the Garden if you'll just let me finish this tour. Right now, I want you to understand when God created Adam and Eve, He included a special area for love- in their minds and in their Garden."

Sonny seemed satisfied so he grabbed Sandra's hand and said, "Let's run up this path and see what's on the other side of the hill."

Off they raced like two young children on their first trip to Disney World. They halted, picked some of the flowers, held them close to enjoy the scent, then gave them to each other and laughed.

I turned to the Archangel and said, "Look at that! They are actually stopping and smelling the roses. I think there's a sermon in there somewhere."

"As we travel up and over the small hills, the sense of love seems to change," Sandra told Sonny as they waited for Gabriel and me.

"I noticed that," Sonny said. "When we first entered, I had this deep love for my family. Since Dad and Curtis are gone, I have only you and Chris. So my love for you two just exploded. As we crossed over this first little hill, I now have this longing in my heart to go tell all my friends how much they mean to me. In fact, if I had my cell phone with me, I would send them all a text message that simply says, 'I LV U.'"

Sandra beamed and said, "I feel the same thing. If I were home right now, I would call everyone who graduated with me from high school and share how much I care about them. Then I would use up all my cell phone minutes calling my friends at Samford. I never realized how special they are to me."

We crossed over another rise and saw the rose garden was intermingled with orchids and irises and a thousand other flowers. "What an amazing sight," she sighed. "Now another love is sweeping over me."

"Yea, I feel it, too," Sonny said. "It's a foreign kind of love- not one we see or experience very often on earth. I feel a love for my lost friends."

There was a bench waiting for them at the top of this hill. They sat down and he continued, "In football, I was taught we were to win- which means we beat down our enemies. We tackle them, push them, shove them- sometimes more than is necessary. I guess we learn to hate our enemies. Then as a Christian I carried the same feelings over to people who didn't go to church- or worse, those who went to church but didn't live a very consistent Christian life. One thing is for certain, I may not have hated them, but I sure didn't love them."

I heard him and knelt down beside him. "You are having some real insight to one of the problems we have in witnessing to a lost world. Sure, we want to see them saved- whether they live down the street or in the far off lands of Iraq. What we fail to see is that our main weapon for evangelism and missions is love.

We need to learn to love folks- especially those who don't sit in our pew nor share our last name."

Sonny nodded his head in agreement. "Whatever God has planned for me in the future- and it seems like He has greater plans for me than I have- this trip to the Garden of Love has helped me understand the power of love. If we are going to win friends, influence people, and win them to Christ- God's love must be on daily display."

We four sat there for a moment, resting in this special Paradise. Our minds shot forward to the days of eternity when we would visit the Garden again. The next time would not be limited to the three humans and one angel- but would include others. Sonny broke the silence, "You know, before my brother Curtis died, he got a glimpse and a taste of the Garden of Love. I was pretty good in sports, but he could out love me any day of the week- with one hand tied behind him."

I patted him on the arm and said, 'I think you do pretty good job of loving people- for a guy."

Sandra wound her arm over his shoulder and said, "I second the motion."

Sonny blushed, then hopped up and said, "It looks like there's one more hill to climb. Race you to the top."

He easily outdistanced us up the path. When he reached the top, he stopped. He didn't turn around to tell us he had won, nor did he continue on over the hill as if he were on a treasure hunt for King Solomon's gold. He dropped to his knees, then gazed at whatever lay beyond him.

Sandra soon stood beside him, anxious to know what new discovery he had found that drove him to his knees. When she reached the top, she gasped, held her hand up to shield the glare, then dropped down beside Sonny.

I talked to Gabriel as we followed the two up the path. "I was fifteen when I had a dream one night. There was a road that led up a hill. It was rocky and I could feel the sharp stones beneath my feet. There were lots of people and they were all headed toward me, so I had to fight my way through them like a salmon returning to his spawning grounds. Finally I struggled to the top and looked straight into the eyes of Jesus. He was hanging on a cross- and my position on the hill allowed me to stare him straight in the eye. He looked at me, and He knew me and He loved me."

I faltered a moment, then said, "I was a Christian at that time, but not much of one. I had been baptized, was faithful in Sunday School and Church on Sunday morning, and lived a good moral life. But when I met the Master face to face- something happened inside of me. Jesus stepped out of the pages of the Bible story book and into my life. He became real. My life changed and I thought it was because of the dream- or vision- or whatever. Now I understand it was the cross and the man on that cross."

We joined the other two and knelt beside them. In front of us was a simple cross. It was not as well fashioned as the chairs we had seen in the hut, nor the prayer bench in one of the gardens. But we knew who had made it- though we doubted he knew what it meant.

It was a cross. Two pieces of wood fashioned together. "Adam made it," Sonny said. "I can't prove it, but I just know it. But how could he know...?"

"The Tree of Life," Sandra whispered. "I doubt if he knew he was making a cross. This may have been something like an artificial Christmas tree. Oh, I get it, it was an artificial Tree of Life."

"Probably," Sonny said. "I think, however, when Adam came to this part of the Garden of Love, he was so overwhelmed with his love for God, he had to do something- make something- leave something. Whether he knew it or not, he made the symbol of the greatest love ever shown. God poured our His love for all mankind on the cross."

+ + +

4004 B.C.

PART 6 THE SERPENT

CHAPTER 39
THE SNAKE IN THE GARDEN

"I wish I could show you all the good times we had in the Garden," Gabriel sighed.

"We?" Sonny asked. "Were you in the Garden, too?"

"Only for special occasions," he answered. "You remember I was still the main messenger. God always sent, uh, what you would call them- Valentines, love notes to His earthly son and daughter. He would often come down and just walk with them in the cool of the afternoon. He is quite a good conversationalist, you know."

"Time just flowed along like a river composed of sweet smells and beautiful sounds and unbelievable tastes. It was really Heaven on earth. Adam and Eve always entertained me. Adam had a sense of humor as clever as yours, Sonny. He would turn to Eve and say, 'You are the only woman for me.'"

Sonny laughed, " I heard a good joke how Eve became jealous. Adam told her she was foolish for she was the only woman on the earth. He awakened during the night and Eve was counting his ribs."

Gabriel said, "He would play jokes on me and write clever little ditties. I remember he wrote, 'Roses are red, Violets are blue, Angels are sweet, What happened to you?'"

"Adam could write?" Sandra asked.

"Well, yes," Gabriel answered, "who do you think wrote all of this down? How do you think Moses knew what happened in the Garden? He wasn't there-he wouldn't be born until 2500 years after Adam and Eve left the Garden."

"Sandra, I wish you could have known Eve before..., uh, before that serpent got hold of her. She was not only beautiful, she was also wise. You think your mother is a good cook; Eve was a gourmet chef. Adam never complained about her cooking. She could make dishes that tasted like fried chicken or pork chops. She loved turnip greens, potato casseroles and fresh fruits. Adam was absolutely useless around the house, a prototype of many men today. It didn't bother Eve. She would bring out a fresh coconut cake or strawberry pie or banana pudding. Needless to say, she gathered her own coconuts, strawberries and bananas in the back yard."

"You still haven't answered how the snake got in the garden," Sonny said.

Gabriel sighed. "The same way he got into Heaven, the same way he gets into the church, and the same way he gets into marriages and friendships and nations. Pride and Envy. Don't you remember Lucifer's faults in Heaven?"

"Pride and Envy!" I exclaimed. "Nothing can keep them out."

The scene behind Gabriel changed from a cloudy green to a screen filled with a sea of colorful butterflies. A symphony played from the water, the wind and the trees. Butterflies were performing an aerial ballet. Adam and Eve sat on a log and applauded the graceful moves of the dancers. As they finished, the gorgeous insects curtsied and flittered off to find flowers or fruit. Eve eyed them admiringly as they floated away so elegantly.

"Oh, Adam," she sighed. "I wish I were as beautiful as a butterfly and as graceful. I wish I had wings so I could fly over the garden and over those mountains to see what lies out there. I'll bet things are so exciting over the hills."

"Eve, you're being silly," Adam said. "You are the most beautiful woman in the world and we have everything we need."

Eve laughed but not as heartily as she had before. Her eyes kept darting toward the colorful creatures soaring above. "Just think how exciting it would be to fly, I wouldn't have to climb the trees to pick the fruit, I could just hover over them- like a humming bird. It would be so much easier. Oh Adam, I wish I had vibrant colored wings. I'll bet you would like me better."

"You would probably like yourself better," Adam teased. "I love you with all my heart, there's no way I could love you more. You are in the same category as God, He is so good to us to give us this Garden. I love Him with all my heart and soul and strength and mind. Don't you?"

Eve was silent for a moment. Her smiled exploded, "Of course I love Him. He has done so much for us. But it wouldn't hurt him to just give me a set of wings, would it?"

'It might not hurt at first, but you could fall and harm yourself," Adam said. "You remember the little robin we rescued yesterday. It had wings but it was too young to fly. But birds are birds so he jumped from his nest and fell all the way to the ground. His mama and daddy were scolding him good. Fortunately, we have hands instead of wings, so we picked him up and put him back in his nest where he was safe."

"Oh, I know," Eve smiled. "I don't guess it hurts to wish."

Adam gazed at his wife then said, "It does hurt to want, however- to want what we do not have is to envy. You remember God told us the story of Lucifer, how he was filled with pride and envy. This caused war in Heaven and Lucifer was kicked out. I sure don't want us kicked out of the garden by allowing him to get in here and trick us."

"Oh, I'm sure God will keep him out. He just wants us to be happy," Eve cooed. "You know, Adam, there is a possibility God has kept some good things from us. We could be happier, you know."

"Eve, we are in a Paradise, Heaven on earth, the Garden of Eden," Adam said in exasperation. "Things don't get any better than this. Besides, my lunch hour is over, I've got to get back to work. We have some cows due to have their calves this afternoon."

He blew her a kiss as he disappeared down the path. It was then we realized he was as naked as a jay bird. So was she. As Gabriel had told us, they seemed as innocent as two children taking baths.

+ + +

Eve sat there for another moment, dreading the work of gathering the fruit. "Lord, I'm going to pray and ask for some beautiful wings. It's not right that those lowly butterflies are more beautiful than I am. And I could use wings to pick the apples off the trees at the very top."

Pop! A cracking sound above her causing her to jump. The noise was like thick ice breaking under an over weight skater. At first she saw nothing out of the unusual. Then the last of the butterflies scurried off toward the river. Wind began to whistle through the trees making an eerie sound, not so much a melody as an unnatural hum. Eve thought about calling Adam back, but she felt she could handle any emergency. Then she looked up and saw a huge butterfly flutter by. Her eyes were filled with desire as she gazed at the creature flying above her. She had seen it many times but now it seemed different- more attractive- more enticing.

Sandra whispered to Sonny, "That's the same creature we saw when we first viewed Eden. Remember, it flew over as they were bathing?"

"Looks like the same one," Sonny said. "It must be some animal that became extinct, like the unicorn."

Gabriel explained, "You need to set your time right. We are now visiting Eden on the afternoon of our previous visit."

"So what we are seeing now precedes the swimming scene and supper at Eve's house," Sonny joked.

"Yes," Gabriel answered. "I wanted you to see the flying creature above Eve. Can you describe it?"

Sandra answered, "Sure. It's unlike anything we have today. The body is long and thin, it has four legs with claws, a slender head, two gorgeous translucent wings, and a long pointed tail."

"Doesn't it remind you of anything you've ever seen?" Gabriel asked.

"Oh, I've got it now," Sonny shouted. "I didn't recognize it because of all the colors. It's a dragon. How about that? There really were dragons on the earth. Could you show us a unicorn?"

"There never were any unicorns," Gabriel answered. "I'm glad you recognized the 'dragon.' It is one of the mysteries of history. All cultures have stories and pictures of dragons, yet there is no such thing. It's truly amazing and unexplainable."

Sandra said, "Well, we understand it now. I heard we all have a recollection of the Garden of Eden built into our memories. If so, we probably also carry a remembrance of the dragon. Brother Chris, isn't it true that almost all cultures also have a flood story built into their history?"

"According to my seminary professors, most people have a Creation and a Flood Story," I answered, glad to have some part in the picture.

"Did the dragon become extinct like the dinosaurs or did he just get left off the ark?" Sonny asked with a grin.

"You'll find out some enough," Gabriel said. "You ought to know the flying creature you see was not called a dragon at this point. Later on that name would be applied to this memory of mankind. At this moment in history, which is 4004 B.C., he had another name, And the popping noise you heard? Satan snuck into the Garden of Eden. God's protection cracked because of the pride and envy of Eve. Lucifer found a willing colleague with the Serpent."

Below us the scene was one of early afternoon beauty. The creature fluttered back and forth among the fruit trees. It didn't have to grab the apples or oranges or pears with his claws, instead his tongue would unfurl and grab the fruit. Once the fruit was safely back in its mouth, the 'chomp, chomp' reminded us of Billie Nelle chewing on the chocolate chunk cookies we had enjoyed that afternoon.

"Could he be the ancestor of us who love to eat too much?" Sonny asked.

Gabriel nodded as he thought through the question, "Yes, you could say that. But let me ask if any of you are smart enough to figure out who he is."

"Well, if it didn't have wings and fly," Sonny said, "I would swear it was a serpent."

"Good," Gabriel said. "Now do you have any idea where it came from- or how it arrived here in Eden- or who it really is?"

Sandra raised her hand, "Oh, I see it now. That Serpent/Dragon is Satan. His entrance into Eden took place when Eve had the same sins as Lucifer: Pride and Envy. That popping sound was when he penetrated the invisible barrier to Eden. Eve's envy caused a puncture in their protection. Since the serpent was the craftiest of God's creatures, Satan made a beeline to him and entered him."

"Correct," Gabriel said.

"That doesn't make any sense," Sonny said. "How dumb could Eve have been. How could she be envious of a butterfly when she lived in Paradise on earth?"

I responded, "Don't you remember how Lucifer had Heaven and was not happy there. He wanted more."

"Is 'More' the root of Pride and Envy?" Sonny asked.

"I'm not sure whether it's the root or the fruit," I said. "Let's just say they go hand in hand."

Sandra asked, "O.K., we are now looking at an afternoon scene in Eden. In a few hours, Adam will come in from work and jump in their swimming pool with Eve. Then they will go to their home and have supper? Right?"

Gabriel and I nodded our heads.

Sandra continued, "Gabriel, the way you have picked and chosen scenes for us, I can well imagine this is the last night in the Garden. Tomorrow must be the day of Paradise Lost?"

The scene slowly faded behind us. Music was playing, most of it beautiful- but a new discordant tone was coming from the dragon above. The fragrances were of springtime but the smell of raw sewage was seeping in. All of our group felt the warmth of love- but it was like a cold night in front of the fire place. We felt heat on one side and a chill on the other. Joy of a hundred Christmases filled us. Peace like a river flooded our souls. But there was another emotion that could not be blocked, *Despair*. An anguish began to creep in like night fog and in the background there was weeping.

+ + +

CHAPTER 40
THE LAST DAY IN THE GARDEN

The sun peeked his bright eye over the horizon that morning as he had for the last 6.5 billion years. Shadows still covered the Garden until Earth's star was high enough to clear the Ararat Mountains to the east. Purple blue shadows melted away before the light as Adam stretched, yawned and prepared to begin another day's work.

Eve was already awake staring at the thatched roof ceiling. Adam nudged her and said, "Rise and shine, my fair lady."

"I don't feel so fair this morning," Eve complained.

This was new to Adam- he didn't know how to handle it. Life had been a bed of roses, in fact, before he built their house, they had slept on rose petals some nights. He had wanted to sleep on the rose bushes, but Eve had laughed and reminded him that even in Eden roses had thorns. So they opted for rose petals. Later he would find stuffing animal skins with cotton was much more comfortable.

Eve, being a normal woman, had often reminded Adam to clean off the table. She didn't have to worry about asking him to clean his clothes off the floor. First they had no clothing and secondly, their floor was dirt. Often she would suggest she had burned the biscuits or overcooked the cabbage or the green beans didn't have enough seasoning. Adam read all of these as hints for compliments, so he would always assure her the biscuits were great; the cabbage was perfect; and the green beans were just as he liked them. Like any good husband who has a marriage lasting longer than the honeymoon, Adam learned to go along and get along.

"So, what's wrong?" Adam asked, eyeing her shapely body outlined under the bedspread made from rabbit skins. "Is it that time of the month?"

"Maybe," she answered in a deep voice. "Maybe I just need an extra hug this morning to get me started."

"No problem," the handsome husband replied as he jumped back on the bed, gave her a hug and began tickling her.

Sonny turned to Sandra and said, "You might need to close your eyes since they may get intimate."

Placing both hands over both eyes, she obeyed, but it was obvious she was peeking through her fingers.

Gabriel coughed, "Uh, it's going to be all right. Eve is just tempting Adam to go along with her plan."

Just as Adam was ready to plant a big kiss on her, Eve brushed him away and said, "No, not now. I don't feel very good. I think I need something for my stomach."

"You want me to hustle out and bring you a grapefruit?" Adam asked with a mischievous smile. "It'll be no problem." He hopped out of bed and headed for the open door.

"Wait," Eve called. "I know just what I need. Give me a minute to brush my hair and I'll go with you." She had made a brush from what looked like a porcupine tail. Stroking her blonde hair, she eyed Adam and winked at him. "I think I'll be fine in just a little bit when I get the right thing to eat."

Sandra was surprised to see Eve reach into a bowl filled with mashed strawberries and spread a little color on her lips. Next she pulled a small cup from a shelf and dabbed something blue on her eyelids. Finally a clay bottle was shaken, and she smeared droplets on her neck, under her arms and on her wrists.

"Women!" Sonny said. "They haven't changed since Eve."

Before the words were out of Sonny's mouth, Adam took a sharp instrument of copper from his shelf, lathered his face and trimmed around his beard and mustache. He then lifted a leather bag, squeezed something from it and ran it through his hair with his fingers. Grabbing a fruit that resembled a ripe banana, he smeared it under his arm pits as modern men apply their deodorant.

"Men haven't changed that much either," Sandra replied.

Eve reached out the window, fingered over several flowers, finally picked a white orchid with a solid red throat and placed it behind her ear. Not to be outdone, Adam found a leather strip with a tooth and hung it around his neck.

Flashing his million dollar smile at her, he offered her his arm and they walked out the front door. Had they donned some skimpy swim suits, they would have passed for finalists in any pageant. His muscles gleaming in the early light would have made him a favorite for Mr. America. With the right two piece bikini, she would have walked away with the Miss America crown, or Mrs. America banner or Mrs. World title. They made a handsome couple as they walked down the path to the fruit orchard.

CHAPTER 41
THE TREE OF KNOWLEDGE
OF GOOD AND EVIL

A mist rose every morning to water the Garden, and today it created a dreamy effect. Flowers still had dewdrops that sparkled like diamonds. Rabbits and squirrels played around Adam's feet then dashed off for games with dogs and cats. The sweet smell of ripened fruit filled the air, and the music was light and airy like a tune played on a flute that sang of Ireland and home and far away places.

"What is this special fruit that will cure your every illness?" Adam teased. "Maybe I need to take a bite to perk me up. I've been feeling a little tired lately after working in the fields all day, then caring for all the animals."

"You'll see," Eve teased. "We've never tried this one before."

"It must be a new fruit you've developed," Adam said. "You spend a lot of time in the fruit garden. I had been thinking I'll bet you could cross breed some of those fruits and come up with something new and exciting."

They passed the fruit trees, coconut palms, the pecan and walnut trees. They went deeper and deeper into the garden and the trees grew closer and closer together forming a wall of protection to keep intruders out.

"Eve, you're not going to eat of the Tree of Life, are you?" Adam asked.

"I know God didn't forbid it, but I also think He will tell us when we need to begin gathering fruit from it and taking it home for supper." He stopped and stared at the huge Tree of Life in the dead center of the Garden. It's unusual shape made it stand out from all the others. The tree was very tall and straight with its two limbs reaching like a cross. We could see the fruit dangling like Christmas tree ornaments. The leaves were silver- the fruit was gold.

Eve said. "I know God will tell us when we are to eat of the Tree of Life. But during the night I had a dream about the other tree..."

Adam stopped and held her by the arm. "No, Eve. Surely you are not thinking of eating from the Tree of Knowledge of Good and Evil. God told us we will surely die if we eat of that fruit."

"Oh, Adam, you didn't let me finish," Eve said. "In my dream an angel came down and informed me we had passed the test. The angel said God only put that tree there to see if we would be obedient to Him for a certain time." Eve clapped her hands and said, "Now the time is up, and God wants us to experience more happiness than we've had before. You know God wants us to be happy."

Adam was silent. He then added, "Eve, we have more happiness than we deserve and we have everything we could possible want."

"Not quite true," Eve smiled. "You want a son or two to help you in the fields during the day, and you want someone you can play with at night. Ha, I saw the ball you made. I've seen you throwing it up in the air or against a wall. It's obvious you want a little Adam, Junior, to play, to work with you."

"Well, yea, but all of that will come when God is ready..." Adam said.

"The angel informed me in my dream that God is now ready," Eve purred. "You will have your sons and I, well..."

"Don't tell me," Adam smiled and raised his eyebrow, "you will be more beautiful."

"Right," Eve answered. "Plus I will be able to fly. Oh, Adam, it's going to be so wonderful: you with your sons- me being able to flutter around and pick the fruit and be as colorful and beautiful as the butterfly."

"I don't know, Eve," Adam stammered. "If God really wanted this, He would come Himself or send a special messenger to us."

Eve winked, "God will send us a special messenger- just wait."

Gabriel and our group were watching and listening to all this conversation. We wanted to shout and warn them of the dangers, but we could not be heard. "Here comes Trouble," Gabriel said as the Serpent/Dragon floated in silently from the west. Jewels in his wings sparkled and glistened in the morning light. His long golden body wiggled slightly as he glided down toward Adam and Eve and the Tree.

"Here it is," Eve announced triumphantly, as she pointed to the Tree of Knowledge of Good and Evil. In all the years, Adam had never been this close before. In fact, he stayed about as far away from it as he could.

"Eve, God has said we cannot eat of this tree or we will die," Adam said as he turned from her and eyed the fruit hanging there.

Sonny and Sandra gazed at the tree, for they had never seen anything quite like it and never had they even imagined the fruit. Sonny said, "Well, I must say it sure doesn't look like any apple I ever ate."

"It's not an apple," Sandra replied as we all zoomed in closer for a look at this infamous tree. "The fruit is about the size of a pear, but I've never seen anything close to this in any book of botany I've studied. It smell like chocolate covered with colored candy., I can smell it. It's like divinity candy. My grandmother used to make this white fluffy divinity that melted in my mouth."

Sonny sniffed and said, "You are right. It's a combination of divinity, candy, fruit and chocolate. Hmm, it's so mouth-watering that I'm tempted to take a bite myself."

"Sin often looks enticing," I sermonized, "but the hangover is terrible."

Adam and Eve were still at a standoff. Adam said, "Eve, I can't help what you dreamed. God has given us this entire Garden, and I don't want us to get kicked out of here as Lucifer was kicked out of Heaven."

"Adam," Eve insisted. "This beautiful flying creature has landed in the tree and it hasn't hurt him. If it were that dangerous, he would be dead by now. God does not want to keep anything good from his children. We were told we could eat any fruit in the garden. Besides, I believe the creature there must be a messenger from God."

The Serpent smiled sweetly and said, "Did God really say, 'You must not eat from any tree in the garden'?"

Eve looked at Adam with the I-told-you-this-was-a-messenger-from-God glare. She turned to the serpent and said, "We may eat fruit from the trees in the garden, but God did say, 'You must not eat fruit from the tree that is in the middle of the garden, and you must not touch it, or you will die.'"

The Serpent waved his wings and laughed, "You will not surely die, For God knows that when you eat of it your eyes will be opened, and you will be like God, knowing good and evil."

Eve turned back to Adam and said, "See we will be like God and we can know Good. God wants the best for us: sons, daughters, more happiness, more good."

"What about the Evil part?" Adam asked.

"There is no Evil to know here in the Garden," Eve answered. "God and Gabriel both have told us the angels had only the knowledge of Good for there was no evil in Heaven. This is just a colony of Heaven on earth."

"But evil crept into Heaven when Lucifer was carried away with pride and envy," Adam argued.

"Lucifer can't get in here," Eve declared. "God has put a protection around Eden. Nobody can get in- nobody can get out. We are safe in the arms of God. We are free and can do whatever we like and eat whatever we want. This serpent here has just verified my dream and brought us a message from God that it is all right to eat of this tree."

Adam grabbed his wife's arm and began to pull her back. "I don't know about this messenger. God usually comes Himself or sends Gabriel. Let's go back to the house and think about it and pray and..."

"Oh, Adam, you are abusing me," Eve sobbed as she jerked her arm free. "God told you to honor and respect me. I've always honored you in every way. I've cooked your meals, kept your house clean, took care of the flower garden and the fruit trees. And I've always been available for you."

Adam reached out his hand and hugged her close to him. "Eve, don't' cry, please don't cry. You know I can't handle that. Let's just wait and God will..."

"No, Adam, God has already let me know this is all right with Him. You sometimes act like I'm not as smart as you. Well, this fruit will make me wise. You can wait if you like, but I am going to taste it." She reached out her hand then turned back to Adam and said, "God is not going to kill us. What kind of God would He be if he killed us for taking one small bite?"

"Eve, don't..."

+ + +

CHAPTER 42
EVE AND ADAM EAT THE FRUIT

*When the woman saw that the fruit
of the tree was good for food
and pleasing to the eye,
and also desirable for gaining wisdom,
she took some and ate it.
She also gave some to her husband,
who was with her, and he ate it.
(Genesis 2:6 NIV)*

The earth trembled and rocked as an earthquake shook the garden for the first time. Dark clouds rolled in and blotted out the morning sun as wind whistled through the trees, bending them and breaking off limbs. Fruit was shaken loose and fell to the ground. Animals who had been playing with each other suddenly snarled. A wolf grabbed a rabbit and tore off its head. A lamb was bitten and eaten by a lion. Lightning flashed and stuck a nearby tree splintering it into smidgens.

*Then the eyes of both of them were opened,
and they realized they were naked;
so they sewed fig leaves together and made coverings for themselves.
(Genesis 3:7 NIV)*

Adam's hair was blown across his face, but he brushed it back and glared at Eve with a nasty lustful look. He grabbed for her but she turned and ran, snatching large leaves from fig trees trying to hold one in front and one behind. Adam dove for her but missed. His eyes were red and his mouth was drooling as he started after her. They rounded a corner in the path beyond sight of Gabriel and all of us. Eve screamed loudly.

Then the wind died, the earth stood still, and there was silence for half an hour in Heaven.

+ + +

The sun did not show his face again that day. As the mist increased around us, the scene was cloudy and foggy. Nearby the trump of elephants exploded as a herd came galloping through the trees. Behind us lions and tigers roared, scratched and tore at each other. Sandra grabbed Sonny for protection for the scene was so realistic.

Birds flew overheard in weird formations with the larger ones diving into smaller flocks for prey. Two ugly buzzards flapped overhead- finally showing their real natures. They had thought they were cousins to eagles, now they showed they are mere scavengers. Others joined the black cloaked birds and they descended upon the dead and the wounded.

Fruit from the Tree of Knowledge of Good and Evil hit the earth and exploded like Chinese firecrackers on New Year's Eve. Ugly seeds burst out and up into the air like a tornado in lower Alabama. Then we watched as the funnel lifted and ascended back into black clouds whirling madly over us. We were stunned to see the clouds hurry off toward the four corners of the earth.

"What was that?" Sonny asked.

I stood silent a moment then turned to the handsome young athlete and his innocent girlfriend. I said, "Sonny and Sandra, you have been privileged to see the beginning of life. Now you have witnessed the beginning of sin."

"You mean there was no sin before this?" Sandra asked.

"Let's see if I can explain," I said. "If a lion eats a lamb, it's not a sin, is it? It's natural instinct. Or if a monkey steals a banana from another, it's no sin- it's just their nature. Up till this time, pre-man and even men outside the Garden would do many wrong things. It was considered natural, not sin. But at this moment all of that changed:

Therefore, just as sin entered the world though one man,
and death through sin,
and in this way death came to all men, because all sinned
(Genesis 5:12)"

"I don't understand this," Sonny said. "Was there no Sin before Adam?"

"It's very hard to understand- but there was right and wrong, and good and bad. Animals and mankind both commit these acts. But they were not Sin. It entered the earth though Adam's disobedience."

"Disobedience is sin?" Sonny asked. "Not doing wrong?"

"Before Adam sinned, it was not called Sin. But once Adam disobeyed, from then on, wrong, bad, evil, wickedness, lust, adultery, idolatry, stealing, lying, all of them become Sin."

Sonny shook his head not quite taking all of that in. Then he asked, "Where are Adam and Eve? God said they would die, but I don't remember- they didn't die did they?"

"Oh, they died all right," I said.

"But I thought they were driven out of the Garden," Sonny said. "Were they driven out in a hearse?"

Sandra couldn't help but smile in the midst of all the chaos happening beneath us. "Sonny, they weren't driven out as in a car, they were driven out like you drive pigs out of your vegetable garden."

Sonny looked perplexed. "But God said they would die when they ate the fruit. Am I missing something?"

I tried to explain. "Sonny, they died that day because they lost their eternal lives. Let me explain. Sandra, did you and your family have a live Christmas tree this year?"

"Well, yes," Sandra answered. Scratching her head, she wondered what a live Christmas tree had to do with Adam and Eve. "We had a white plastic one for years and before that we had a hideous silver one. When I was in high school, Daddy bought an artificial green one from Wal-Mart. But this past year, mother insisted we have a live tree. So the three of us and Sonny hiked back through our woods and found a beautiful fir. We chopped it down and brought it home. Daddy made a stand for it, and we placed it before the window in the living room."

"I helped decorate it," Sonny said. "It was real, it was a live tree."

"Sorry to disappoint you young students," I said. "But the minute you cut that tree from it's root, it was no longer 'alive.' Oh, it looked alive and smelled alive, and all of you said it was alive. But it was dead as a doorknob when it was cut from it's source of life."

"So Adam and Eve looked alive and smelled alive, but when they disobeyed God, they were dead; for they chopped themselves off from life?" Sandra asked.

"Correct," I said. "Adam and Eve were dead in their sin. Because of them sin entered in and we all now die."

Shrieks and screams continued to vibrate in the Garden below us. Gabriel wiped a tear from his eye as he gazed at the chaos below him. "I really don't want you to see all that happened that dreadful day. You are better off without having to witness nature at it's worst."

Sonny whistled, "Wow, this was worse than nine-eleven when the Twin Towers went down. Hey, I guess you could say the Twin Towers of Humankind fell that day because of the terrorist, the dragon or serpent or whatever it was."

"It was Lucifer," Gabriel said. We followed his gaze as the dragon flashed a big smile as his forked tongue shot back and forth in merriment. What was disaster to man was entertainment to Satan.

+ + +

THAT EVENING

Gabriel reached and took their hands again. "We need to fast-forward from the morning to the evening." The scene dimmed. Clouds looked like smoke of a California wild fire hanging dense over the trees. Down the path to their home, our group moved, only to see a huge tree had toppled onto the house, smashing it along with the table and chairs. A few flowers remained on the bushes but most had blown away. The scene was more like pictures of World War II than images from the Bible.

A loud thumping sound was heard as we turned to see if the elephants were returning due to the fact the footsteps were so loud. Instead we were surprised to see the Triune God walking heavily past the debris and litter. Although we could not see His face, we were sure there was no smile.

Sandra poked Sonny and said, "Listen, He is weeping."

"But he's dragging an animal by the tail," Sonny added.

Adam and Eve had sewn some of the fig leaves to make some outfits that would be appropriate for a tacky party. They had hidden in a patch of bushes as if their camouflaged uniforms would prevent God from seeing them.

With a loud voice that roared like thunder, God had yelled out,

"Adam, where are you?"

I turned and said, "I think God knew where Adam was, but somehow I believe Adam had no idea of his place and position right now."

Then the man and his wife heard the sound of the LORD God
as he was walking in the garden in the cool of the day,
and they hid from the LORD God among the trees of the garden.
But the LORD God called to the man, "Where are you?"
He answered, "I heard you in the garden,
and I was afraid because I was naked; so I hid."
And He said, "Who told you that you were naked?
Have you eaten from the tree that I commanded you not to eat from?"

The man said, "The woman you put here with me--
she gave me some fruit from the tree, and I ate it."
Then the LORD God said to the woman,
"What is this you have done?"
The woman said, "The serpent deceived me, and I ate."
(Gen 3:8-13NIV)

"Passing the buck," Sonny whispered to Sandra.

We heard Adam's weak confession about hearing God- but being afraid because he was naked. A few leaves covered his private parts, but his arms and shoulders and face were bare and smeared with mud and blood.

Eve didn't have the beauty pageant winner look either. Her outfit looked like a Muu Muu after the cow had mooed all over it. Leaves and trash stuck in her hair where the white orchid had been earlier that morning.

The Triune God spoke harshly toward the one He had so adored,

"Who told you you were naked?"

God scanned the garden His private property. Nothing was to be seen but the corpses of dead animals and the trampled leaves of trees and vegetables. Gabriel and his group knew God was aware of who had caused the fall- He was only waiting to see if Adam and Eve knew who it was.

God asked again,
"Have you eaten from the tree that I commanded you not to eat from?"

Many a mother has asked a child if they have gotten in the cookie jar or sampled the chocolate cake, while knowing the answer by seeing the chocolate smeared around the mouth. The evidence was on the face of Adam and Eve. The sweet brown stains of forbidden fruit were obvious.

Adam had seemed to be Superman or some great hero until this point. Instead he dropped his eyes, stared at his feet, kicked a twig away and mumbled, "The woman you put here with me, she gave me some fruit from the tree."

He stopped, kicked the twig again, looked up at God, cut his eyes toward Eve, then looked down again and confessed, "And I ate it."

God's gaze turned toward the once beautiful Eve and almost sobbed as he looked at her and all that remained of the Garden. The hand, which had

created *Adam from dust and Eve from a rib, slowly was raised up to His eye where He wiped away a tear.*

"What is this you have done?"

Eve tossed her hair back defiantly. Showing disgust to Adam for not defending her, she spat out, "The serpent deceived me."

She gazed into the sky to see if the dragon serpent would fly, if so she could place all the blame on him and possibly be set free. When she did not see him, she said softly,

"And I ate."

+ + +

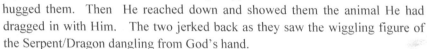

CHAPTER 43
THE CURSES

The Triune God put his head into both hands and sobbed. Finally He reached out and pulled them close to him as if He were about to give them a scolding and send them to bed without any supper. He hugged them. Then He reached down and showed them the animal He had dragged in with Him. The two jerked back as they saw the wiggling figure of the Serpent/Dragon dangling from God's hand.

God shook the Dragon/Serpent as He said.

Adversary
Angel of Light
Devil
Dragon
Enemy
Liar
Lucifer
Murderer
Prince of Darkness
Prince of this World
Roaring lion
Satan
Serpent
Tempter
Wicked One

"Because you have done this,
Cursed are you above all the livestock
and all the wild animals!
You will crawl on your belly
and you will eat dust all the days of your life.
And I will put enmity between you and the woman,
and between your offspring and hers;
he will crush your head, and you will strike his heel."
(Gen 3:14-15NIV)

As God gave the snake a shake both wings snapped loose and fell to the ground. There they withered up quickly, losing their brilliant colors until they looked like two ancient spider webs. Then He put the curse on the serpent of having to crawl on his belly and eat the dust from which Adam had been made. With that the legs of the dragon shriveled up and fell to the ground like dead twigs from a tree in the winter time.

Swinging the wingless, legless Serpent/Dragon over His head, God threw him out of the Garden and over the mountains. Where the Garden had been completely surrounded by trees and mountains before, now we saw a huge opening. It was hard to tell if this were the entrance or exit to the Garden.

"All hope was not lost," I said. "God did tell Lucifer about the Messiah who would come some day and crush his head."

"What did He mean by the serpent would strike His heel?" Sonny asked.

I said, "I don't know unless when they drove the spikes into Christ on the cross they drove one through his feet and heel."

Turning to the once beautiful Eve, God stated,

> To the woman he said,
> "I will greatly increase your pains in childbearing;
> with pain you will give birth to children.
> Your desire will be for your husband, and he will rule over you."
> (Gen 3:15-16 NIV)

Sandra expected a whine or a complaint but there was none. Instead a smile flickered across the mud-stained, tear-stained, chocolate-stained face. Eve was almost grateful as she murmured, "Children, I'm finally going to have some children. Adam, we'll have that boy…"

God turned his full attention to Adam and slowly shook his head.

> "Because you listened to your wife and ate from the tree
> about which I commanded you, 'You must not eat of it,'
> Cursed is the ground because of you;
> through painful toil you will eat of it all the days of your life.
> It will produce thorns and thistles for you,
> and you will eat the plants of the field.
> By the sweat of your brow you will eat your food
> until you return to the ground,
> since from it you were taken;
> for dust you are and to dust you will return."
> (Gen 3:17-19NIV)

Eve turned to Adam and buried her face in his shoulder. He patted her head with one hand and scratched his beard in unbelief with the other. Just a few hours earlier he had jumped from his bed so alive just as many a young man will jump into their chariots or cars or airplanes down through the years. One drink, one drag, one slip of the steering wheel then the vehicle and the man are out of control. There is the crash and the misery that follows.

Eve pulled herself loose and looked to see if anything was salvageable from their little house. Nothing had survived. Plates and pots were broken, some by the falling tree- some by the trampling beasts. Stooping she picked a single bloom and held it up for Adam to see. "It's a forget-me-not," she *sighed. "We'll take it with us so we shall never forget the days in the Garden, the happiness, the joy, the peace."*

An icy wind whipped through the gate to the garden. They both clutched their leafy garments and shivered. God saw their misery, so he reached down and produced a dress and coat for Eve made of animal skins. "Real fur," she said as she tried it on. Then she slipped her feet into two warm leather shoes.

+ + +

God handed Adam a leather robe and an overcoat made of fur. Two boots were added along with what looked like a Russian wool hat. He took their hands and led them gently from the Garden. The cold wind whistled around them as they caught their first glimpse of snow. The sad faces of the two began to shine, and they were like two children enjoying the first snow of the year. They laughed and walked down the darkening path. Eve threw a snowball at Adam, then ran for her life. Adam chased after her.

God stood in the entrance of the Garden for a moment, His eyes glistened as the first two made in His image headed for the shelter of the nearby woods. He reached down and pulled His sash up to wipe a tear away from his eye.

"I knew Jesus wept over Jerusalem," Sandra said softly. "I never imagined God wept over the Garden of Eden. I thought He just got angry."

Gabriel and our group stood silently as we watched the well clothed couple run toward the darkening woods. "Well, looka' there," Sonny said excitedly. We could see a thin trail of smoke rising from a log cabin on the edge of the forest. "God does take care of His children."

Two cherubim flew down from above. They held a flaming sword to prevent Adam or Eve or anybody else from entering the Garden to eat of the Tree of Life.

"Hey," Sonny shouted. "Those are Cherubim. Lucifer was one of them, I thought they all got thrown out of Heaven."

"Not all the Cherubim nor all the angels followed Lucifer," Gabriel said. "I, for one, preferred Heaven over Hell."

+ + +

From heaven the LORD looks down and sees all mankind;

from his dwelling place he watches all who live on earth--

he who forms the hearts of all, who considers everything they do.

(Ps 33:13-15NIV)

4004 B.C.

PART 7 OUTSIDE THE GARDEN

CHAPTER 44
GOD ALWAYS PROVIDES

S now continued to fall until the scene was straight from a Currier and Ives Calendar- Christmas in Vermont. We would not have been surprised to hear the jingle bells of a one horse open sleigh. Instead we heard voices from the cabin.

"I'm so sorry, Eve, for what I did to you," the voice of Adam said.

Eve was silent for a moment, then said, "Hey, your sin was nothing like mine. I let the serpent tempt me. Oh, Adam, I was so foolish. I had the best husband in the world. Life was a paradise and I was not content unless I had wings. So, you forgive me and I'll forgive you."

"Lord, forgive us for we knew not what we were doing," Adam prayed. "Thank you for the warm cabin and warm clothes. Thank you for making us strong and giving us the ability to do good, hard work. And, Lord, I specially thank you for Eve. Amen."

Eve's voice cracked a bit as she added, "And dear Lord, thank you for the chance to start all over again."

Sandra patted Gabriel on the shoulder. "I really like this happy ending. It's not like they lived happily ever after, I just thought they didn't live happy at all after the Garden."

"So they got kicked out of Eden," Sonny said. "What next?"

"They did not get kicked out of **Eden**," Gabriel replied. "They were driven out of the **Garden.** Don't you remember I told you the Land of Eden was about the size of a hundred mile rectangle?"

"Oh yea, I remember. Eden was a big area in the mountains somewhere," Sonny answered. "I remember you saying something about a hundred miles, I thought that was the size of the Garden."

I answered, "The Bible is very clear. God planted a garden in the east of Eden."

"But so what?" Sonny said. "Once they were out of the Garden, weren't they in the real world?"

"Not exactly,' Gabriel answered. "The Land of Eden was a protected property. It was ringed with mountains and sat at the bottom of what you would call a natural bowl."

"Why did God do that?" Sonny asked.

"You'll find out soon enough," Gabriel said. "Once they were outside the Garden, Eve was able to have children. In a little over two years she presented Adam with two sons, Cain and Abel."

"Throw it to me," a voice yelled as a spring time scene came into view. Fruit trees grew around the small cabin and flowers bloomed near the front door. Two teenage boys dressed like cavemen were playing ball with Adam in the front yard.

"It's your turn, Abel," the father called as he tossed the almost round ball toward his younger son.

Sonny looked closely at the flying object and said, "I don't believe that ball would ever be accepted in the Big League or even the Little League. It looks like some goat skin wrapped around cotton."

"Good perception," Gabriel said.

"But it's my time to catch the ball," the older son whimpered. 'You always do more for Abel because he's your baby!"

"Hush, Cain," Adam demanded. "Both of you are getting equal turns."

'But I'm the oldest so I ought to get more," Cain complained. Turning toward the invisible spectators, he kicked a rock and said, "It's not fair."

It was easy to see the differences in the two boys. Cain was more like his mother, fair skinned, thinner, more delicate, almost fragile. Abel was the spitting image of his father, dark skinned, dark eyed, dark hair. His muscles already were beginning to bulge and he stood several inches taller than his older brother.

"It's all right, Dad," Abel called. "You can toss the ball to Cain more. I've got to go take care of the flocks. Plus, tonight is the time for our sacrifice to God. I can hardly wait to give some of my sheep back to the Lord and thank him for being so good to us." He turned to leave. "Good-bye, Dad. And good-bye, little brother," he laughed as he patted Cain on the head. Cain shot a wicked glance at Abel as he left.

"Don't you need to tend the fruit trees?" Adam asked Cain. "Plus, I notice some beans and tomatoes need picking in the vegetable garden."

"I don't feel too good," the son answered as he rubbed his tummy.
"You will feel worse if you don't go do your chores," Adam snapped.
"You had better bring your best for the sacrifice tonight to God."
"Yea, yea," Cain mumbled as he grabbed a hoe and started toward the gardens.
He walked slowly toward the east, grumbling and kicking a stone. Picking a larger rock he held it in his hand and smashed it into a tree trunk. That seemed to perk him up so he snatched it up and threw it harder. Adam watched his wayward son, shook his head and walked toward the cabin. "Eve, we'd better get everything ready for the sacrifice tonight. We'll need some candles and we'll need to get our best clothes ready. Do you know where those boots are- the ones God made for me?

+ + +

THE SACRIFICES

As the scene faded, Gabriel glanced at his two young students and me, then said, "I really wish I could bypass this next scene…"

"We know what happened," Sandra said sadly. "You know, I always felt so sad for Eve through this. But it's past history."

"Worse, it's modern history," I said softly. "Brother killing brother, men envious of other men- will it ever stop?"

Gabriel smiled in his genuine way and said, "You know the answer to that one. Yes, it will stop when we all get to Heaven. And when Lucifer and his gang get their just deserts. But let me show you what happened behind the scenes."

This time the scene was nighttime, a huge fire roared outside the cabin. There was laughter, and one could feel the joy and love returning to the first couple. Adam cried out, "Abel, you're the youngest, so you go first. Bring your sacrifice."

Abel walked past his older brother, went to the fire, and held out a handsome lamb. The white wool glistened and reflected the orange and red and yellow of the flames. He held the animal over his head and prayed, "Oh God, thank you for your blessings. I thank you for our comfortable home, for my good parents, for my, uh, little brother. You have given to us so I gladly give to you, these portions of the firstborn of my flock. Amen."

Taking a knife he quickly cut the lamb's throat and slit it open. He cut out the fat portions and tossed them into the fire. Sizzling, they filled the night with smells of barbecue and all the trimmings. Then he laid the little lamb on the altar, where it was soon burned.

Adam and Eve applauded their son like parents cheering when their offspring knocked a homerun or scored a touchdown.

"Cain," Adam called out. "It's your turn. We save the oldest until last."

The older son lugged a leather sack behind him to the fire. "God, I give you this, uh, sacrifice. Thank you for your, uh, blessings, and Mom and Dad. And, oh yea, my little brother, for I am older than he is." He almost hissed the last few words before he said, "Amen." Pulling a few onions from the bag, he tossed them on the fire. Looking back at his father for approval, he received none. He then reached inside and produced what seemed to be some old apples and a pear. These were thrown on the fire, making a hissing sound. Instead of the tantalizing fragrance of meat, there emerged the putrid smell of rotten fruit and burned leaves. Fishing around in the sack to see if anything else was there, he pulled out a large rock. He looked at the fire and the altar, but he decided not to throw it in- instead he put it back in the sack and said, "That's all."

Adam and Eve were shocked at the small sacrifice as well as the manner of their oldest son. He didn't seem any more thankful than a turkey at Thanksgiving. Adam finally broke the silence, "That's all?"

Cain nodded his head and hauled his sack back toward the shadows. It was easy to see Eve wanted to comfort him or correct him or both. Instead she clapped her hands, and said, "Good boy, Cain." Adam didn't make any response to the older boy. Instead he brought forth a young heifer from his flock. The animal was heavy but Adam was strong. The animal, slain by the knife of Adam, gave his life for the group. "Father, we bring our gifts to you as a sacrifice for our sins. We are sorry and ask your forgiveness. We thank you for your goodness and ask for your blessings. Bless my two sons, Cain and Abel. And especially bless Cain. Amen."

Abel walked over to his parents as we watched the flame light up the sky. Over head the moon was full and stars glittered down upon their little kingdom. Cain turned his back on his family and walked toward his fruit orchard- dragging his sack behind him with the rock inside.

In the darkness of the woods, God confronted the spoiled son,

"Why are you angry? Why is your face downcast?
If you do what is right, will you not be accepted?
But if you do not do what is right, sin is crouching at your door;
it desires to have you, but you must master it."
(Gen 4:6-7 NIV)

Gabriel looked at the rerun of this tragic moment. "Cain trembled before the Lord as most men do when confronted. Alas, also as most men do, he didn't pay any attention to the Lord's instruction. It seems so simple, 'If you do what is right, you will be accepted. But if you do not do what is right, sin crouches at the door. Sin and Satan desire to have us, but with God's help we can master evil.'"

As Gabriel lectured, Sonny and Sandra saw a dark figure slip out from behind one of the trees. He was tall, dressed in a black robe. His pony tail gave him away.

"That's Beelzebub," Sonny shouted. "So he's got to get in his two cents worth. Cain, don't pay any attention to him. Cain, trust in God, not in this guy-he's a devil!"

We watched as Beelzebub sympathized with Cain, patting him on the back. Cain told the fallen angel, "They've never treated me fairly. Abel, the younger son, gets all of the attention and it's obvious he's more physical than me. He makes me so angry that sometimes I want to smash him like I crush a tree stump. Of course, it doesn't hurt the tree stump, it just grows back. But it makes me feel better."

"That is all that's important," Beelzebub cooed. "It's what makes you feel good. Your brother has cut you down and rubbed salt in the wounds too many times. A good knock on the head will bring him to his senses."

+ + +

3980 B.C.

Cain

CHAPTER 45
CAIN TEACHES ABEL A LESSON

Night faded into morning before us. A rooster crowed then the cows began to moo for their breakfast. Birds were chirping. It was just an average day in Eden. Oddly enough, Cain was first out of the house. On his face was a smile, a wicked smile. Dashing cold water over his face, he dried off with a towel made of lamb's wool. Then he went back inside where the smell of cooking cereal drifted through the air.

Abel

Abel was next, he yawned a bit, fell to the ground and did one hundred pushups. Hopping up, he bowed his head and said, "Thank you Lord for a new day." He then went inside for his meal.

After a while they came out together. Cain was unusually chummy this morning. "Abel, you're looking mighty good. I'm sorry about last night with the sacrifice thing. You know it's been a bad year for crops. All we get for water is the mists that rise. But I've found something out in my vegetable garden I want you to see."

"Thanks, Cain, but you hear the cows calling to me for their breakfast, and I've got the sheep and..."

"Please, it won't take long," Cain pleaded with his younger brother. "You are always such a good learner. I promise you will learn a good lesson from this."

"Well, okay," Abel grinned. "We really need to spend more time together and become better friends and brothers."

Sonny and the others watched the two brothers walk down the path to a new garden, not the Garden of Eden which was Paradise, but a garden that would soon become a Hell on earth. We noticed Cain dragging his sack behind him, the rock inside bouncing over the bumps in the road. They disappeared over the top of the hill and when Gabriel started to move us there for a closer look, Sandra cried out, "No, please. I don't want to see this. I'll have nightmares the rest of my life over that last day in the Garden: the horror, the tragedy. Please don't make me look at the catastrophe of this scene. I know too well what happens." Though we could not see, we could hear the two young men laughing and joking on the other side of the hill.

Then we heard Abel cry out, "Cain, what you doing. No, Cain, no!"

There was the sickening thud of a stone smashing against a tree trunk or perhaps someone's head. Then came a laugh and words, "Yea, that'll hurt a little, Big Brother. From now on, quit making fun of me. I'm just as good as you are, even better. I'm the oldest and the wisest. From now on, you bow when I come around."

Silence.

Cain laughed a hesitant laugh, "Come on, Abel, that was just a smack on the head. You're tough- all you'll have is a sore spot and a headache. Come on, get up. You've learned your lesson."

"Abel, get up! Please! Oh Lord, what have I done," screamed Cain as he came running back down the road toward the house. God stood in the middle of the road and asked,

"Where is your brother, Abel?
"I don't know, he replied, "Am I my brother's keeper?"
The LORD said, "What have you done?
Listen! Your brother's blood cries out to me from the ground.
Now you are under a curse and driven from the ground,
which opened its mouth to receive your brother's blood from your hand.
When you work the ground, it will no longer yield its crops for you.
You will be a restless wanderer on the earth."
Cain said to the LORD, "My punishment is more than I can bear.
Today you are driving me from the land,
and I will be hidden from your presence;
I will be a restless wanderer on the earth,
and whoever finds me will kill me."
But the LORD said to him,
"Not so; if anyone kills Cain,
he will suffer vengeance seven times over."
Then the LORD put a mark on Cain
so that no one who found him would kill him.
(Gen 4:9-15 NIV)

Cain's eyes glared up at God as He touched his head with His finger-winced as if he had been burned, then without a thank you, he turned and ran down the road toward the east, past his fruit trees, toward the mountains.

Eve heard the commotion and came to the front porch only to see her oldest son running down the road. Adam appeared, "What's happening?" Eve said, "I feel something awful just took place. There goes Cain running away. Where is Abel? Where is my baby son? Abel, where are you?" Adam tried to calm her down. "Eve, everything's okay. They're just two brothers having difficulty. I saw them walking down the road a while ago with their arms around each other."

"Then why doesn't Abel hear my cry?" Eve called as she rushed up the road where the two were last seen together. This time Gabriel did zoom in to the scene. The morning sunset now flooded the sky with the pink-gold sunrise of a new day. A flock of birds flew gracefully past-although a buzzard was already circling high overhead.

Eve was kneeling with the bleeding head of Abel on her lap much like Michelangelo's famous Pieta of Mary with the dead Jesus in her arms. Sobbing, Eve's tears were falling onto the crushed face of her youngest son. Adam stood at the top of the hill, so stunned by this act of murder he could not move. Finally he ran to his bleeding son and tried to breathe life back into him. Finally he wailed, "He's dead, my youngest son is as dead as the lamb he slew last night."

Suddenly Eve shook her fist into the air and cried out, "Why, God, why? I know I sinned and we were punished. But we have tried to live your way since we left the Garden. We have prayed, we have sacrificed. Now why did you let this happen?"

Bursting into tears again, she paused, grabbed her breath, shook her fist once more toward Heaven and said, "God, I never want to speak to you again."

Weeping was heard both from Eve and Adam as the scene faded.

Sonny and Sandra stood in the darkness of the hour. Finally Sandra said, "That broke my heart. It was bad enough for I knew Cain killed his brother, but I didn't realize it just about killed his mother. Adam didn't handle it well, either." She turned and asked Gabriel, "Is this how the Garden ended? Did Eve ever come back to God?"

"I'll show you," Gabriel said.

+ + +

CHAPTER 46
ADAM AND EVE MAKE A COMEBACK

S lowly the scene below lightened. We were on the
edge of the vegetable garden. Before us was an
earthen grave. Somehow we knew years had gone by
since Cain killed his brother. Adam had his head low-
ered in humility- it was obvious he was praying.

"Lord, this is Adam and my wife, Eve.
We hope you haven't forgotten us.
It's been years and years since we talked.
We've come out to Abel's grave today to weep.
We realized we had quit worshipping and started weeping.
I thought we were weeping for Abel,
but we were only weeping for ourselves."

Adam started crying and choked up, unable to go on with his prayer.
Eve took his hand in hers and continued.

"I found something by the grave today.
I didn't plant it there
and our son, Seth, he's too young.
It was a forget-me-not.
Then I realized You put it there.
A forget-me-not from you, God."

Eve's eyes were glistening and a snip of a smile
crawled across her face. Adam was still pretty upset,
but he cleared his throat and continued.

"You didn't forget our dead son, Abel.
I know now you took care of him.
Somehow you've taken him back to the Garden, back to Paradise.
Someday, we'll see him again."

Finally a small smile came back to Adam. He hugged his wife and lifted his hand toward God. Eve stammered, then took Adam's hand in hers. She prayed:

"Lord, I held the little forget-me-not close to my heart,
then I remembered when you put that curse on us,
You also gave us a promise.
You promised the serpent would bruise the heel of my son-
but you also promised my son would bruise his head.
That's what happened to Abel.
The old serpent of sin and death bruised my son.
He died.
But my son had faith in you- and faith won out.
Faith is stronger than sin.
Faith is stronger than death."

Adam smiled at Eve the way we had first seen him look at her when they bathed in the Garden that day. Love once more flowed between then like electricity. He prayed,

"And, Lord, we look down the tunnel of time,
and we believe there's more.
We believe Sin and Satan and Suffering will get worse and worse,
and affect more and more sons and daughters
until one day...."

Eve held the little forget-me-not up to the sky and to the sun and to the Lord,

"There will come from the son of a woman
One who will truly be your Son.
Somehow He will die as our son died,
A righteous sacrifice.
And He shall be able to promise all the believing sons who die.
Today- You Will Be With Me in Paradise."
"That Son, Your Son, will be a New Adam.
He'll bring about a new creation.
Then, Oh Lord, we who are faithful shall all return to the Garden of Eden.
Amen and Amen.

+++

4004 B.C.

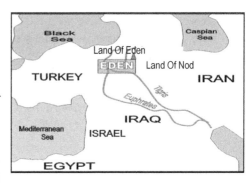

CHAPTER 47
CAIN FINDS A WIFE
IN THE LAND OF NOD

"That would make a wonderful movie," Sandra sighed as the
scene slowly faded from our view. "I'm so glad you allowed us to see this side
of Adam and Eve. As I told you before they were merely one dimensional characters with absolutely no personality. I assumed they were simple minded and I
had them in the category of Judas and Jezebel. They were traitors to all mankind
and womankind. But, now, I see they made a mistake..."

"They sinned," I reminded her.

"Sure they sinned, but it seems so mild compared to the sex perverts we have
today, or the drug dealers, or parents who abuse their children. All they did was
nibble on some forbidden fruit..."

"They sinned," I reminded her again.

She sighed, looked at me and said, "You're right. We have deceived ourselves by saying we tell little white fibs and we commit sins-that-aren't-all-that-
bad."

Sonny remarked, "Preacher, you told us one time that the average American
couldn't name a single sin he or she had committed that day. Sin is something
other people do."

"Adam and Eve have shown us the horrible results of sin," I said. "Abel
lived a righteous life, gave a righteous sacrifice and got killed although he did
nothing really wrong. He was the result of someone else's sin- that of his brother, Cain."

"Wait a minute- that sounds like Jesus," Sonny realized. "He lived a righteous life, gave a righteous sacrifice and was killed as a result of our sin."

I said, "Glad you saw the comparison."

"Hey, Preacher, wait a minute," Sonny said. "You and Gabriel did a good
job of summing up Adam and Eve, but you've got two big questions unan-
swered about Creation."

"And they are..."

"Where did Cain get his wife?"

"That's easy," I grinned. "He got her from the land of Nod."

"Oh, that's right," Sonny said then thought for a moment. "Hey, that's not a good answer. If Adam and Eve were the first man and woman, and Cain and Abel were their only children, where did some woman in Nod come from? I've got you this time, Preach."

"At first glance, we've got a problem," I agreed. "Adam was the first man:

> *"The first man Adam became a living being";*
> *the last Adam, a life-giving spirit.*
> *(1 Cor 15:45NIV)*

"So," Sonny asked. "What are you trying to say?"

"He was- the first man created in the image of God," I answered.

"Still, I don't understand," Sonny said. "You are confusing us."

"I'll make it simple," Gabriel said, "I've already given you the answer. When did Homo Sapiens arise?"

"No clue," Sonny said.

"Two hundred thousand years ago," Sandra said.

"And how long were Adam and Eve in the Garden," Gabriel asked.

Sandra gasped, "Two hundred thousand years! So Adam and Eve were the first Homo Sapiens!"

"Exactly! They were the perfect Homo Sapiens, made in the image of God," Gabriel said then shrugged. "The others didn't turn out so well."

"The others? You mean the Neanderthals, Homo Erectus, etc?" Sandra asked.

"They never developed into the Image of God and they never once worshipped Him,' Gabriel said sadly. " A good analogy would be the Jewish people. God wanted them to be His chosen people, chose them, protected them, gave them enough miracles to fill the Old Testament. Then guess what happened? They never fulfilled God's purpose. So He let our Jewish brothers go their way. The 'chosen people' or better, 'His children," then became those who chose Him through faith in His Son."

Sonny scratched his head and asked, "So we did not come from apes?"

"No. If you read 'Genesis One' carefully, it is quite obvious man was created after the animals," Gabriel commented.

"Ha, got'cha," Sonny said. "But you told us in 'Genesis Two,' God made the man first, then the animals, and Adam had to name them."

"That is true," Gabriel said. "But it's only true for the animals of Eden. My goodness, do you know how many land animals had evolved by that time in the world? Not to mention the fish, birds, insects and a jillion other things that had come and gone over the years."

"The animals of Eden?" Sonny asked. "Do you mean God didn't put every kind of animal in the Garden?"

"No, He only put the animals He had designed in the beginning. Just as he only put the completed man there," Gabriel answered. "But be patient, you'll understand this…"

"Yea, in due time," Sonny said. "I'm not sure if 'due time" is earth time or heaven time, or a time you made up."

Gabriel chuckled. "Let's follow the villain Cain and see what happened to him."

+ + +

CAIN"S WIFE

A white and green scene appeared below us. As the panorama came into focus, we realized we were watching trees take shape. Like a Christmas scene, snow hung on the branches and covered the ground. Hugging his skin garment tightly, Cain appeared slowly making his way toward the top of a mountain. Standing there with raised swords were angels stretching across the mountain tops as far as we could see. From this perspective we could see the land below us was bowl-shaped. Far, far away we saw other mountains that surrounded Eden. To the North East stood another snow covered mountain, Mount Ararat. Below us we saw the remnants of the Garden. It was obvious restoration was taking place. Trees were growing back and flowers were blooming again. All of the animals had calmed down to the normal food chain variety. The Cherubim still stood guard at the gate with flaming sword. Not far from the entrance to the Garden, a tiny square with a smoke curl could be identified as the cabin home of Adam and Eve.

"We've gone back to the day after Cain killed Abel. If you look closely, you can still see the blood on his hands and on his, uh, garment, whatever he called it," Gabriel said.

"Looks like a Tarzan outfit to me," Sonny said. "Or maybe a little like a caveman tux."

Cain seemed astounded to see angels guarding the top of the mountain.

Sonny interrupted, "I'll bet those angels were put there to keep folks in Eden and out of Eden."

"I'll bet you're right," Sandra said, "but I don't bet."

"Actually if you look closer, you will see their wings, and you will understand these are Cherubim," Gabriel said. "These are the Guardian angels."

Cain was not frightened by the angelic host, for he had talked with God and no Cherub was about to scare him. One held out his sword to keep Cain back, but Adam's prodigal son simply pushed it away. Two other swords quickly appeared on each side of Cain's neck.

The angel who seemed to be in charge demanded, "You are not allowed to leave this land. Besides aren't you the human who killed your brother?"

Another pushed his face forward and glared, "He is the one. Let's put our sword through this murderer."

Cain did not bat an eye. He reached up and pushed his hair back from his face to show them his forehead. Immediately the angels jumped back, lowered their swords and invited him to pass through them.

"The mark God put on Cain!" Sonny shouted, "I've been wondering about that," Sonny said. "This was to keep someone from killing him, but there was nobody around to do him in except his mother and father. Hmm, they may have considered it. Exactly what was the mark?"

"Can you guess?" Gabriel asked.

"I don't have the foggiest," Sonny answered. "Our practice football shirts have 'Property of the University of Alabama' on them. Was it something like that?"

"No."

"Was it some kind of secret symbol, like the all seeing eye of the Masons, which is on our one dollar bill?" Sandra asked.

"Something like that," Gabriel answered.

"Think hard," I chimed in. "What symbol would protect Cain?"

"In the old vampire movies, it was a cross," Sonny said as he crossed his fingers and held them toward an imaginary monster.

'That's it," I said. "The mark was a cross to keep Cain safe and to help him get in and out of Eden. It also pre-viewed the fact a cross would be our passport to heaven."

"To get out of this world and to get into the next one," Sonny said.

Cain did not even look back at Eden nor the angels as he crossed over the mountain. Below him was a dry, arid val-ley looking much like the Mideast today except a layer of snow covered every-thing. Some trees grew around a lake and a number of small mud brick houses were scattered around a village. Cain trudged down the slopes. Often rocks would slip beneath him and crash down the path before him as the rock had crashed into his brother's skull. If there was remorse, it didn't show. His face was downcast but determined.

'He's not running from his parents," Sonny said. "He's running from God. He is afraid of how God will punish him for his awful act."

Horsemen rode toward the little town as snow swirled behind them. Some dogs barked as they ran out to greet the men and their animals. Scrubby gardens grew behind the houses. Cain stopped to examine one that needed water, weed-ing and a worker. A snarling dog caught his scent, let out a yelp and rushed from the street to the stranger by the garden. Cain held him off with a stick but soon a man appeared. Only a little over five feet, he was not as tall as Cain. His face was hairy and dark while Cain had a straggly beard and was blonde. He was built like a fire plug and Cain was thin as a rail. A leather helmet sat atop his grizzly hair and was decorated with bones and bits of feathers. Cain was bareheaded. Where Cain wore only a simple animal skin draped like a caveman, the man was heavily clothed with layers of skins and furs. Some were dyed red, some yellow, and others were a deep purple.

Tiny black eyes glared at Cain, then the man reached for his sword. Animal like sounds spewed from his mouth, and it was quite obvious he was asking who he was, what he was doing here, and was he prepared to die.

Again Cain's bravery amazed us. He never shook with fear, showed any sign of running, nor did he say a word. He pulled the hair back from his forehead and let the angry man stare at the cross burned onto his head. Seeing the mark, the man immediately threw down his sword and fell to the ground, bowing down before him.

"I need to get me one of those marks," Sonny said.

Cain walked over, patted the man on the head, then beckoned for him to rise. Keeping his eyes downcast, the dark man struggled to his feet. Cain reached out his hand and raised the man's face toward his. He then held out his open palm in the manner that would become the universal sign of peace. Again the man bowed then held out his open palm. No sword this time.

Cain spoke, "I'm hungry," and rubbed his tummy and pointed to his mouth. The man answered in some grunts indicating they had food.

"Whoa," Sonny said. "I thought they all spoke the same language?"

""That was just before the Flood," Gabriel explained.

"The Flood really happened?" Sonny asked, then thought of the display of his lack of faith. "Oh yea, they all spoke the same language after the flood, because they were all Noah's kids. Let's see, mankind split up at the Tower of Babel, right? Then they learned Chinese or Latin or English."

Sandra chuckled at the wit of her good looking boyfriend.

Gabriel didn't answer as he turned to watch the taller, thinner Cain follow the small muscular man into the house. An older woman stared at him through a wrinkled face. It looked as if a smile had never even thought about appearing there. However, a young girl, probably fourteen or fifteen, smiled at him. He smiled back. This was the first girl he had ever met, and it was love at first sight. Dark eyes were set in a darker face than Cain was accustomed to. Her sleek black hair parted in the middle and fell nearly to her waist. Her short nose was cute as a button as it stood guard just above her pink lips.

She wandered over to him, reached out her hand and ran her fingers through his hair and said something in a sing-song voice to the old woman. The old woman grunted and spat in the fire.

The girl let her fingers do the walking across his face, then she traced a line around his lips and smiled again. Cain did not kiss her but it was obvious he desired her.

The man shouted something and the old woman picked up the pot cooking over the fire. Looking back at him, the girl went over and placed some pottery plates on a skin that lay in the middle of the one room. A hole in the ceiling let out most of the smoke.

Cain was offered an animal skin holding something wet and almost white. Deciding it was some kind of milk, Cain took a good drink, wiped his mouth and said, "Good."

"Guut!" the man grinned. "Guut!" He pointed a finger at himself and said, "Arkap."

Cain caught on and pointed at the man and said, "You Arkap." Pointing to himself he said, "Cain."

A bigger smile revealed several missing teeth, but the man grunted, "Kaan." He seemed quite pleased with himself so he pointed to the young girl and said, "Barjah!"

Hearing her name, she smiled at her father then back at this stranger. Cain looked at her then said softly, "Barjah."

Soon the meal was served and Cain had no trouble eating. It was similar to the food of Eve, except it lacked the seasoning and that special chef's touch she had. However, there was something he had never tasted. Pulling a piece from his mouth, he examined it. It was meat. Holding it up, he said, "Good."

Arkap's face broke into a thousand smiles, "Guut!" He pulled a piece of meat from his mouth and said again, "Guut!"

After supper, Arkap took Cain and Barjah outside, where the rest of the village had already gathered. They had heard of this strange fair-headed man and wanted to see him and touch him. Arkap, acting as if he must be the chief, went to the center where a fire burned. He motioned for all of them to sit. Then he brought Cain before them as if he were showing off a prize catch from the hunt. Loudly he proclaimed, "Kaan."

They mumbled, then clapped their hands and stomped their feet. It didn't take Cain long to take full advantage of the situation. Realizing they thought he was some kind of god, he pointed his thumb to his chest and said, "Cain."

They all repeated "Kaan."

Arkap again took center stage, pointed to the golden-haired god who had appeared to them and shouted, "Kaan Guut!"

Cain caught on quickly, pointed to himself and yelled, "Kaan Guut!"

Breaking into a religious frenzy, the villagers jumped and waved and yelled over and over, "Kaan Guut! Kaan Guut! Kaan Guut!"

Then Cain pointed to the high mountains behind them and made a motion of climbing over them. They let out a sizable "Ahhhh." It was obvious they had never crossed over the mountains. Or perhaps they had tried and been pushed back by angels with swords or rockslides or avalanches. Cain held up his open palm for peace then all the tribe held out their open palms. Arkap held his hand higher and shouted again, "Kaan Guut!"

They joined him in the chant, "Kaan Guut! Kaan Guut! Kaan Guut!"

A medicine woman then swooped in toward them. Covered with a black mask, she wore a loose fitting garment covered with buzzard feathers. Around her neck hung more bones, hollowed rocks and the skull of a baby. Dancing around the fire, she threw her arms skyward worshipping some god.

Sonny and Sandra almost froze when she shouted, "Baal! Baal! Baal!"

Cupping his hand toward Sandra, he said, "Did you hear what she said? They are worshipping Baal. That's Beelzebub. Here this tribe is in the shadow of Eden and they worship the devil."

"I warned you,' Gabriel said. "The human race went to Hell in a hand basket very quickly after they appeared. If I were to take you around the whole world at this time, about 4000 B.C., you would not find a single group, a single person worshipping the God of Creation."

"Was Cain a kind of missionary?" Sonny asked.

"He was supposed to be," I answered. "But he wasn't much better than we are. He had the cross and knew the way to Eden- but he didn't show anybody the way."

Now the dancing witch grabbed a young woman from the crowd and pushed her up to Arkap. The girl pretended to be afraid and acted as if she did not wish to be close to the hunter. Then the old woman ripped off the girl's animal skins and pushed her closer to Arkap. He laughed.

"Is that his wife?" Sandra asked.

"Don't think so?" Sonny answered.

The medicine woman then threw the girl down on the ground and danced around Arkap in very suggestive ways. As she pranced she removed his hat, then his sword and belt. Now drums were beating and the people were pounding the ground with their feet. Fire from the center leaped higher and kept tempo with the drumming. Chanting began, "Arkap! Arkap! Arkap!" The warrior continued laughing as the woman began removing his skins and furs. Sandra said, "I think I know where this is leading." Covering her eyes, she refused to watch.

Sonny was spellbound. Gabriel explained, "This was their worship. Sex was a part of their praise service- as was sacrifice. Different men and women were chosen each night to entertain the others."

"Sounds like Hollywood," Sonny said.

"Unfortunately, there's not a lot of difference," I said. "We haven't come that far in civilization. People will pay big bucks to go to a movie to watch a young man and woman jump in bed. 'Sex is only entertainment,' they say."

Completely naked, Arkap stood beside the fire and over the girl. Chanting arose again obviously encouraging them to get on with it. As he learned over, smoke billowed up and concealed the view from the humans. Though we could not see, we could hear the shrieks of laughter and applause and the name, "Baal, Baal. Baal."

The scene faded as time passed. Gabriel explained that he wanted us to see what happened later. Sure enough the smoke swirled, and the sounds squeaked as we moved forward about thirty minutes. The picture cleared, Arkap was clothed and the girl was nowhere to be seen.

Now the old witch came dancing forth again, the bones and rocks and baby skull clattering as she shook herself around the flames. Several of the other old women now joined in, even the sour faced one who had been preparing the meal for Arkap. Again the drums began a slow roll as the witch woman pulled Barjah into the circle of light. Her clothes were quickly removed. Then Cain was pushed forward by Arkap and the other men. It didn't take long to strip off his animal skin.

"I hope this is their idea of a marriage ceremony," said Sandra.

"Yes, it is," Gabriel replied.

Shouting "Baal! Baal! Baal!" the entire tribe was now standing, clapping their hands, stomping their feet and laughing loudly.

"Looks like we've got a double feature tonight?" Sonny said.

"Sonny," Sandra tried to snap at him but couldn't help giggling. "We can at least be civilized."

"They're sure not," Sonny said.

Cain's eyes began to burn with desire as he looked upon the young girl from Nod. Smoke billowed up and the scene disappeared.

+ + +

CAIN HAS A SON

"The Bible says Cain lived in the land of Nod. He lay with his wife and she gave birth to Enoch," I added.

"Enoch was the one who walked with God?" Sonny asked.

"No, that was a different Enoch, one of Seth's line. You remember Adam and Eve had another son," I explained, delighted to show off my knowledge of Bible history. "It was several generations before the Enoch arrived that you remember. He did walk with God, he fathered a child, Methuselah."

"I remember him," Sonny said. "He lived longer than anybody. Let's see if I can remember, it was 969 years. I remember for I used that for the combination to my locker my senior year, 9 6 9."

"We believe he died the year of the flood," I said.

"He did die the year of the flood," Gabriel said. "I ought to know because I was there."

"Why did people live so long back then?" Sandra asked. "If I remember, Adam lived about as long as Methuselah."

"Adam lived a long, long time in the Garden," I laughed. "But when he and Eve came out, time really began for him and he lived 930 years."

"But how? Now if someone lives to 100 years old, it's almost a miracle," Sonny said.

Sandra said, "We had to study that at Samford. People are actually living longer today than they have in years. There are 55,000 people in America over 100 years old. Japan has 30,000. There are way over 340,000 centenarians living in the world, and more are being added every year.

"Who knows, Sandra, our great grandchildren might live to be 900 years old," Sonny said.

"Probably not," Sandra laughed. "You must remember all of those long livers lived in Eden, which was protected by God. There were no diseases, no automobile accidents, very little murder, people did not eat meat."

"It was only in Eden where people did not eat meat," I informed them. "The fallen humans outside their gardens quickly began to eat meat. They did not know much about sanitation, so they developed diseases and died off early."

"No meat in Eden?" Sonny asked. "Then I'd probably be happy just to live four or five hundred years and enjoy my steak and hamburgers. By the way, I thought you were going to show Noah's ark."

"In due time," Gabriel grinned. "Let me set the stage for Noah and the flood."

+ + +

3504 B.C.

PART 8 NOAH AND THE ARK

CHAPTER 48
ADAM AND EVE HAVE A VISITOR

The Visitor

I need to fill you in on a little history before we witness the flood," Gabriel lectured. "Do either one of you remember the name of Adam and Eve's third child?"

"That's easy," Sandra said...

"It's Seth," Sonny filled in the blank before she could finish. "It is easy because Eve mentioned him in her prayer by Abel's grave. Plus, we learned it in Sunday School, or Vacation Bible School, or maybe, Brother Chris, you mentioned it in a sermon, or..."

"Enough," Gabriel shook his head at the talkative athlete. "Seth was their third son. There were other sons and daughters but they are not named. Seth becomes the main blood line through which God carries on his work."

"What happened to Adam and Eve?" Sandra asked. "We saw where they turned back to God. Were they ever able to forgive Abel?"

"Were they *able* to forgive *Abel*?" Sonny hummed. "Sounds like an idea for a country song to me."

+ + +

The scene grew lighter beneath us. An older man was lying in the bed, moaning as he tried to rise. "Adam, it's time to get up," a cheery voice echoed from a back room. "What would you like for breakfast this morning? Oats with cow's milk or oats with goat milk?"

"Forget the goat milk," Adam replied, "they are too much trouble to milk. Eve, I must be getting old- it's hard for me to get out of bed each morning."

"Old? Why, you're not old?" Eve laughed as she came through the door. "You'll only be five hundred on your next birthday. My goodness, time

flies when you're having fun. It just seems yesterday we left the Garden- but it's been five centuries."

Adam rose, stretched, stooped to the floor and did fifty pushups. He pulled a robe on over his undergarments and looked out the window. "Who's that stranger coming down the road?"

Eve looked through squinted eyes, "It's not Seth. And it's not our grandson, Enos, nor his son Cainan. It might be Jared, our great, great, great, great grandson with his new son, Enoch. Whoever it is, looks like his wife and some children are with him. Let me hurry and put out some more plates and fix something to drink."

"No goat's milk," Adam shouted as she left. He stood at the door and watched the little band grow closer. Finally he walked onto the front porch and held his hand up to shield the sunshine. "Shalom," he cried out as they stood before him.

Adam studied the face of the people, then looked closely at the man who wore a hood over his head and most of his face. "You must be some of my grandchildren from over on the west side of Eden," he said. "To be honest, I can't remember who you are."

Eve came to the front door and stared at the group. "No, Adam, I don't believe these are any of my grandchildren. I know all of them plus their birthdates. They have strange clothes. They must be..."

The man with the hood raised his head and looked into the eyes of Adam. With a cracked voice, he said, "Father, forgive me for I have sinned. Mother, forgive me."

Adam and Eve stood in shock. Eve lifted her hand to her mouth then stooped to look at him closer. He pulled the hood back, parted his hair and revealed a cross burned into his forehead. Eve leaped from the porch, grabbed him in a hug and cried, "Cain, oh my son, Cain, you've come back."

Adam stood still for only a second before he joined his wife and gave big bear hugs to both of them. He prayed, "Father, oh Father, thank you. You have brought our prodigal son back home." Stepping away from him, Adam said, "Oh Cain, we thought you were dead. We waited year after long year for you to return."

"We prayed for you every night," Eve said. "After a hundred years, we just gave up. There's a little grave in the garden we made for you. It's beside your brother. Oh Cain, we are so glad to see you."

"First," Cain stated as he stood back. "Will you please forgive me for murdering my..." he chokes back tears. "my brother? I am so sorry. I should have stopped and told you I only meant to hurt him- I never meant to

kill... Oh Father, I didn't know it was possible to kill a human."

Adam stretched both arms around him and said, "Cain, oh my oldest son, Cain. Of course we forgive you. Have you asked God to forgive you?"

"I begged for forgiveness every step up the mountains and over into the land of Nod."

"You went over the mountains?" Adam asked. "No wonder we never found your body. We looked all over Eden. We even thought you had found a way to get back into the Garden. We tried but the Cherubim always kept us out with their flaming sword."

Eve looked puzzled. "How did you get over the mountains. We were told that no one could leave and no one could enter. We don't even know if there is anyone out there who wants to come here. This is our Eden- this is our World."

"There is much more out there, Mother. But it's in bad shape," Cain told Eve. He pushed the woman with him forward. "I want you to meet my wife, Barjah."

Eve eyed the woman. She was covered in layers of skins and furs and probably had been prettier in her earlier days. Now she was plump and pleasant. Her lips were covered with a bright red substance; her eyes accented with heavy black lines. Eve hesitated only a moment before she threw her arms around the woman and hugged her. "We are so glad to know you."

Through the furs, Eve felt lumps around Barjah's neck and assumed it was a necklace. "Oh, let me see," Eve said excitedly as she examined the two strange objects. "What are these?" she asked as she turned them over and over. "I've never seen anything like ..."

"These are my god and goddess," Barjah smiled. "This one is Baal, he is the god of war and protects us from our enemies. The other is Astarte. Because of her I have many children and many, many grandchildren."

Eve dropped the necklace as if it were a snake. "Uh, we don't worship gods and goddesses here, we worship the Creator God."

"I know," Barjah continued. "I worship Him, too. Cain told me about Him. So we make sacrifices to all three of our gods. He told me about your three gods in One, perhaps it is really your one god plus my two."

"That's not the way it works!" Adam stammered, then realized this was his daughter in law and mother of some of his grandchildren. "We are glad you are here. Let me meet my grandchildren and great grandchildren. Is this all of them?"

Cain beamed, "Oh no, I have many, many others. I built a city, Father, and it is named Cain. Scores of people live there. I told them of you and Mother and the Garden. They all wanted to come and live there, but I told them it is impossible. The gates were closed. Also, the Cherubim won't allow them to come over the mountains."

He looked down, wiped a tear from his eye, then asked, "Has God opened the gates so we can enter the Garden again?"

"No," Adam answered quickly. "We've found we can get along very well out here with faith and hard work. Come on in. Bring your family. Oh Cain, it's so good to see you again, I can hardly wait for you to meet your brother, Seth. You'll love him- he is just like Abel."

They entered the door of the little cabin God had made for his first couple. Slowly the picture faded with sounds of happiness.

Sandra was the first to speak. "I love happy endings. I'm so glad Cain came back and apologized. Most of all, it's good he got forgiveness from his earthly father and his heavenly father."

"The ending is not as happy as you suppose," Gabriel said sadly. "Cain was able to use the mark on his forehead to re-enter Eden, and it served as a passport for his wife and a few of his children. You remember I told you how people lived a long time in those days because there were no diseases?"

"Yes sir, I took note of that," Sonny said.

"But there was another kind of disease, a spiritual virus, that crept into Eden when Cain returned," Gabriel said.

"The idols, the god and goddess," I said. "They looked like two charms on a necklace but there was nothing charming about those two heathen gods. Men are always looking for something to worship instead of the True God. In Eden they found a few 'open-minded' believers among Seth's children and grandchildren. It only takes a drop of HIV blood to contaminate an entire human body. One person can share the virus with many others. That's what happened in Eden."

"Did Cain and his wife stay in Eden,? Sandra asked.

Gabriel responded, "They stayed a short time in earth days, but it was long enough for a bunch of the women to want Astarte goddesses. Many of the younger men wanted to increase their virility and their manhood by worshipping Baal.

"Eve never worshipped Astarte nor did Adam ever bow to Baal. However, because they had disobeyed God and had eaten the forbidden fruit, they died."

+ + +

CHAPTER 49
ENOCH AND METHUSELAH

Enoch

L et's see," Sonny calculated, "Adam was 500 years old when Cain reappeared. Did he die soon after that?"

"Not too soon," I said. "Adam lived to be 930 years old!"

"What about the rest of the folks there. Did all of Eden go bad?" Sonny asked.

I answered, "Of course not. God always has a remnant. You remember Adam saying the strangers might be his great, great, great, great grandson with his new son, Enoch?"

"Yea, I wanted to ask you about that," Sonny said. "I'll bet he is the Enoch who walked with God. Preacher, you told us about him, how he and God would walk together every afternoon. Then one day God said to him, 'Enoch, we're closer to my home than yours, why don't you just go home with me?'"

"I probably used it as an illustration for a funeral," I confessed. "I don't know if I told you Enoch did not live very long. He was only three hundred sixty five when he went with the Lord."

"We should remember that easily," Sonny said. "Three sixty five, he lived one year for each day in the year."

"However, he had a son during his 'short' time on earth who fathered the man who lived the longest," I said.

"Got it," Sonny said, "Old 969, Methuselah. Did he have any important children or grandchildren?"

"Funny you should ask," I said. "He did have a grandson who was rather famous- his name was Noah."

+ + +

A WICKED WORLD

The LORD saw how great man's wickedness on the earth had become,
and that every inclination of the thoughts of his heart
was only evil all the time.
The LORD was grieved that he had made man on the earth,
and his heart was filled with pain.
So the LORD said,
"I will wipe mankind, whom I have created, from the face of the earth--
men and animals, and creatures that move along the ground,
and birds of the air--
for I am grieved that I have made them."
But Noah found favor in the eyes of the LORD.
(Gen 6:5-8NIV)

The smell reached us before we could see the village. Putrid garbage mingled with cheap perfume. Loud coarse laughing from men and shrill giggling from women. Weeds grew in the streets and vines crawled over the mud brick houses. There was a lot of cursing and little work. Skinny priests stood in silent watch before two huge idols to Baal and Astarte. Scrawny temple prostitutes stalked the street, openly propositioning men and women and even children.

"Where are we, Sodom and Gomorrah?' Sonny asked.

"No, but the city is some kind of sneak preview to those wicked twin cities. This is 2348 B.C.," Gabriel answered. "You may not recognize the Land of Eden, or what is left of it below you."

"What about the Garden of Eden?" Sonny asked.

"Still there," Gabriel answered, "but not open for business."

A woman screamed and swung her purse at an old man, who only laughed and stalked her. She showered him with obscenities, as he grabbed her and jerked the purse away. She yelled for help, but a few young ruffians saw her and laughed. No one came to assist her. Screeching, she clawed her fingernails into her attacker's face. His laughter turned to rage as he pulled a knife and plunged it into her chest. Blood spurted onto the dirt street. Taking the purse, the robber turned and walked away as he rummaged through her handbag. He hummed a tune. Shouting for assistance, the woman struggled to rise but fell back into the pool of blood.

Two priests walked down the street, cackling at some dirty joke. When they saw the victim, both grabbed their robes so they would not get bloody. They passed by on the other side of the road. As they vanished the young thugs rushed out toward the fallen woman. Before they could steal anything from her, a group of old hags hollered at them and told them to get away. When the boys refused, the women threw rocks at them until they left. Then the old women slithered up to the woman who was not yet dead. Instead of aiding her, one grabbed her cloak and another snatched her shawl. The other, bent over with old age and rheumatism, fell to her knees and pulled off the shoes of the unfortunate woman.

"How disgusting," Sandra said. "They act like wolves or hyenas. Aren't they even going to bury the poor soul?"

As if answering her question, a short squatty man slowly made his way down the street. An emaciated donkey pulled a pitiful cart behind. The man picked some trash from one house, rifled through it, pulled out a saucer with only a slight crack, and put it in the bag over his shoulder. Seeing the woman was now dead, he approached carefully. He looked around to see if anyone would claim her or at least ask for her body. No one appeared and no one cared. The squatty man poked around her dress until he found where she had sown a miserable coin in the hem. Pulling it out, he examined it and poked it in the bag. Struggling, he picked the woman up and dumped her in the cart. With that, he went to the next house looking for trash.

"He must have been a combination garbage man and funeral director," Sonny said. "Those folks make modern America look like Utopia. Who are they?"

"These are the descendents of Adam and Eve through their son, Seth," Gabriel answered.

"So Heaven on earth became Hell on earth rather quickly," Sonny said.

Sandra said, "Don't forget it's been over fifteen hundred years since Adam and Eve were driven out of the garden. That's about the same amount of time since the Barbarians sacked Rome."

"Looks like we know where the Barbarians came from," Sonny said.

"Without God, men turn into animals," I said.

+ + +

2348 B.C.

CHAPTER 50
METHUSELAH LIVED UNTIL THE FLOOD

Methuselah

Moving from the city and the smell, we saw dark, swirling clouds hanging overhead. An old man was hobbling down a dirt road. To the side was a forest and directly in front of him was a giant boat.   A long, gray beard stretched down the front of his robe, and long gray hair fell from beneath a dark hood.. He carried a walking cane as he approached some young men. They turned to taunt him.

> *Instead of stepping aside for the elderly they joined hands so he could not get around them. "Hey you old S.O.B.," one jeered. "You should have died years ago."*
>
> *Another joined in, "Pew, he smells like he died and they forgot to notify his body."*
>
> *Loud, rough laughter erupted from the bunch. One grabbed the old man's stick and hit him hard across the back of his legs causing him to fall. They then attacked like a pack of wild dogs, scratching, biting, tearing. Finally they found his money bag, jerked it open and shouted, "Hey, the old S.O.B. is rich, let's take his money and go get drunk."*
>
> *Before they could turn, an ax handle hit the backside of the one with the purse, causing him to fall and drop the money. When the fallen looked around, there were four men standing with different tools in their hands. The older one shouted at them, "Get out of here, you young thugs and leave my grandfather and us alone."*
>
> *The ugliest one sneered, "We're not afraid of you and your sons, Noah. You're just a bunch of fools, building a boat in the desert. There is not any rain, there's never been any rain, and there's never going to be any rain. Yah, yah, yah."*
>
> *The littlest one puffed up like a bantam rooster and crowed in a cracked voice, "You've been working on this dumb boat for over a hundred and twenty years. You're stupid to build a boat in a desert."*
>
> *Noah and his three sons advanced toward the rebels. They quickly picked*

up their fallen buddy and raced back toward a town. *"We're going to tell our daddies on you,"* they yelled.

"You tell your daddies they need to get right with the Lord. So do you," Ham yelled at the rebels.

Shem was not so evangelistic for he yelled at them, *"We don't care who you tell. The whole land of Eden is beyond repair. All of you are going to drown in the flood, unless you repent."*

"Flood," they all howled and shrieked. *"They'll have snow in Hell before they have rain in Eden."* Laughing they strutted back toward town. Loud music was blaring from the village mixed with vulgar laughter.

Methuselah was picked up by his three great grandsons. His injuries were not bad. *"Thank you Shem, Ham and Japheth,"* he said as he brushed himself off. Noah hugged the old man, then said, *"Come on Grandpa, let's get you over to the ark where you'll be safe. The young hoodlums are getting worse and worse. Last night a crowd of over a hundred came with torches to burn the ark. Fortunately God protected the ark as he once protected all of Eden."*

The old man sighed as he walked beside his son, *"The Land of Eden is an evil place, Noah. Frankly I'm glad God is going to clean it up."*

"What about the world outside of Eden?" Shem asked. *"You remember Great Grandpa Adam told you how his son Cain went over the mountains, married and came back."*

"He brought the devil back with him," Methuselah said. *"I don't mean his wife, she was probably innocent enough in her belief that you can worship God, Baal and Astarte equally. But we have a God who has told me we are to have no other gods before Him."* The old man stroked his beard then added, *"And we are not to have any other gods along beside Him."*

"It won't be long until there won't be any gods beside, over or under him," Ham laughed. *"When the flood comes, God is going to clean up our Land, Eden. All those pieces of wood and clay and metal they worship back in the village are going to be long gone."*

"Well, I'm 969 years old. Until today I had dreamed of boarding that ark with you men and your wives. I wanted to step out on clean land and a clean world someday. But God has other plans," the old man said. *"Let's see, now, I was 849 years old, when you began this big boat. So you must have been building on it for 120 years,"* Methuselah said. *"Did you make the Ark large enough for all the men and women of Eden to get on board."*

+ + +

Noah

CHAPTER 51
NOAH BUILDS AN ARK

"Yes, Grandpa. But as you know not a single one of the folks wants to get on board the ark. So, I'll have to obey the Lord and figure out a way to gather all the animals on board. I haven't figured that one out yet," Noah answered.

The group of men looked to see if any animals have shown up. There were none. Noah looked admiringly at the huge ship as they neared it. "We have finished the ark, made it just like the Lord commanded." Banging his hammer against the side, he drove in the last peg. "Made it of pure gopher wood, or as some call it, cypress. It is 450 feet long, 75 feet wide and 45 feet high."

THE ARK
450 feet long, 75 feet wide and 45 feet high

Sonny had been quiet for some time, but he had to blurt out, "Wow, that's the length of a football field and a half and taller than a four story building. I had no idea it was so big. Tell me again why they can't find something that big on Mount Ararat."

"Because it didn't land on Mount Ararat; it landed in the Ararat Mountains," Sandra sighed. "Gabriel, can we look inside? I would love to see what it was like."

"Sure," Gabriel nodded. We walked across the open door, which we remembered was like the one we had entered into the cross back in CROSS+ROADS. We gazed up to the roof some forty-five feet above us. Two doves flew past us into the ark then spiraled upward toward the top.

"Looks like the doves are getting some test runs in today," Sonny quipped.

"Look at the size of this thing," Sandra said. There were stairs on either side of the entrance that led to the floors above. To the left and to the right a long hallway stretched into the darkness. Stalls of various sizes were built on either side of the passageway.

"Looks like a floating motel," Sonny said. "Is there going to be room enough for all the animals? We studied there were millions of kinds of insects. There's no telling how many animals there are."

"God has it all figured out," Gabriel said. "When he gives a command, we obey and the results are always up to Him."

"Where are Noah's family going to live- in one of the cages?" Sonny asked.

"No, they have beautiful living quarters on the top deck. Plus there are some windows up there," Gabriel answered.

Methuselah stood outside the open door when Noah said, "Grandpa, it's time to call the animals in. The people have had an invitation for one hundred and twenty years to get on board but they refused. They prefer their gods and goddesses and their immoral lives to the ark. They prefer to live in a pig pen than to live in God's boat,"

Methuselah said. "My father, Enoch, walked and talked with God. God gave him instructions for me to tell you about the animals."

"Maybe we should round up a few horses to get them," Shem laughed.

"Sounds good to me," Ham and Japheth agreed.

Sonny asked, "How did they get all those animals on board? Some of them must have lived in Africa and the polar bear was surely up around the North Pole."

"Just watch," Gabriel said.

+ + +

CHAPTER 52
THE ANIMALS BOARD
THE ARK

M*ethuselah motioned Noah and his three great grandsons to follow him.*
Sonny said, "Can we get a better view? This I want to see."
Gabriel floated his group to the very top of the ark. We drifted toward the end where the men had entered the woods. Before us was the Garden of Eden! A door made of green foliage was guarded on both sides by Cherubim. As Methuselah, Noah and the sons approached the closed gates, the flaming sword went out. The giant Cherubim spread their wings over the top of the gate, then used their powerful arms to lower the gateway.

Methuselah took the hand of Noah and raised both their arms toward Heaven. Then he yelled out, "Animals, come forth!"

Gabriel and our group had a ringside seat to the first Barnum and Bailey Circus. Sonny told Sandra, "I'm putting my money on the elephants being first." Sure enough, trumpeting could be heard ringing through the old Garden. However, to their surprise two sheep, a ram and an ewe, were the first to emerge. Regally they marched out and headed for the ark. "I should have known," Sonny said. "The preacher told us once that the sheep were the first animals to be created and the goats were the last. He even divided us in church- sheep on the right, goats on the left."

Sandra looked up and said, "That's Biblical you know. When Jesus comes to judge the world, "He will put the sheep on his right and the goats on his left." Matt 25:33 NIV.)

"Really?" Sonny asked. "Then I need to start sitting on the other side of the church.

"Which side of the church you are on doesn't matter," Sandra said. "It matters whether you are on the Lord's side- sheep are on His side, goats are not!"

Below a steady stream of animals emerged and marched like an army on parade before us. Two by two they entered the Ark and seemed to know just where their living quarters were. Two skunks came waltzing out. Sonny said,

"Whew, I'd hate to be locked up with them for a …. How long were they in the ark?"

"Almost a year," I answered.

The last pair had to be driven reluctantly from the garden. Sure enough, it was two old goats, a billy and a nanny. At first they tried to turn and run back into the safety of their Garden home, but Shem had a long staff, and he prevented their return. They tried to bolt to either side, but were prevented. Finally, they stopped at the edge of the door to the ark and refused to budge. Methuselah came behind them, picked up a stick and said, "Get on board, you old goats!"

I laughed and said, "Sounds like an invitation at a Revival for Senior Adults."

The goats looked at the old man, then they bowed their heads as if to butt him, but he popped them with the stick and they scampered on the ship.

Noah's wife and daughters-in-law walked past them, waving and speaking to the old man as if he were their own grandpa. "See you on board," one of them yelled, then the women disappeared into the boat.

Thunder shook the ground and made the boat sway. Lightning flashed across the sky like the tongue of the serpent. "Grandpa, say a prayer for us before we all get on the ark."

The old man resembled the painting of God by Michelangelo in the Sistine Chapel as he raised his walking stick and his head toward Heaven and the swirling clouds.

"Oh God, you who made Adam and Eve, we thank you for making us.
We praise you for blessing us.
Oh Lord, we have labored in your vineyard for over nine hundred years, yet instead of a great harvest, we see the chaos of spiritual drought.
We pray once more for our neighbors, but now they are in your hands.
I praise you for my grandson Noah,
his three sons, Ham, Shem and Japheth, and for their wives.
Keep them safe through the flood
And deliver them into a new world.
Amen

Noah beamed at the old man, then said, "Grandpa, you go first into the ark before my boys and me."

"Oh no," Methuselah shook his head, "you go first."

Noah did not care for this but to be respectful to the old man, he and his sons walked across the open door and stood inside waiting. Rain began to fall. The boys laughed out loud for they had never seen rain. The old man lifted his head up toward the clouds as the shower became a downpour.

"Better get on board, Grandpa," Noah yelled. To his surprise two hands reached down through the clouds and took hold of either side of the door to the ark. The heavy door creaked as it slowly began to rise. Noah rushed across the door and reached out to the old man, "Grandpa, give me your hand. Quick, the door is closing."

A beam of light shot through the clouds illuminating Methuselah for a minute. His face glowed. "This ark was not made for me. God has plans for you and your children and your children's children. From you will come one who is the Door, and He will invite men and women to come on board his Ark of Salvation."

"No, Grandpa," Noah yelled as the door was closing. He reached an arm out, but the old man refused to take it. "My father Enoch walked with the Lord and was no more." He clutched his heart but he laughed, "I'm not going to swim with the Lord and be no more, but I am going to die a peaceful death, knowing my grandsons are safe on the ark."

Noah was barely able to peek out the opening in the door. But he saw the old man smile and hand him a leather packet. Then he slowly sank to the ground. From the edge of his eyes, he saw one of the Cherubim leave his post at the Garden Gate, come and pick up Methuselah and take him back into the Garden.

The hands of God pushed the door shut and sealed it.

+ + +

CHAPTER 53
WHICH WAS FLOODED?
THE EARTH
OR THE ERES, EARTH, LAND OF EDEN

As the song says, "The rains came down and the floods came up." Rain descended on Eden for the first time. Great fountains of water spewed upward as the earth opened deep crevices. Soon a foot of water had risen on the ground. Shouts and screams exploded from the village. The three young punks headed a mob of motley looking priests and prostitutes. Old men and women fought with each other to be first to the ark. Young men and women snarled at each other and even pushed children aside. They banged on the door, screeching out for Noah to let them in. They begged for forgiveness, they pleaded for entrance. The brown water swirled higher and higher as trash and garbage floated by. Some climbed to the top of their houses while others scampered up into the trees.

When the three guys who had attacked Methuselah could not beat the door open, they fled to the mountains surrounding Eden. Soon gangs of folk were desperately fighting the rain and mud trying to reach the top of the mountain. They hoped they could find safety on the other side, but when they reached the pinnacles, they encountered angels with drawn swords. They tried to wrestle their way past, but they were not equal to the heavenly host. Now the rain was pouring in sheets like one gigantic waterfall. Rivers of water and mud pushed them back down the mountainsides.

One man clung to a tree near the top of the mountain and cried out, "Lord, I'm ready to follow you. I'll do anything, anything."

But it was too late.

+ + +

THE *'ERETS* (EARTH OR LAND) IS FLOODED

Thunder boomed and lightning flashed unceasingly across the sky. For forty days it rained and the waters gushed forth from beneath the earth.

"Problems, Brother Gabriel," Sonny said. "How did Moses know all of this to write it down?"

"If Adam wrote the story of the Garden, who do you think wrote the story of the flood?" Gabriel asked.

"Well, it had to be Noah or one of his sons," Sonny answered.

Gabriel asked, "Do you remember seeing Methuselah give Noah a leather packet just before God closed the door to the ark?"

Sandra's eyes lit up as if she had just discovered the secret of perpetual motion. "I know! I Know!" she said. "The leather was a book. Adam wrote down details of their life in the Garden."

"And outside the Garden," Sonny added. "but who carved the history after Adam?"

"First, it wasn't carved," I said. "It was written on parchment- leather pages. The answer to your question should be logical. Adam lived up until the birth of Enoch, so..."

Sandra filled in the blank. "Enoch added to the manuscript. When he left this earth to walk with God, he gave the story to Methuselah."

"And Methuselah knew his 969 years were coming to an end, so he passed the book on to Noah," Sonny beamed. "So it was Noah who wrote down the story of the flood. Where did it go then?"

"It had to be his son, Shem, who was still living when one of his descendents was born- Abraham," Sandra said. "Then Abraham handed it down through Isaac and Jacob until it came to Joseph."

"Pretty close," I said. I had been this route before so I was able to fill in the next link in the history of the Bible. "The book then went to Levi, not Joseph. Levi was the father of the priesthood, so he and his descendents became the guardians of the book, or as we call it today, the Bible."

"What about Moses?" Sonny asked. "I thought he wrote all this down."

I beamed, "You are right. Moses was given the writings of Adam, Enoch, Methuselah, Noah, Shem, Abraham, Isaac, Jacob and Levi. Levi's descendents kept it up to date until the time of Moses. Under the inspiration of God, Moses wrote the first five books of the Bible. Genesis was unique because it was before his time. So, he gathered his facts from the parchments passed down to him. Moses even wrote Deuteronomy, but one of the Levites added the story of his death."

Gabriel nodded his head then added, "The most important information you have heard is the fact that the Bible was inspired by God, written down by his chosen men, and to all of us today it is..."

Sonny leaped forward, "The sword of the Lord which is the Word of God. Angels used it in the War in Heaven, so we had better learn to use it in the war on earth."

"Pretty sharp for a jock," Gabriel said.

Sonny grinned then became thoughtful and said, "You told us Adam could write, but what about all the others?"

"They could write," Gabriel said a little sharply. "This is 2348 B.C.- the Egyptians and the Babylonians already have writing. What language do you think was used for writing?"

Sonny answered, "I know! The preacher at the little church I attend in Tuscaloosa told us."

I listened and hoped I could obtain better respect for the unknown preacher who taught that anyone who believed in Evolution would go to hell. "And what language was the Old Testament written in?"

"The same as the New Testament- the King James Version," Sonny exclaimed

We all laughed, including Sonny. Finally I said, "That would have been a real miracle since the King James Version of the Bible was not written down until 1611 A.D."

"Just kidding, Preacher, it had to be Hebrew," Sonny said. He thought a moment and asked, "But I thought the whole earth was flooded."

Gabriel said, "The whole Earth, or the whole Land of Eden was flooded."

I was glad to show off my knowledge of Hebrew and asked, "Do you know that the Hebrew word for "Earth" is "'erets?"

Sonny shook his head and answered, "Preacher, that's a wasted question. There's no way I know the Hebrew for 'Earth.'"

"Then you need to know the word 'erets' can also mean 'land or country.' In Genesis 6:17- God said, 'Everything on earth ('erets) will perish.'"

Sandra said, "I get it. That verse could be translated that everything on the 'land' would perish- and it could further mean, everything on the Land- the Land of Eden would perish!"

I smiled and said, "You got it. It was the 'erets' that was flooded: the Land of Eden with all of Seth's descendents."

"Why didn't the rains flood other lands?" Sonny asked.

"I told you and showed you that Eden was in a hollow bowl, surrounded by mountains," Gabriel answered. "Most folks think it was a universal flood. Some even say it was when the Black Sea broke in from the Mediterranean."

"I'm not sure the preachers are going to buy the 'erets' bit," Sonny said.

"I remind you again, the truth is not for sell," Gabriel snapped. "They weren't there and I was. You have seen it. God flooded the Land of Eden and washed away the sinful people. He then saved those who were obedient and who had faith enough to get on board the ark."

"Noah and his family may have been cleansed though the flood, but they didn't stay clean," Sonny said.

'erets can be translated as earth, land, county, ground, nation, world..
Strong's definition.

"You're right," I added. "A lot of church folks think a good baptism in water cleans them up, and they never have to worry again. You and I know the only permanent cleansing comes from the blood of the Lamb."

"So it rained forty days, the waters rose for one hundred fifty days. Then the flood began to recede for another one hundred fifty days," Gabriel said.

"It was almost a year," Sonny added up.

A blue blur appeared, and we saw the ark floating on gentle waters. There was no more thunder nor lightning. Everything was as peaceful as the bathing pool in the Garden. The top of Mount Ararat could be seen in the distance, and other mountains also poked up through the quiet waters. Noah had a window open. He, his wife, his sons, and his daughters-in-law were looking out at the blue sky and the blue water. For those who had never seen an ocean, it was a gorgeous sight.

Thunk! A sound was heard as the ark hit land beneath the waters.

"That sounded like Mount Ararat to me," Sonny grinned.

+ + +

---

*Footnote on the Hebrew word, *'erets, "Earth or Land."*
'Erets can be translated as earth, land, county, field, ground, nation, world. (Strong's definition.)

- In Genesis 1:1, it is Earth, *"In the Beginning God created the heavens and the earth ('erets)."*

- In Gen 4:16, it refers to a particular area or a Land.
"Cain went out from the Lord's presence and lived in the Land ('erets) of Nod,"

- Genesis 2:5-7 seems to refer to a Special Creation of the Land of Eden:
"and no shrub of the field had yet appeared on the earth ('erets) ... the LORD God formed the man from the dust of the ground and breathed into his nostrils the breath of life..."

- Therefore, I chose this definition of 'erets as *"Land"* for the flood account:
Gen 6:17: Everything on earth ('erets- referring to the Land of Eden) will perish.

I am aware this interpretation is highly debatable-
but this book is one of fiction, and it does offer a possible understanding of Eden and the Flood.
The Author

2347 B.C.

CHAPTER 54
THE ARK LANDS

Gabriel smiled back and said, "That's pretty close. You just heard the sound of music to Noah's family. They touched land in the mountains of Ararat."

> *and on the seventeenth day of the seventh month*
> *the ark came to rest on the mountains of Ararat.*
> *(Gen 8:3-4NIV)*

"Several days go by," Gabriel said. "You remember God sent out a raven first. Then he released a dove that flew out and turned around and flew back."

"Maybe he sent out a homing pigeon by mistake," Sonny said.

"Not funny," Sandra said.

"Finally, he sent a second dove who brought back..."

"An olive leaf," Sonny beamed. "I know that one."

Gabriel continued, "He sent the dove out again, but this time the dove did not return. They waited until the earth was dry, except for a beautiful lake you can see there now, Lake Vann. It's all that is left of Eden."

> *Then God said to Noah,*
> *"Come out of the ark, you and your wife and your sons and their wives.*
> *Bring out every kind of living creature that is with you--*
> *the birds, the animals, and all the creatures that move along the ground--*
> *so they can multiply on the earth and be fruitful*
> *and increase in number upon it."*
> *So Noah came out, together with his sons and his wife*
> *and his sons' wives.*
> *All the animals and all the creatures that move along the ground*
> *and all the birds-- everything that moves on the earth--*
> *came out of the ark, one kind after another.*
> *Then Noah built an altar to the LORD*
> *and, taking some of all the clean animals and clean birds,*

he sacrificed burnt offerings on it.
The LORD smelled the pleasing aroma and said in his heart:
"Never again will I curse the ground because of man,
even though every inclination of his heart is evil from childhood.
And never again will I destroy all living creatures, as I have done."
As long as the earth endures, seedtime and harvest, cold and heat,
summer and winter, day and night will never cease."
(Gen 8:15-17, 20-22 NIV)

Sonny, Sandra and I stood in awe as we heard God's voice call out from Heaven. Then, just as any good movie would end, a Rainbow curled upward from the east, reached high into the heavens and plunged down in the west.

We followed the colors, then watched amazingly as three hands reached from the end of the rainbow: one red, one yellow, one blue. The hands reached toward a tropical island floating in a vast sea. Three hands slipped beneath the green mass and slowly lifted it up the rainbow toward Heaven.

+ + +

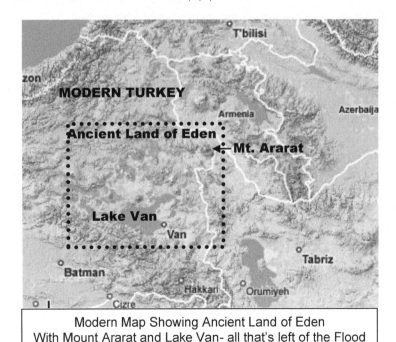

Modern Map Showing Ancient Land of Eden
With Mount Ararat and Lake Van- all that's left of the Flood

CHAPTER 55
A LAST LOOK AT THE GARDEN

How about that?" Sonny said. "That island is the Garden of Eden. No wonder man hasn't been able to find it. It ascended into Heaven just like Jesus."

As it came closer, Sandra exclaimed, "The gate to the Garden is open. Look, you can see the Tree of Life shining like a million watt bulb. It's like a cross atop a mountain for everyone to see."

"Who is that old fellow waving to Noah," Sonny asked. "It's Methuselah. I'll be, the old man died and went into the Garden. Hey, there's somebody with him.."

Gabriel answered, "That man with him is his father, Enoch."

Sonny beamed, "I get it- Enoch walked with God. I thought he went up on a mountain and floated into the sky. He just walked with God beside the Garden until one day God said, 'Come on in.'"

Sandra waved, "There's Adam and Eve. They're young again and so happy. I suppose it's true, everyone is thirty years old in Heaven."

I almost choked in tears as a man younger than thirty came into view. I said, "Now this is the good part. Do you recognize him, Sonny?"

"Can we get a little closer, Brother Gabriel?" Sonny shaded his eyes from the bright sun hanging over the ark. "Well, I'll be! That's Abel. He's my kind of hero. Abel offered a righteous sacrifice to God, a blood offering. His brother, Cain, only brought veggie leftovers not fit for the homeless."

Sonny waited for a round of applause for making an A on his Bible history test, but everyone was silent. We were all moved to tears as Adam and Eve ran down the road to meet their son, Abel. They hugged and kissed and laughed and gave everyone a sneak preview of how Heaven is going to be one great Homecoming.

A hooded figure stepped from the shadows of the trees inside the Garden. Adam's family did not see him at first- they were too busy celebrating. The man came near and stood in silence."

"Who in the world is that?" Sonny asked. "It must be Seth since we never saw him. Hey, pull up your hood, reveal yourself! I want to see if you look like your mama or your daddy."

Eve saw him first, then Adam, finally Abel. We all looked at the quiet figure standing outside the family circle.

Sandra squealed, "How wonderful! Sonny, you can see him now. Recognize him? Don't you remember the mark on his forehead?"

"It's Cain! It's Cain who killed his brother and had a cross put on his head." Sonny shouted. "Cain, you made it. Good for you!"

"He's running up to his brother Abel," Sandra almost cried. "Now, they're hugging each other."

Cain stepped back from his brother, bowed down and fell on the ground in repentance. Abel held out his arms in the shape of a cross, said something to him, then lifted Cain up in his arms and hugged him again and again and again.

Sonny watched the Garden disappear into a cloud in the sky. We all could hear the voice of God:

> *"To him who overcomes,*
> *I will give the right to eat from the tree of life,*
> *which is in the paradise of God."*
> *(Rev 2:7NIV)*

Gabriel pulled the two young people close to him, hugged them and said, "I think it's time to go home."

+ + +

PART 9 EASTER SUNDAY

CHAPTER 55
CHURCH

Easter had never been so meaningful, so glorious. Sonny and Sandra sat side by side in church on Sunday morning. Of course, I was so full of the Holy Spirit, I glowed as I told of the Christ. At the front door, One eyed Jack told me he had stayed awake for the entire sermon. "Preach, it was almost as if you had been there and seen the nails and the cross and the blood. Your message was so emotional- it was like you were there when they crucified our Lord. And when you got to the part where the stone rolled away and Jesus rose up from the dead, well, I just couldn't help myself. I just stood up and shouted, 'Glory!' Brother Chris, if I didn't know better I would swear somehow you have had a dream or a vision of our Lord, and you want to share the good news with us!"

"You're exactly right, One-eye," I said as I hugged the old man. Looking over my shoulder, I saw Sonny and Sandra next in line, so I winked at them and said, "Yep, it was just like we really saw the Lord."

They ate at Sandra's home. Cooking was a talent Mrs. Hall possessed and used extravagantly. Mr. Hall was a good example of being married years and years to the best cook in town. Pleasantly round, he sported a balding top, eyes that sparkled like Sandra's and a warm personality that would make even the devil feel at home. Mrs. Hall was the beauty queen of CROSS+ROADS when she was a teenager. Tall and thin, she moved with the poise of a queen. Her hair was still golden, her eyes blue, her smile would knock any man down at twenty paces or more. The two loved each other in such a way that Sonny could hardly wait to finish school, marry Sandra and start his own family.

"I need to warn you," Mr. Hall eyed Sonny. "Sandra may have her mother's good looks, but she can't boil water."

"Daddy, that's not true," she laughed as she threw a sofa pillow at him. "I'll have you and Sonny Miller know I made an A plus in Home Economics."

"You need to tell Sonny Miller the reason for your A plus was that you used your mama's recipe for coconut cake filled with fresh strawberries and toasted pecans," he teased.

"You forgot I had the ingenious idea of adding double chocolate chunks," she returned.

"I remember. She gave me a slice and I almost asked her to marry me," Sonny said. "I would not care if she were Colonel Sandra and she used Kentucky Fried Chicken recipes- that daughter of yours can cook. Mrs. Hall, I need to warn you, you better hold on to your blue ribbon from the county fair for cooking. If Sandra ever wants to challenge you, we may have a new winner."

Mrs. Hall smiled as she finished putting the glazed honey ham on the table. "We women are not in competition like you men. You grow up playing games and having to win, and be first or you get your feelings hurt. We women are interested in dolls and play house. No winners, we just learn to love."

Sonny thought a minute, then said, "A wise man told me the same thing not too long ago. Mr. Hall, do you believe we can play football in Heaven the same way girls play house?"

"Don't know about that, " Mr. Hall said as he wobbled down the dining room table. "But I'll have to tell you this, Mr. Sonny Miller and Miss Sandra Hall; your mother wins a gold star for being a loving wife and a loving mother every day." With that he reached over and kissed her smack dab in the mouth. "I tell her how much I love her. But if she ups and dies on me, since I can't cook a lick- I'll have to bring someone home from the funeral with me."

They laughed as they were seated at the table. All sat and inhaled the aromas of baked ham with pineapple rings with plump red cherries inside them. The bean casserole with piles of fried onions sent fragrances across the table. Snuggled in were bowls of fresh corn, homemade potato salad, creamy mashed potatoes. A bowl of white gravy looked like Aladdin's lamp with a smoke shaped Genie drifting upward.

Fresh rolls tried to hide under a towel in the bread basket, but it was in vain. They peeked out and sent the sweet smell of fresh baked bread in all directions. If that were not enough, one of Mrs. Hall's coconut cakes sat on the buffet, guarded by a fresh pecan pie and a huge bowl of banana pudding.

"Heaven is going to have to go some to beat this," Mr. Hall grinned as he reached out to take his wife's hand. All four joined hands and automatically bowed their heads for the blessing.

"Lord, you have been so good to us and we are most thankful," Mr. Hall began. "I could go on and on praising you for your blessings, for my wife, my daughter and my son in ... uh, my daughter's boyfriend, Sonny. If I took the time to thank you for your son, Jesus, His death on the cross, and His wonderful

Resurrection, well, I would have to pray for eternity. But, Lord, a prayer like that would make the food grow cold, and that would be a sin." Three sniggers of laughter were heard as he prayed on, "So, thank you Lord for everything and especially for this food. Amen."

He looked at Sonny and said, "I can't let Sandra's mama pray a blessing. She gets so carried away with all the missionaries and sick folks she won't quit. The only way I've survived these years is while she's a praying, I sneak some food and eat it. If not, I would be a mere shadow of myself."

Mrs. Hall retaliated, "Your shadow is so big that we don't need an umbrella for the patio."

Sandra yelled, "Bravo!" and applauded her mother. Then she reached over and hugged her dad. "God sure blessed me with the two of the finest parents in the whole United States of Alabama."

She noticed Sonny sadden, so she released her dad and hugged him. "I know holidays must be pretty hard on you, Sonny. Your mom died when you were young. Your brother had a stroke but managed long enough to move here and get saved before he, he, uh, went to Third Heaven."

"Third Heaven?" her Daddy said. "Wow, that guy is up there in Seventh Heaven, right alongside his daddy. Sonny, your brother and dad were a real inspiration to all of us who knew them, who loved them, who miss them. I know you must be sad."

Wiping a tear from his eye, Sonny replied, "There's nothing to be sad about, really. I just miss them. But I know they are saved, satisfied and sanctified in third... uh, Paradise."

"Paradise, Third Heaven, Seventh Heaven," Mr. Hall shook his head. "I don't know a lot about all of that. I just know I'm saved and ready for my Lord's return."

Sonny leaned toward his future father in law and said, "I know and you know, faith in Christ is what really matters. Now, will somebody pass me some of that ham, before I become a shadow of myself?"

+ + +

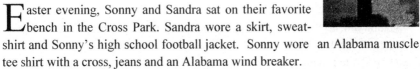

CHAPTER 56
EASTER EVENING
AT CROSS PARK

Easter evening, Sonny and Sandra sat on their favorite bench in the Cross Park. Sandra wore a skirt, sweatshirt and Sonny's high school football jacket. Sonny wore an Alabama muscle tee shirt with a cross, jeans and an Alabama wind breaker.

Lights illuminated the twelve foot cross. The same flowers bloomed sending out the sweet smells of Spring as they had three nights before. In three short days they had visited Eternity, took a whirl wind tour through History, and experienced both the beginning of the slow and natural creation of Angels and Life. Plus, they had been where no man had been for over six thousand years; they had walked in the Garden of Eden. They had witnessed the creation of Adam and Eve. They had felt and smelled things no body will understand until the Fourth Heaven after the final judgment when once again, Eden will be restored and the Tree of Life will give fruit again. Men and women will enter into a place unbound by time and space.

Sonny ran his fingers across Sandra's hand, then did the wedding march up her arm, as he hummed and sang, "Here comes the bride, big fat and wide. Here comes the groom, skinny as a broom."

"I am not going to be fat, Sonny Miller," she laughed. "Since I do cook like my mom, it may be the groom who is big, fat and wide and the bride who is skinny as a broom."

"Doesn't rhyme," Sonny smiled.

"Don't care if it rhymes or not, I will be glad when I finish college next year, and you have your last year of football at Alabama."

"May not be my last year of football," Sonny sighed. "If Gabriel is correct, and we haven't found him to be otherwise so far, I'm headed for the pros and big bucks."

"I hope all that doesn't go to your head."

"No way. The number ones in my life are you and God." he said. "Plus, it's going to be interesting to discover how God will open doors for you and me to share the secrets of creation with a doubting world."

"Some won't like it," Sandra stated. "The Six Day Creationists will hate us. They insist that their way is right and everybody else is wrong. Plus, there are many who are adamant that the flood had to wipe out everything and everybody except Noah, his family and all the animals on the ark."

"Yea, I know," he sighed. "But soon the time will be right. Creationists are so busy trying to get the atheists and scientists to agree to Intellectual Design, many of them will welcome the truth."

"But a lot will refuse the truth. Since we don't have any evidence left of Eden, they will swear our stories are not true," Sandra mused. "Of course we know they are looking in the wrong place. They have scoured the Near East looking for a garden that is third Heaven now- and we call it Paradise."

"It's the same way with those folks who spend money to go look for the ark on Mount Ararat; they ignore the fact the Bible never said it landed there. They believe it's there, and they are going to continue to take looks and write books about the ark." Sonny laughed, "Reminds me of a man looking under a street lamp. Someone came by and asked what he was looking for. 'My car keys,' the searcher said. They looked together and the second man finally asked, 'Are you sure you lost them here?' 'No,' the searcher replied, I lost them up the block in the dark, but the light is down here.'"

Sandra laughed, then placed her hand on his bronzed cheek. "The light is down here now, I hope people can discover and accept the truth- science and religion can work together to explain Creation."

The young football player stretched his arms, wiggled his neck, then strummed his fingers and pointed to the cross. "Someday there may be a monument placed here."

"What do you think it will say?"

"Well, it depends on who places it here. It could read, 'Here is where Alice fell down the rabbit hole- and where Sonny and Sandra came tumbling after."

Laughing louder, Sandra said, "I hope not. That will make us look like something from a fairy tale."

"Everybody is not going to believe us, Sweetheart," Sonny said in a rather quiet manner.

"The Good News is unlike the old days- we probably won't be arrested, tied up, bound to the cross, and burned at the stake," Sandra replied.

"We'll have Gabriel to protect us, I hope. Where is he now?"

"He told us he had to go away for a while."

"Where did he go? Here on earth? Back to Heaven? To visit another world in another galaxy where God also is creating life?"

"He didn't tell us the answer to that one. But I do know if there is life on another planet, they, too, would have the same Creator. They would also need an Adam and an Eve. Plus it would then necessitate the Son to go and redeem them from their sins."

"You think His name will be Jesus?"

"Depends on what language they speak," she grinned. "He might be named Hharuggart. But I don't think he will have ten feet and three heads. He will be 'in the image of God,' and so will they."

"You suppose they have their own history and their own Second and Third Heavens?" Sonny asked.

"Probably not, there's just One God." she said. "We know more about eternity than any two people on earth. Well, except for Brother Chris. But we still don't know everything. We only have a hint at the Triune God. Frankly, I think it's much more complicated than red, and blue and yellow. I figure God revealed that to us because we could understand it. Had Gabriel taken Joseph and Mary on the tour of Eternity, He might have revealed Himself to them in a far different way. I do know He never expects more of us than we can do. He never demands we understand more of him than our brain can comprehend."

Sonny wiped his hand across his nose, posed it under his chin like a modern day replica of the "Thinker." He thought for a while then stood up, stretched and walked over, and looked up at the cross. "Cross, you are so simple, yet so complicated. You are nothing more than two pieces of wood fitted together. I was taught the vertical is 'Loving the Lord your God with all your mind, heart, soul and strength.' A few nights ago we saw the horizontal beam reached out around the world with the command to 'Love our neighbors as ourselves.' I have come to understand it is easier to say than do, easier to preach than to practice."

Stepping back to take it all in, he said, "So simple, yet so complicated. Here, two roads crossed, a city was born, a church arose, a cross was erected, a vision was given. Today the roads of Evolution and Creation cross, and clash, and crash: fact versus faith, science versus religion, and schools versus the church."

Turning to Sandra, he took her hand and pulled her up beside him. "You and I have been given data that could make the two cease their warfare, and instead, walk side by side triumphantly into the future."

Sonny thought a moment then asked, "What about my professor's view where we all emerged from two molecules in a pond?" "Your professor has a bigger problem than you," Sandra answered. "He is trying to convince you that inanimate objects can produce animate objects, or to put it another way, inorganic material is able to fabricate organic life. There was a time when the best thinkers doubted we even existed. 'How can you prove a man exists?' they asked back in those days. What if we are all just an illusion, a dream?"

COGITA ERGO SUM

Sandra let Sonny think that about for a moment. Finally she said. *" 'Cogito, ergo sum,' 'I think, therefore I am.'* Rene Descartes made this basic statement in philosophy- it means, 'I can think, therefore it's a fact that I exist.'" "Well, that's dumb. Anybody ought to be able to tell we exist. Why do you have to prove it?" "That's Science's way of dealing with issues. You can't just say something is obvious or true. When Descartes presented his famous statement that settled their questions. If a man didn't exist, he couldn't think, therefore because he can think- it proves he exists."

"Huh," Sonny said. "Then why don't scientists just realize only a God who thinks could produce something as complicated as a human being. You told me once even Darwin made some statement about an eyeball so complicated it would be impossible to just happen."

"That's right here in one of my books," Sandra said as she reached into her back pack. Thumbing through the pages she said, "Here it is,

'To suppose that the eye with all its inimitable contrivances
for adjusting the focus to different distances,
for admitting different amounts of light,
and for the correction of spherical and chromatic aberration,
could have been formed by natural selection, seems,
I freely confess, absurd in the highest degree.'
* *Darwin, Charles. The Origin of Species, p. 167.*

"Didn't that disprove his concept of Evolution?" Sonny asked.

"Nope, evolutionists believe in evolution like we believe in God. Later on in the same chapter of his book, he explained how he believed the eye evolved anyway and that the 'absurdity' was illusory. Had Darwin had the knowledge about the eye and its associated systems that we have today (which is a great deal more than what it was in his time), he may have given up his naturalistic theory on the origin of living things. Plus, his idea of a cell was nothing more than a glob or protoplasm. Today we know the cell is extremely complicated and made up of over three billion parts that have to work together."

Sonny sighed, "Evolution is so complicated. If you just think about it, only a thinking God could have thought up mankind."

"Sonny, that's it," Sandra cried out. "It's exactly the answer I've been looking for. Let me see if I can translate it into Latin, so it will sound much more scholastic.

'Cogito, ergo sum eventus reputo'"

"I get the *'cogito ergo sum'* 'I think, therefore I am,'" Sonny said. "But what is this 'eventual one potato, two potato, three potato?"

Sandra laughed and hugged him, *" 'Eventus reputo.'* It means 'The result of a thinker."

"So?"

"Put it all together in English."

Sonny pondered then said, *"I think, therefore I am the result of a thinker."*

+ + +

CHAPTER 57

I THINK THEREFORE
I AM THE RESULT OF A THINKER

The Thinker

That's it! Now I know the subject of my doctoral thesis: *'Cogito, ergo sum eventus reputo,' 'I think therefore I am the result of a thinker.'* I see why Gabriel took me on the journey back to the Garden. He knew when I saw the Big Bang, the Beginning of Life, and Adam and Eve, I would put it all together. There is no way all of this could have happened even by Intelligent Design. It takes far more than just an Intellect. We are the product of a God who thinks and plans and creates. Oh, it's wonderful. I can hardly wait to get back to school."

"So," Sonny said. "because men can think, they exist. But also because we can think, it proves someone who can think produced us, or in our case someone created us."

Sandra exclaimed excitedly. "I see where my research will lead. Only thinking life can produce other thinking life. Example, thinking rats can produce more thinking rats. Humans produce thinking humans; therefore, it has to be someone who can think who created us. For years I had realized the brain is amazing, and evolution does not seem to be a fit answer for it's many functions. Do you realize the brain can think, it manages our muscles, nerves, blood. It also can remember things from the past and can even predict the future."

Sonny coughed and said, "I think you're getting a little carried away- predict the future?"

"Yes. Say you are driving and you need to make a left turn. You see a car coming and you can predict if you have time to make your turn or wait until it passes."

Sonny said, "Hey, you're right. I can predict what defense a team will use, and come pretty close to telling you what play the offense will run.

"The brain can imagine and it can create. That's pretty good evidence it is the result of a Creator God."

"But can't a machine make machines that do things?" Sonny asked.

"Only a programmed machine can produce machines that function. You are right, we live in a day when computers can do almost anything AFTER they are programmed, Sandra explained. "This is a whole new revelation in dealing with life. I'm going to have to do a great deal of thinking about this. I love it,

> 'Cogito, ergo sum eventus reputo,
> I think therefore I am the product of a thinker.'"

Sonny hugged her and said. "Now if scientists will just use their brains to think instead of worshipping at the shrine of Evolution, they will open their minds to see the truth of your discovery."

"Still wish Gabriel was here beside us," Sonny sighed. "I would feel much more comfortable when we encounter real spiritual warfare."

"Not to worry, Big Boy," Sandra rubbed her fingers across his bicep. "You're pretty tough. Remember our guardian angels that Gabriel forgot to show us?"

"Yes, but..."

"No buts, please. Maybe our guardian angel is strong enough."

"Strong enough for attacks by little red-eyed imps, but I'm not sure they can hold off the 'Big Boys,' and I'm not talking about me."

"Then, guess what?" Sandra smiled, turned him toward her and put her face up next to his, "Maybe he will just send us another angel."

Sonny kissed the end of her nose, took a deep breath and said, "If you are talking about Sandra Hall, then I'll agree he has sent me an angel." He put his arms behind her back and pulled her up against him, tight and then a little too tight.

"Whoa, Romeo, put on the brakes," she smiled. "This is Easter- we are in the park for all to see; and we have taken a vow of chastity. Besides, I've got to get home. We are both due back to at school tomorrow morning. I've got to go pack and so do you. Then we have to get a good night's sleep. You will pick me up at five o'clock Monday morning and chauffeur me back to Birmingham. Deposit me at Samford. Then you, James, will travel on down to Tuscaloosa and spring practice."

+ + +

"Cogito, ergo sum eventus reputo,
I think therefore I am the product of a thinker."

Temptation

CHAPTER 58
TEMPTATION

Sonny drove his old car back to her house where they had eaten the Easter meal.

"I would invite you in for a snack," Sandra said. "But unfortunately there was this monster football player who was invited to lunch. He stayed all afternoon, snacking on this and that. Then my mother insisted he eat supper where he actually picked up the honey glazed ham and chewed on the bone."

"Did not," he laughed.

"Then the monster finished off all the food, including the coconut cake, the last piece of pecan pie, and guzzled down banana pudding as if he had not eaten in three weeks."

"Do you know what dorm food tastes like?" he asked.

"Yes, I do. Samford is a good school, but the cafeteria food is prepared in the first level of Hades. You can't chew it; you can't swallow it; and you sure can't digest it. If it were not for care packages from my mom, I would be a mere shadow of myself."

Sonny laughed so loud, he snorted, "Please tell that mother of yours to put me on her Care Package Mailing List."

"You are already on her cookies and cake of the week mailing list. Do you want to move up to her daily list?"

"Either that, or I might someday marry the daughter," Sonny said, then became quiet.

Sandra picked up the lull, coughed, remembered he had never actually asked her to marry him. To break the silence she asked, "Do you have everything packed?"

"Yep, got my jeans and tee shirts already in my suitcase your dad gave me for graduation. And best of all," he paused, waiting for her to ask him what his best of all was. She didn't so he continued, "Best of all, I've got on my Whole Suit of Armor."

Patting him on the shoulder like a mother telling her toddler he had just done a good potty, she said, "Good for you. I'm proud of you. You sure you have all of it?"

"Yep, in modern terms, I've got on my belt of truth. I use the word *belt* because a *girdle* of truth sounds like something an overweight woman would wear. Got on my Nike shoes to carry the Gospel back to Alabama. My shield of faith is in good condition; my helmet of salvation is secure, and I never leave home without the Sword of the Lord," he said as he reached in his pocket and held out his New Testament, "Which is the Word of God."

"Didn't you forget one?" she asked.

He fumbled his hands back and forth across his body, trying to remember if one piece of armor was missing. "Oh yea. My brassiere of righteousness!"

"Sonny Miller!" she shrieked. "God is going to get you."

"Oops, I'm sorry, that's the feminist version of the Bible that has the Lord's Prayer beginning with "Our Mother, who art in Heaven..."

Sandra shook her head playfully and said, "Oh, you men. For your information, it is the Breastplate of Righteousness. It's necessary to protect ..."

"Your breasts," Sonny interrupted then lifted one eyebrow, grinned a little sneer, and acted as if he were tapping the ashes from an imaginary cigar. "Hey, you pretty little thing, let's see if your breastplate works."

With one arm he turned her toward him, then kissed her. "Mmm," she said, "that's nice." His hand brushed against her breast, and since she didn't remove it, he held it softly and kissed her even deeper. Since no security alarm went off, he placed his other hand on her leg, just below her skirt and began to inch upward.

"No trespassing," she laughed, as she pushed both hands away. "You remember God should have put that sign on the tree in the garden. Look at all the trouble Adam and Eve caused. So we'll just have to limit our 'love-making' to kissing, but no handling."

He blushed a bit because he had stepped over the line, but she pulled him toward her and kissed him again. The fire within him blazed up, the countdown began, ten, nine, eight, six, five, four.... He stopped then said, "It's getting more and more difficult to wait until marriage."

"I know," she answered. "Well, no, I don't really know how difficult it is for you guys- but from what I've learned, you have some pretty heavy sex drives. It's like a river. Sometimes it floods. Billy Graham was correct in advising us to channel the river. We have to control its force to bring about good, or else it can cause vast destruction. Do you know how many children are born today outside of marriage?'

Sonny pulled back from her. There was sweat on his brow and a look in his eyes, she had never seen before. Same eyes, but behind them there was a drive, a glare which was almost scary. He wet his lips, thought a moment and said, "What if I said, 'If you love me, you will ...'?"

She cut him off, "Then I would say, '*IF* you loved me, you would not ask me to do anything immoral."

Sonny breathed deeply, gazed at her and said, "You are so beautiful, and I am so human. You are right, but true love waits. True love, Christian love, never asks the one you love to do anything immoral."

"I love you, Sonny Miller."

"And I love you, Sandra Hall," he gazed lovingly at her. "There's something I want to know?"

"And what would that be?"

"Why do you think God could choose me for the special honor of sharing his truth about Adam?"

Sandra laughed again. It was hard to believe someone so athletic, so sharp in so many areas could change a love scene into a 'Why me?' question.

"Maybe you are the new Adam. But I am not going to be the new Eve and tempt you to sin with me."

"Yea, as we joked in our boys Sunday School class one day, 'It wasn't the apple on the tree that led to sin, it was the pair on the ground.'"

"Shame on you," Sandra laughed. "God knows the reason He has chosen you and me to bring the news to the world when the time is right. And he has chosen you and me to wait for that special experience until that time."

"What about lust?" Sonny suddenly asked. "Didn't Jesus say it was just as bad to lust as it was to commit adultery?"

"No, He did not," Sandra answered. "He said in Matthew 5:28, 'But I tell you that anyone who looks at a woman lustfully has already committed adultery with her in his heart. (NIV)'"

"So," Sonny blinked his long, black eye lashes at her, "if I have already committed adultery in my heart, what's the difference in going 'all the way.'"

"The difference is 'all the way.' You may pass a jewelry shop and want to reach in and take an expensive watch 'in your heart.' But you remember Christians don't steal and you don't commit the crime. As one of our counselors told us girls, who, by the way, also have lustful thoughts, 'you can't keep a bird from flying over your head, but you can keep it from building a nest in your hair.'"

"I like that," Sonny giggled. "I guess every guy just wants to see how far he can go."

"Yep, and it's up to us girls to determine how far that is."

"Wait a minute," Sonny pondered. "Since I just lusted, and you insinuated that you lust on occasion, isn't that just as bad a sin as committing the act?"

"No Sir-ree," Sandra came back strongly and looked at the handsome hunk sitting beside her. "It is wrong to lust after a woman. But lust comes in different degrees. It's one thing to kiss your girlfriend and touch her and burn with desire. Then when she tells you to back off, you obey. Well, that's a sin of about one on a scale of ten. Now if you go home, pull out the porno magazines and then lust after all those, uh, harlots and have that same deep, burning lust for your girlfriend, that moves up to about a five."

"Closer to a seven or eight," Sonny corrected her.

"If the girlfriend tells you to back off, and you continue with your act, then you have moved from lust to adultery."

"Is that a Ten?" he asked. "Then what is rape? What is sexually assaulting a child? What is sodomizing a little boy?"

"Yuk. Those are on the Big-time Sin list and you don't even want to think about them. You may want to think about how God is going to punish those, uh, uh, demonic animals."

He kissed her softly again and made sure his hands were at the ends of his arms and not in the wrong place on her body. Opening the car door, he took a sniff of the spring breeze, the smells of small town, the honeysuckle growing profusely by the fence at the front of Sandra's home. He loved the smell, the sound, the experience of Easter. As he walked around the car he heard a dog bark in the distance and remembered how God had carefully designed the dog over millions or years. Red tulips danced by the sidewalk and he remembered God planned it all to provide flowers and trees and bushes. They had experienced a trip given to no other person. An arrow of guilt shot through him. If his passion had continued and he had surrendered to the lusts of the flesh, he could have spoiled God's plan for him. Pausing, he wondered how many bushes God burned before he caught Moses attention. Then he pondered how many other young football players, or scholars, or band members, or just plain Joes, God had attempted to catch their attention, but the enticing sounds of sin had blocked out His voice.

Thanking God for the high honor of his calling, he then rejoiced of having someone like Sandra for a girlfriend now and a wife someday. "Hmm," he thought. "And she will be the mother of my little Sonnys and Sandras."

Opening the door, he bowed as some nobleman of old, escorting the queen from her carriage. Taking his arm, she laughed as they walked up the walkway, tickling him and watching him wiggle away from her, only to circle in again.

They stood at the door. Dark masculine eyes immersed in long black eyelashes looked down upon her twinkling blue eyes. "One question before I go," he said.

She pulled back a bit so she could observe his olive skin and that gorgeous mouth filled with solid white teeth. "Yes," she said wondering if he were going to pop the question. She had made her decision the day she saw him walk up the Sunday School in that silly hat and oversized coat. "Well, one question, then."

"I'm afraid you'll say. 'No.'" he grinned,

"Well, you never know till you ask," she purred. Reaching down she felt for the ring finger where she hoped she would soon wear an engagement ring.

"If you say, 'No,' I won't think less of you," he teased. "And I won't stop loving you."

"You'd better not stop loving me… ever. So go ahead, Sonny boy, what you got on your mind?"

"O.K. This is the question." He paused for dramatic effect, winked at her, grinned that million dollar smile at her, then asked. "Do you really think Adam and Eve ran around butt naked all that time and never lusted after one another?"

Sandra dropped her mouth, gave a shocked, embarrassed look, grabbed her purse and gently popped him on the shoulder with it. She laughed, "Get out of here, you dirty young man."

Howling with laughter, he jumped off the porch, saluted her, blew her a kiss and said, "I'll pick you up at five a.m. to drive you to Samford University before I motor on down to Tuscaloosa."

+ + +

CHAPTER 59

THE ANGEL BACK AT THE HOUSE

The Angel

When Sonny arrived at what he still called, "his dad's house," he pulled his car up the graveled driveway and realized how much he missed his dad and brother. Inwardly he wished he had gone back in time to when they were alive and had seen them one more time. Even better, if he could just have seen his mother again: to look at her and remember all she had done for him. She had given him life. He looked across the yard at the clothes line he and his brother had put up in the backyard. The lines still swung between the posts, but he noticed the posts looked like small crosses.

Stars blazed down from the Heavens, and he realized he had walked among them and saw them born, or more truthfully, saw them created. A meteorite streaked across the sky then exploded. "Gabriel, I wish that you were here to help me," he said aloud. Still gazing at the heavens, he mumbled, "Dad, I wish you and Curtis were still here with me to help me enjoy life and fulfill my mission."

There was no need to lock his car. First there were no thieves out here in the country, second he had nothing to steal. Walking around the car, he visualized how in a few years he would play professional ball and drive a new car. He prayed he would be sensible with the money and not waste it, but use it to help the Lord and to help folks.

As he started up the front steps, he was startled to see someone sitting in the rocking chair, slowly swaying back and forth. At first, he thought it was some crook waiting to rob him or hurt him, but as he watched, the man in the chair had a glow about him.

"Is that you, Gabriel?" he cried out happily. "Man, I'm glad you came back, it's so good to ..." He stopped. "You're not Gabriel!"

The man in white stood. White hair flowed over his ears and down to his shoulders. His eyes were darker than Gabriel's, his nose broader and his chin longer. His gown was white but seemed a bit dingy compared to that of the Archangel.

"I, I don't know you," Sonny said as he extended his hand.

The stranger flashed a big smile, like that of a used car salesman, and said, "We have never met. I though Gabriel may have told you about me."

"No, not that I remember," Sonny stumbled. "But we have been a lots of places. We are the original 'Been There, Done That' folks."

"I know," the stranger replied. "I'm an angel. But as you can tell by my attire, I'm not an archangel. My name is Myianel." Laughing he added, "I'm not as high up as Gabriel or Michael or Raphael."

Taking his hand, Sonny shook it and said, "Glad to know you. Funny how all of you angels have names that end in '–el.'"

"It's really not funny," he answered, "El is the word for God, and we were all named for him. Some changed their names- especially those who were in the fall."

"Yea, like Lucifer or Satan or Beelzebub," Sonny smiled.

"But you notice Beelzebub kept the 'el' in his name, 'Be-*EL*-zebub?'" the angel informed him. "I figure he might want to become a Lord himself, or perhaps, find a weak spot and crawl back into Heaven."

"He and Lucifer actually think they could overthrow God?"

"Sure, they thought they were victorious at the crucifixion. Don't you remember? It was all a trap to exterminate God's precious son. And if the son is eliminated, what's to keep someone else from taking the throne?" Myianel replied.

"Interesting," Sonny said. "What brings you here?"

"I'm afraid we have some bad news," the angel said. "But we can make good news of it if you will just follow our instructions."

"Bad news?" Sonny asked, "What bad news? God is on His throne and all is well with the world."

"God expects obedience from his chosen ones and perfection, really."

"Hey, none of us are perfect," Sonny stated, as he had many times when he had told a little white fib, or got the answers from a test before it was taken. Sonny's mind darted back to earlier that evening when he was right on the edge of adultery, hoping the angel did not know about that.

A small smile appeared on the angel's face. "I think I know why you forgot the 'brassiere of Righteousness.'" He laughed but it was not the jolly sound like that of Gabriel, it was more the cackling of an old crone. Maybe some angels were the messengers of good news and some were the angels of bad news. If so, perhaps he didn't have much to smile about.

Sonny tried to laugh it off. "Yea, I was just kidding her, you know. Girls can be so gullible and naïve. And, we guys, you know, we laugh and kid around. I used the 'brassiere of righteousness' with some prayer buddies of mine one night at college. They thought it was hilarious. But I know it's the Breastplate of Righteousness and I truly know how important it is to resist Satan. If that breastplate is not in place, or if is has holes in it, you can be wounded."

The angel nodded his head in agreement with all Sonny was saying. "That's what I'm here to talk to you about. We have discovered a small hole in your armor. If it were on the side or at the back, it probably could be patched easily. But this hole is right over the heart."

"Where?" Sonny asked and looked down at his shirt trying to find a rip, a hole, a scar.

Laughing a little sharply, the angel said, "Oh, you can't see it- but we can. We find the weak spots quickly. As you know, Lucifer will find your weakest point and attack you right there."

"Oh, I wish Gabriel were here," Sonny mumbled. "He would be able to tell me how to fix it."

"A band-aid will not do," Myianel replied rather coldly. "No, a simple patch will not do for you. Maybe it would work for others, those not chosen for such high places. In your case, you need to cure the cause of your problem."

"I've tried to live a clean life," Sonny sputtered. "I don't cuss, nor drink, nor smoke. And I was kidding Sandra about going all the way."

"Good for you," the Angel answered. "Of course, you realize the Pharisees could claim all of that and a whole lot more. They read the Scripture more than you, prayed more than you, went to church more than you, and were, in their eyes, far more righteous than you. Yet, these were the ones whom Jesus attacked and called, 'Hypocrites.'"

"I've never been a hypocrite! No! No! Ask my preacher. Ask Sandra."

"Do you wonder why Jesus attacked the hypocrites so openly, so often, so viciously?"

"Not really. I guess it was because they didn't believe in him?"

"They were assailed because they thought they had invented the Breastplate of Righteousness. They were so religious, so good, so pious, so self-centered. So Jesus had to take them down a peg or two. Never would a Pharisee commit adultery, yet they would stone an adulteress quickly. Then even tried this one day when they dragged a woman to Jesus."

"Yes, I remember, he said, 'Let he who is without sin, cast the first stone,'" Sonny smiled. "The law was rough on the adulteress, but rather easy on the adulterer."

"The hypocrites thought because they did not sleep with a harlot or their neighbor's wives, they were all right," the angel said in a voice that slowly began to rise. "But these same 'religious" men would watch the young ladies walk by and just imagine how wonderful it would be to grab a girl by the hair, drag her into a side room of the temple. In their mind and hearts, they would undress her, throw her down upon the beds intended for religious purposes and force themselves upon her. In their minds they would lust until the fire reached down into their loins. But as long as their body was under control, they thought all was well with God. They had kept the law."

The angel eyed Sonny then continued, "You seem to know the Scripture, Let's see, how does it go, Oh yes, in Matthew chapter five, verse twenty-eight. "

*'But I tell you that anyone who looks at a woman lustfully
has already committed adultery with her in his heart."
(Matthew 5:28 NIV)*

His eyes squinted, his smile stooped, as he asked, "Who do you think Jesus had in mind when he said this in his Sermon on the Mount?"

"The Pharisees?" Sonny replied.

"Exactly, give the boy an A plus for his knowledge of the Bible." The Angel walked to the edge of the porch and looked down at the toolbox sitting there. Sonny had meant to take his brother's tools and put them in the barn, but he remembered how Curtis loved to sit on the porch in the afternoon with his dad. They would talk and whittle. Sometimes they would take out the hatchet and chop down a stick of wood so they could carve it into a whistle or a toy for someone. He felt like the tools needed to stay on the front porch as a memorial to his brother and dad.

"There is a hole in your armor, Sonny Miller. A dangerous tear that will cause you to fail in the future in your task," the angel stated as he looked over the objects in the tool chest.

"What sin is that?" Sonny asked. "I'll repent. I'll give up anything, anything for my Lord. I'll do anything for God. Anything he tells me to do."

"I'm glad you said that," the angel said as he picked up something, turned to Sonny, but held the tool behind his back. "Because I'm asking you to do something that will prove your faith and be used in the future as a testimony of your obedience to God."

Sonny backed up a step or two away from the angel. "What is my sin?"

"Lust," the angel smiled and his eyes almost danced. "Lust. Something we angels can never know. God made us incomplete- you know. We have the same plumbing as you mortals, but one of our parts can only be used to eliminate liquids from our body. Yours can be used for the greatest pleasure of man- sex."

"But I haven't really lusted," Sonny backed further away. "What happened tonight was, uh, normal. Normal men have passion- it's a built in drive. It is what causes species to breed and reproduce. I have never used my body for..."

"But tonight, Sonny Miller, you lusted. You would have gone all the way with Sandra Hall had she not stopped you."

"No, no, I don't think I..." Sonny halted. "God would have stopped us."

"God doesn't always stop what we start," the angel said softly. "So you remember what the Bible says about lust being adultery in the heart. Do you recall how Jesus said that we have to deal with that sin?"

"Uh, not really," Sonny said. "But if you give me a chance, I'll go call Brother Chris and get him up here then he can tell you and he can help you."

+ + +

CHAPTER 60
IF YOUR HAND OFFENDS YOU...

The Angel moved toward him, with his hand holding something behind his back. "I think you do remember what it says. I know that Scripture very well and used it often in the days of the Inquisition. It is Matthew Five, verses twenty-nine and thirty:

> *If your right eye causes you to sin, gouge it out and throw it away.*
> *It is better for you to lose one part of your body*
> *than for your whole body to be thrown into hell.*
> *And if your right hand causes you to sin, cut it off and throw it away.*
> *It is better for you to lose one part of your body*
> *than for your whole body to go into hell.*
> *(Matthew 5:29-30 NIV)"*

As the words soaked in, Sonny remembered he had heard this strange teaching and never understood it. It didn't make sense for a man to gouge out an eye or cut off his hand. He also recalled that some of the monks would turn their backs on society and live in caves. Brother Chris had told of one who castrated himself so he would not lust.

Immediately his hand went down to the front of his pants, and he shook his head refusing to believe what he was hearing from an angel.

The angel laughed a sinister laugh. "No, it's not that part of your body you must surrender. The Bible is clear. 'If your right hand causes you to sin, cut if off and throw it away.'"

As he drawled these words out, Myianel brought his hand out from behind him. Sonny gasped and stepped back again. "No, no," he cried. "This isn't fair."

The moonlight glistened off the blade of the hatchet. Sonny recognized it immediately and remembered the times he had chopped small limbs from trees, or hacked kindling for a winter fire. As the angel came closer, Sonny could see the dark stain of blood where his father had used it the last time. Brother Chris and his family were going to come for Sunday dinner. His dad had grabbed the hatchet, gone out into the chicken yard, grabbed the young rooster by the neck.

Taking him over to a log, he had put his foot on the back of the screeching bird and then, "Whack." The little axe had plunged down and severed the head from the body. Part of the blood was still there.

"God, Father God," Sonny screamed up at Heaven. "You didn't tell me all of the contract. Why didn't you choose someone else? I don't have the faith of Abraham. I don't even have the trust of Isaac."

"You must be obedient," the angel scowled. "Take the hatchet and chop off your right hand. That is the hand that fondled Sandra Hall's breast this evening That is the hand that led you to the very edge of adultery. That is the hand that unless removed will reach out to some young cheerleader who would die to go to bed with you. Your hand will feel her body, and she will guide it to places where hands are not to go until you are safely and securely married in the sight of God."

He thrust the hatchet into the hands of the young football player. "Like so many hypocrites today, you claim you will go where He wants you to go, do what He wants you to do. But you are do-nothings, and you go nowhere except places of pleasure. When you chop off your hand, you will prove to the world you are a man of faith."

"But my football.."

"Your football has become *Foot Baal*, the god that the Israelites worshipped in the Old Testament. He is the one you know as Beelzebub, Lord of the Flies, second in command to Lucifer. And when he has the opportunity, he will take over first command and lead the rebellion back into Heaven."

"Oh God, send Gabriel!" Sonny moaned, feeling the weight of the hatchet in his hand. His brain was spinning completely out of control. His reasoning was saying to let somebody else have the honor of sharing God's secret creation. His faith was shouting, if you really love the Lord, you will do whatever He says.

"Can I have time to pray about it?" Sonny asked.

"No! You must decide now. God told Abraham to take his son and sacrifice him. What would Abraham have done if God had given him the easier task of simply cutting off a hand or a foot?"

"I don't know. I don't know." Sonny was crying. "Let me call Sandra. She'll help me decide. If I am to be her husband, she may not want a one armed beggar."

"No! Now!" The angel was screaming at him. "You can't have Gabriel or the preacher or some woman to hide behind. You must make your decision or the whole deal is off. Unless you chop off your lustful hand, you will forget everything you have been taught- it will be erased. The minds of Sandra and the Preacher will also be cleared. None of you will recall these few days. Science and Religion will continue to clash. Each will try to overrule the other until war will actually break out among them. And it will be all your fault."

Sonny slowly put his right hand on the arm of the rocking chair where his dad had sat on those pleasant evenings. He could hear all three of them laughing and joking and enjoying being together, just as the Triune God enjoyed being three in one. Taking the hatchet in his left hand, he juggled it a moment, then righted it. Instinctively, he lifted the index finger of his right hand to the blade to make sure it was sharp. When it cut, he wanted it clean- not a mangled mess.

Bowing his head, he prayed, "Lord, not my will, but thine be done. If this is what it takes to help save a world, then I am surely no better than your son, Jesus. He gave his life. I'll have one hand, two legs, a head, a brain. But nobody can chop off my faith."

He closed his eyes and raised the hatchet back as far as he could. Opening them quickly he looked again at his right hand that had thrown so many footballs and baseballs. The right hand that had shot the basketball into the hoop. The right hand that had strayed beyond the No Trespassing Sign with Sandra that very night He eyed the spot where he would inflict the cut. Steadying his right hand as best he could, he raised the hatchet once again, closed his eyes, breathed a prayer and brought the blade down with all the power of a well muscled young man who played football at the University of Alabama.

WHACK!

He heard the crunch. The blade slicing through flesh and bone. He hoped that he had cut it off completely and wondered how he could keep from bleeding to death. Maybe he could put on a tourniquet to keep enough blood in his body as he drove to the hospital ten miles away.

What if he bled to death? What would Sandra think? What was he thinking? How could he bleed to death if he were doing God's will? God would provide, yes, in the Old Testament. He heard himself saying aloud, "In the Old Testament, when Abraham was ready to sacrifice Isaac, he raised the blade,..."

Sonny's eyes were still closed although his brain was going full speed.

There was no pain!

There was no pain at all. Had God given him some kind of anesthesia to deaden the hand? What was going on.? Eyes closed, he repeated aloud, "Abraham raised the knife..."

"And God provided a ram," a deep voice finished the statement.

Sonny's eyes shot open and he looked up to see Myianel, looking angrily at someone. The someone smiled at Sonny and said, "I was busy, but Gabriel told me something like this would probably happen, so I hustled here as fast I could."

Sonny looked at the giant muscular man in the white robe wondering who this could be.

"I'm Michael, the Archangel," the smiling face explained. "I had to hurry to get here just in time."

"You're too late," Sonny said sadly. "Unless you can heal my hand."

"Take a look, Sonny Miller," Michael smiled.

+ + +

Michael

CHAPTER 61
GOD ALWAYS PROVIDES A RAM

Sonny looked down where the hatchet was still clutched in his left hand after he had plunged it down to cut off his right hand. But his right hand was in tact! It was still attached to his arm! But over his right wrist, where the hatchet had landed, was the hand of Michael. The blade was buried in the flesh of the angel.

"I don't understand," Sonny said as he dropped the hatchet. It fell out of the deep cut in Michael's hand. Immediately, the wound began healing into a scar. Sonny saw many scars in the angel's hand.

"It's always wise to check out angels, especially angels of light," Michael said as he grabbed the strange angel around the neck.

"Brother Chris warned us that Satan could become an angel of light.".

"The Bible also tells you how to test the spirits," Michael said as he tightened his grip around Myianel's neck.

Snarling, the angel shrieked, "Let me go, Michael."

"Sure, I'll let you go," Michael said, "If you will say, 'Jesus is Lord.'"

"Jesus is a Fake and Phony, and I hate him and I hate you."

"Whoa, brother, that's no way to talk." Michael looked at Sonny and said, "Those fallen angels can't say 'Jesus is Lord of my life.' and they are not going to make Him Lord. They hated Him up there and they hate Him down here. Plus they hate all of us who follow Him."

"Who is this angel?" Sonny asked as he eyed the one who had almost talked him into cutting off his right hand.

"He told you- you just don't speak Hebrew." Michael answered. "This guy is very proud of himself. Myianel is just one of his name. 'El' as you know means 'God or Lord.' 'Myian' means 'Flies.' He is the Lord of the Flies."

Michael reached over, grabbed the hair of the fallen angel and jerked it off the imposter. Off came the hair, the mask and the white robe. Standing there naked and black was the demon from Hell.

"Beelzebub!" Sonny shouted. "He was there when we entered the cross. He swore he would get us. He was there when Cain killed Abel." Looking down at his wrists, Sonny said "I almost chopped off my hand…"

"Don't underestimate the power of God, Sonny Miller." Michael touched the young athlete's eyes and said, "Look."

As his vision cleared, bright images began to appear all around the yard. Light after light emerged, some glowing bright, some fluttering. As he watched their shapes began to form. They were angels! Hundreds and hundreds of angels! Michael reached over, put his arm around Sonny and said, "Any every one of those angels would gladly have their hand chopped off for you."

Sonny said, "They all have on helmets."

"Helmets of salvation," Michael proclaimed. "Notice the breastplates of righteousness." As he said this, golden armor shone brilliantly on each one of them. Yet, if you notice, angels have to have the belt of truth, shoes that help them carry the messages. Bet you never thought Angels have to have shields of faith. How do you think they keep Satan's darts from piercing them- and you."

Silently and thankfully, Sonny took it all in. "Look at those swords! Michael, are those swords as powerful as I think they are?"

"It's about the only way you can take on devils, especially big ones like Beelzebub."

"The Swords are the Word of God, aren't they?" Sonny asked.

"Give the young guy in the tee shirt another A-plus. You got it right," Michael laughed and all of the hosts of angels in the yards and in the sky laughed merrily with Michael and at Beelzebub. The archangel put his mighty hand on the one God had chosen and asked, "Do you know how they defeat Satan?"

Sonny thought for a moment then said, "I'm sure they use their armor of God, but I remember a verse from James. Let's see, it's something like:

> 'Submit yourselves, then, to God.
> Resist the devil,
> and he will flee from you.
> (James 4:7NIV)'"

"I guess my best protection is to submit myself completely to God." Sonny paused, then bowed his head and prayed, "Dear God, I'm doing what you commanded. You didn't say submission is an option or a good idea, you made it a direct order. So from now on with Sandra or any other girl, I'll keep my hands in my pockets and my gun in its holster. Amen"

There was a roar of laughter from the angels as red, yellow and blue lights flashed on and off among them. Michael cackled out, "Well, that's one way of putting it."

Sonny grinned, "I mean it. And resist the devil- Satan and Beelzebub I resist you." He aimed his finger at Beelzebub and shouted, "I resist you!"

Nothing happened. Sonny turned to Michael and said, "The Bible promises when we submit ourselves to God and resist Satan, he will flee."

"Yep. That's what it says ," Michael agreed as Beelzebub sneered at them. "But you have to really submit and you have to really resist."

Beelzebub crackled a hideous laugh, turned his naked bottom toward Sonny and Michael and waggled it at them.

"Sometimes, you have to help him to flee," Michael said. The archangel took his big foot and kicked the demon in the rear end. Like a launched space-ship, the devil flew off the porch, across the front yard, up into the sky, and blazed into the distance like a sky rocket.

"Teach you to moon an Archangel," Michael said, then smiled. "So I sent him to the Moon. He can't do much harm up there unless some astronauts come along." He thought for a moment and said, "Now I remember. Beelzebub was one of the last I booted out of Heaven. Wonder if I'll have the honor of kicking him into Hell?"

Sonny's eyes were filled with tears. "Michael, thank you, thank you, thank you. Satan is so sneaky and tricky and wicked. I don't know if I can make it by myself."

Michael put his well-muscled arm around the young athlete. "You don't have to make it by yourself. You have a guardian angel; you have a good girl-friend and a good preacher. Best of all, the Lord Himself promised He would be with you, to the ends of the world."

Sonny gazed at the hundreds of angels surrounding his house. He realized they were not pale nor effeminate as they are usually pictured. Instead they re-sembled the starting lineup of the Green Bay Packers. Most of them proudly wore scars; all of them wore smiles, and love radiated from each of them like beams from floodlights.

"Which one is my guardian angel?" Sonny asked Michael.

"I thought you would never ask." Pointing to one of the cherubim close by, he beckoned him to come to them. "Sonny Miller, I want you to meet Son-e-el, your guardian angel."

Sonny gasped in surprise. He thought he was looking in the mirror, because standing in front of him was an exact duplicate of himself. Reaching out to shake his hand, Sonny said, "I didn't know angels came with dark hair and dark eyes."

Son-e-el shook his hand, then grabbed and gave him a bear hug. With twin-kling eyes and a mischievous smile, he said, "We angels come in all colors."

"So, you've been watching over me all these years?" Sonny asked.

"Never left your side. Except tonight when Beelzebub slipped up on me, tied me down and kept me away from you. I'm sorry, he fooled me just as Lucifer fooled a lot of Cherubim in Heaven. But just like the Lord Jesus, I will be with you unto the ends of the earth. You won't be able to see me any more than you can see love, joy or peace, but I'll be there for you."

Sonny threw both arms around Son-e-el. Then he hugged Michael who was so big it was like trying to hug a redwood tree. He waved a thank you to the hundreds of angels filling the yard. He said, "Excuse me," and dashed into the house. Inside they heard drawers opening and slamming shut. In a moment he came running out the door, waved at the angels and Michael and said, "I've got to make a call."

+ + +

Sandra Hall

Sonny Miller

CHAPTER 62
ONE LAST QUESTION

"Sonny Miller, I hope this is important," Sandra said to him. "Good thing you called on my cell phone so you didn't wake mom and dad. Why do you need to see me so late at night, and why did you insist that I meet you here in the Cross garden?"

Looking around them, their eyes took in the sheer beauty of the flowers, trees, and shrubs. They enjoyed the sweet smell of home. No one could ever persuade them life was just a series of accidents, mutations and evolution. In their minds they once again roamed the paths of the Garden of Eden, breathed the heavenly aromas, gazed at the spectacular sights. They were both homesick, and would be until they hiked the green hills of Heaven.

"It's a pretty important question," Sonny said as he held her hand.

"O.K. What's so important?" she asked.

Reaching into his pocket he pulled out a small black box and handed it to her. Nervously she opened it and saw the light from the full moon explode into a thousand dazzling colors. "It's a ring!" she said, "It's beautiful! Yes! Yes! Yes!"

"It was mom's engagement ring. Dad made pretty good money back in those days, and he wanted to give her something to show her how much he loved her. Before she died, she told Pop to save the ring and someday give it to Curtis or me, whichever one got married first."

He took the ring, slipped it on her finger and asked, "Sandra Hall, will you marry me and have my babies?"

Sandra smiled her million dollar smiled and said, "Oh yes. I will marry you-AFTER we graduate. And I'll gladly have your babies, AFTER we are married."

Sonny kissed her and held her close- and he was pleased that he didn't feel a single ounce of lust- only love. Looking around he sighed, "It's nice to visit Heaven and the Garden. But it's also nice to have a little sneak preview here on earth."

Sandra pulled the ring off to examine it closely. "Sonny, there's something inscribed inside the ring."

"I hope it's not my mama's name."

"No, but it is so beautiful and meaningful. Your dad was quite a guy.

"What does it say?" Sonny asked.

"*Amo, ergo sum*," Sandra said. "I love, therefore I am."

+ + +

God sat on his great white throne, looked across Heaven and gazed over the Garden. The Tree of Life still glowed and the river still flowed. Then He looked down on the two young humans he has chosen.

A golden glow appeared and said, "Good selection, Father."

A crimson heart pulsated and whispered, "So these are the two who will help prepare the world for my return. I'm ready, Father."

All was silent in Heaven for a while- then God smiled a rainbow smile.

THE END

REASONS I BELIEVE IN GOD, CREATION AND INTELLIGENT DESIGN:

*Author's Note: The three main characters wanted to make a statement regarding their personal belief in God, the Creation and Intelligent Design.

CHRIS CHRISTIAN:

I'm a preacher so my reasons for belief, or faith, are obvious:

1- The Bible says God created the universe and life.
That's good enough for me.

2- To me the Bible dates do not conflict with Science.

3- I have personally felt God, talked to God, and had God talk to me.
Nobody can disprove what is a fact in my life.

Bro, Chris

4- Creation tells me there has to be a Creator, and we are His Creatures.

5- People's lives have been changed by a belief in God and Christ.
I have seen "New Creations," where God literally created new lives.
Murderers, thieves, addicts, you-name-it, have been changed into good moral citizens by their faith in Christ.

6- Everything in the Universe has a Purpose.
From the hummingbird to the buzzard, from minnows to whales, from mayflies to meteors, from mustard seed to man- everything has a reason and a function.

7- There is a Beginning and an End.
Not only did we have a beginning, all of life appears be heading toward some final destination. I believe that is the Return of Christ, the last Adam.

8- Jesus is the Answer to man's Sin, his Purpose and his Final Destination.
Man is a sinner- evolution offers no remedy.
Only Christ offers forgiveness.

REASONS I BELIEVE IN GOD, CREATION AND INTELLIGENT DESIGN:

Sandra Hall

SANDRA HALL:

I know I'm only a college student- but God gave me a mind and I plan to develop it to the fullest. My plans are to obtain my Ph.D. in some area of Science, and I want to teach on a college level. Here are some things I believe:

1- The Law of Cause and Effect.
My intelligence will not let me believe that something (the universe) came from nothing except maybe a big bang. Every Effect demands there had to be a Cause, and I believe this was God.

2- Someone had to make the Universal Laws.
All the laws of physics, chemistry, even mathematics had to have a law maker- they did not make themselves.

3- The basic cell contains three billion parts including the complicated DNA. It does not make sense to believe this happened with no outside help.

4- The human being is too complicated to have made itself.
As intelligent as we are today, and with our sophisticated methods, man cannot create life. How do you expect chemicals and electrical reactions to attain what man cannot achieve?

5- There are limits to variation.
We can breed and cross pollinate till we drop,
but we can't make a beanstalk that can talk nor a pig that can fly.

6- Mutations almost always corrupt, not create.

7- Fossils do not show that one kind of organism has ever changed into another.

8- Evolution cannot explain morals.

9- All life points to a Common Designer.

10- I think, therefore, I am the product of a thinker.
Cogito, ergo sum eventus reputo,
I think therefore I am the product of a thinker.
Only a thinking God could create a thinking man.

SONNY MILLER ON CREATION & INTELLIGENT DESIGN

Hey, I'm just a football jock- and I don't claim to be a brain. So my reasons are very simple for believing that God is the Head Coach behind everything.

THE PARABLE OF THE FOOTBALL GAME

Once two teams played for the national championship. Since this is my story, I'm going to make one of the teams Alabama, naturally, and the other could be any body, but let's say, uh, Notre Dame. So the two teams meet in the Superdome on New Year's Day- and they both play as hard as they can and Alabama wins. So they're number one. Roll Tide!

Sonny Miller

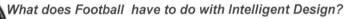

What does Football have to do with Intelligent Design?

1- THE PLAYERS had to come from somewhere. Some daddy or over-athletic mom started grooming their son to be a ball player. Wait, first they had to birth him. And somebody had to give birth to them- yadda, yadda, yadda, all the way back to Adam and Eve.

So- the players did not just make themselves, nor did some strange invisible force named evolution mold them and make them by accident that day.

2- THE RULES were formed by somebody,
The rules that govern football are specific and not just chemical and electrical reactions.

3- THE FOOTBALL is not the result of two bubbles beside a prehistoric ocean. It didn't make itself by starting with a couple of molecules, changing into a pig, cutting out a strip, sewing itself together, blowing itself up and saying, "I am a football- nobody made me, I made myself."

4- THE FIELD. If it had been left to design itself, it probably would look more like a pine thicket or a weed patch than one hundred yards of expensive turf with lines drawn at just the right yardage. The goal line could hardly have been the result of trial and error, nor were the goalposts some mutation of a palm tree.

5- THE PLAYBOOK. Football plays are designed for all the team to work together for the desired effect. Someone had to draw up the plays.

6- THE DESIRE. You can mix people and rules and footballs and fields together for a million years- and still have nothing but some guys taking naps on a grassy lawn. Where does the desire come from? To win, to do our best for our school, for our parents, for our God. You can make your guesses, but for me, my desire to do my best comes from the fact I am made in the Image of my God.

CREATION TIME LINE
(Used In This Book)

DATE BC	EVENT
2348 BC	**The Flood** *Methuselah Dies, Noah Family Survives*
4004 BC	**Adam and Eve Sin** *Driven From Garden*
200,000 BC	**Homo Sapiens Created in Image of God** *Garden of Eden, Adam and Eve*
3 Million–30,000 BC	**Pre-man** *Last Pre-man Extinct in 30,000 B.C.*
230-65 Million BC	**Dinosaurs**
530 Million BC	**Cambrian Explosion** *Almost all forms of life appear*
4.5 Billion BC	**Creation of Life Begins**
6.5 Billion BC	**Creation of Earth**
13.7 Billion BC	**Creation of Universe Begins** – *Big Bang* *Lucifer and Followers Cast out of Heaven*
15 Billion BC	**War In Heaven**
25 Billion BC	**Creation of Seraphim** *(Winged Praise Angels)*
50 Billion BC	**Creation of Lucifer and Cherubim** *(Winged Guardians of the Light)*
100 Billion BC	**Creation of Gabriel and Angels** *(Messengers)*
ETERNITY No Beginning- No End	**GOD** God is not created, He has always existed as the Triune God: Father, Son and Spirit.

בְּרֵאשִׁית	בָּרָא	אֱלֹהִים אֵת	הַשָּׁמַיִם	וְאֵת	הָאָרֶץ
b·rashith	bra	aleim ath	e·shmim	u·ath	e·artz
In Beginning	Created	God	the Heavens	and	the Earth

BOOKS BY BOB CURLEE

- FROM HAYSTACKS TO SKYLABS
- CROSS+ROADS I, THE GOLD NUGGET
- CROSS+ROADS II, WHO'S IN THE CASKET?
- THE GARDEN OF EDEN
  (THE SECRET OF THE GARDEN OF EDEN)
- BRIAN HAS LEFT THE BUILDING
- THERE WILL ALWAYS BE A JUDSON
- CITY SET ON A HILL
- BROTHER BRYAN
- DANCING WITH THE DEVIL
- THE SECRET OF THE VIRGIN MARY
- TED BUNDY, JOHNNY AND JESUS

*Some books are available at Amazon books,
  also some are at Kindle.

**Bob Curlee may be contacted at
  bobcurlee1492@yahoo.com.

Drop me a note by Email-
  I'd love to hear from you!

Bob Curlee

97084945R00163

Made in the USA
Columbia, SC
14 June 2018